Circulation & Urbanization

Ross Exo Adams

SAGE

Los Angeles | London | New Delhi
Singapore | Washington DC | Melbourne

Los Angeles | London | New Delhi
Singapore | Washington DC | Melbourne

SAGE Publications Ltd
1 Oliver's Yard
55 City Road
London EC1Y 1SP

SAGE Publications Inc.
2455 Teller Road
Thousand Oaks, California 91320

SAGE Publications India Pvt Ltd
B 1/I 1 Mohan Cooperative Industrial Area
Mathura Road
New Delhi 110 044

SAGE Publications Asia-Pacific Pte Ltd
3 Church Street
#10-04 Samsung Hub
Singapore 049483

Editor: Robert Rojek
Assistant editor: John Nightingale
Production editor: Swales & Willis Ltd,
    Exeter, Devon
Copyeditor: Swales & Willis Ltd, Exeter,
    Devon
Proofreader: Swales & Willis Ltd, Exeter,
    Devon
Indexer: Swales & Willis Ltd, Exeter, Devon
Marketing manager: Susheel Gokarakonda
Cover design: Wendy Scott
Typeset by: C&M Digitals (P) Ltd, Chennai,
    India
Printed in the UK

Library of Congress Control Number: 2018943446

British Library Cataloguing in Publication data

A catalogue record for this book is available from
the British Library

ISBN 978-1-4739-6330-6
ISBN 978-1-4739-6331-3 (pbk)

At SAGE we take sustainability seriously. Most of our products are printed in the UK using responsibly
sourced papers and boards. When we print overseas we ensure sustainable papers are used as
measured by the PREPS grading system. We undertake an annual audit to monitor our sustainability.

For Arno

Contents

About the Author

Ross Exo Adams writes and teaches on the relationships between architecture, urbanism, geography and political theory. He is Assistant Professor of Architecture at Iowa State University.

reviewers:

Acknowledgements

Like so many intellectual endeavours, this book came into being through a combination of intention and interjection. So many people, events, books, artefacts, arguments and fragments of knowledge, the whole of which I count as a kind of core knot that holds this work together, entered into this project through chance encounter. Realizing this is both arresting and reassuring – arresting in how a book reveals itself as an intellectual map of those with whom I have shared friendships and those who have inspired me; and reassuring in the widespread generosity that such a map reflects, especially in times when academic work is an increasingly individuated and entrepreneurial form of labour.

The guidance, support and advice from many people and institutions, over the course of many years, stands in sharp contrast to this tendency. I would like to thank all those who have contributed to the development of this work either intellectually, pragmatically, emotionally or all of the above. Rory Rowan deserves special thanks for all the lengthy discussions, comments and critiques of this work that he offered as it first took shape. Friends and colleagues who in one way or another left an indelible mark on this work: Adrian Lahoud, Pier Vittorio Aureli, Douglas Spencer, Platon Issaias, Aristide Antonas, Neil Brenner, Nikos Katsikis, Milica Topolovic, Thanos Zartaloudis, Maria Giudicci, Joana Rafael, Tom Vandeputte, Murray Fraser, David Cunningham, Christopher Gonzales Crane, Jacob Dreyer, Sami Jalili, Raphaëlle Burns, Marko Daniel, Tom McCarthy, Anne Hultzsch, Pedro Alonso, Timothy Ivison, Julia Tcharfas, Marina Lathouri and Dubravka Sekulic. Special thanks to Reinhold Martin and Alex Loftus for their exhaustive and inestimable readings of this text at a pivotal moment of its development as well as to Stuart Elden for all of his help and support throughout the writing of the manuscript. Much appreciation to John Nightingale and Robert Rojek at SAGE for their work in organizing the production of this book, as well as to Louise Smith and Caroline Watson for their scrupulous copy-editing work. To the unnamed reviewers of this manuscript, who provided sharp and thoughtful feedback, I am in your debt. Thanks as well to Bas Princen for allowing me to grace the cover of this volume with his incredible photograph.

Many others have been significant interlocutors in the development of this work, inviting lengthy conversation, opening space for me to share parts of it or situating it in new and unexpected contexts. To Francesco Sebregondi, Dele Adeyemo, Christina Sharpe, Andrea Bagnato, Nida Rehman, Azadeh Mashayekhi,

Susan Schupli, Claudia Aradau, Martina Tazzioli, Anita Rupprecht, Shehab Ismail, Eyal Weizmann, Hamed Khosravi, Danilo Mandic, Jelena Stojkovic, James Scott, Ayala Levin, Abdoumaliq Simone, Kenny Cupers, Max Viatori, Albert Pope, Antonio Petrov, Charles Rice, Rania Ghosn, El Hadi Jazairi, Renia Kagkou, Martín Arboleda, Mariano Gomez Luque, Álvaro Sevilla Buitrago, Paolo Tavares, Beth Hughes, Davide Sacconi, Emily McCarthy, Emma Letizia Jones, Alex Vougia, Mark Campbell, Parveen Adams, Ilona Sagar, Connor Linsky, Elia Zenghelis, Teresa Stoppani, Giorgio Ponzo, Matthew Gandy, Maros Krivy, Emily Scott, Tianhui Hou and Boya Guo, Anooradha Iyer Siddiqi, Rachel Lee, Stephen Graham, Marwan Ghandour, Deborah Hauptmann, Felicity Scott, Samaneh Moafi, Godofredo Pereira, Lorenzo Pezzani, Montserrat Bonvehi: I have learned a great deal from you all. Included in this particular list are the many brilliant students I've had the pleasure to think with at Iowa State University, the Bartlett, UCL and in the Architectural Association, whose intuition and energy continues to inspire new approaches to my work.

A special note of gratitude must be mentioned for the academic generosity displayed by those who have edited my work, either professionally or as guest editors. You have not only helped me develop clarity in my writing, but you have also helped bring this project into conversation with different intellectual milieus, broadening its scope and opening it out to new valences of thought. Thanks to Cynthia Davidson, James Graham, Nick Axel, Jack Self, Natalie Oswin, Stephanie Wakefield, Bruce Braun, Phillip Steinberg, Elaine Stratford, Kimberly Anne Peters, Nadir Lahiji, Helena Mattsson, Catharina Gabrielsson, Ed Wall and Tim Waterman.

As a project that grew out of my PhD research, it is fair to say that this book would not have been possible without the generous support that the Royal Institute of British Architects (RIBA) provided through the LKE Ozolins Studentship as well as a bursary from the London Consortium. I would like to thank those in both institutions for taking a chance with me. Thanks also to the Arxiu Municipal de Barcelona, the RIBA, the Canadian Centre for Architecture and the MoMA Archives for access to and support in navigating their archives.

Of course, it is equally impossible to imagine this book without the dedicated support, patience and endless wisdom of my dear friend and former PhD supervisor, Mark Cousins, whose impact on this work is immeasurable. Mark's support over the years extended far beyond the rigour and diligence of the best of research advisors. It is fair to say that the years spent working with Mark have been life-changing in many respects and he holds a unique place in my heart. Most especially, I would like to acknowledge the presence of Ivonne Santoyo Orozco in this project. Ivonne, my longstanding intellectual partner, has consistently pushed my work beyond what I could have imagined, refining trajectories, listening and arguing for countless hours, exposing me to new material and supporting me in times of doubt: my gratitude is beyond words. Along with Ivonne, I would like to warmly thank my family (both immediate and extended) for their continued patience, love and support over the past years helping me work through this project.

Introduction:
What Is Urbanization?

'Ruralize the urban: urbanize the rural: . . . Fill the Earth.' This proclamation appeared on the frontispiece of Ildefonso Cerdá's seminal work, *Teoría general de la urbanización* (*General Theory of Urbanization*), published in 1867. It captures the intoxicated zeal with which Cerdá sought to persuade his colleagues that he had discovered not a new type of city, but a system for the co-organization of life and infrastructure that would do away with the city altogether. In its place, an edgeless, centreless grid of fluid circulation and administered domesticity would extend across the Earth, accommodating a calculated distribution of population and services. The '*urbe*', as he called it, was indeed not a city at all, but a template on which to constitute new relations between life and technology, nature and capital, justice and subjectivity, territory and private property, movement and security. Not only would the *urbe* displace the city – it was a medium that would, by its very spatio-technical disposition alone, render the state and politics redundant.

Those who have ventured into the depths of Cerdá's rambling and somewhat hyperbolic *Teoría general de la urbanización* (1867) tend to overlook these central objectives, likely reading them as the by-products of his inflated, self-congratulatory and unbounded positivism. Instead, readers of his work seem more intent on uncovering those more familiar ideas that reaffirm the history of modernist urbanism: Cerdá is celebrated for his ideas that, we are told, predate those of prominent figures such as Le Corbusier, Ludwig Hilberseimer, Constantinos Doxiadis and even early urban cyberneticians, placing him as an unproblematic figure in a well-established canon. The two most dominant narratives that have emerged around Cerdá ignore his theoretical work almost entirely: urban designers view his 1859 *Eixample* (Extension) of Barcelona as a paradigm of sustainable urbanism, and architectural and urban historians often celebrate him as the socially conscious Haussmann.[1] Although such readings of his work are no doubt useful, they conceal a far more profound, challenging and intersectional reading, one increasingly relevant today, as contemporary discourses, from architecture to sociology and geography, circle ever closer to questions of the urban. Admittedly, Cerdá's claims to have single-handedly invented 'urbanización' (a neologism he coined) are both remarkable and easily dismissible. Yet the copious pages and volumes he devoted to describing this process and the order of space it produces perhaps deserve a closer, more interpretive consideration. For what they reveal, I will argue, is not so much an invention as a careful documentation of sorts of a truly new order of space coming into being to which Cerdá is witness. Indeed, between his abundant statistical mapping of his contemporary city and his exhaustive theorization of a planetary urbe to come, Cerdá's many teorías do more to describe the logic and social, political, legal and economic relations of a real spatial order that he sees emerging all across Europe, than to prescribe it in its concrete specificity. Text, statistical analysis, mathematical formulae and speculative spatial diagrams, together, articulate the emergence of urbanización in what could be the world's first theoretical account of a space-process that has, today, encircled the planet. Indeed, it may be that Cerdá's writings, diagrams, calculations, plans and policies all stand as a network of objects that speak to an order of space new to the world in the nineteenth century – a set of artefacts that reveals, in other words, that urbanization has a history.

However, this is not a book about Cerdá per se. Rather, it is an attempt to distance ourselves from many of the silent assumptions we tend to make about the urban. Although it may be hard to take some of Cerdá's claims seriously at face value, this book begins by taking one of them as its central hypothesis: that the urban was in fact 'invented'. It asks its readers to imagine what it could mean to consider the urban as one of the many anonymous projects and products of modernity, one whose historical emergence is neither sudden, nor infinitely complex; neither chronologically localized nor transhistorically ingrained in the human condition. To this end, Cerdá's work serves more as a way into a project that interrogates a broader set of historical relations between space and power that both prefigure the emergence of the urban and inhere within its seemingly endless reproduction. His work allows us to risk posing a question whose audacity is evident in the way it appears both trivial and perplexing, as commonsensical as it seems unanswerable: What is urbanization?

This book is thus a call for a wholly new understanding of a unique space (the urban) and the processes of its self-expansion (urbanization): it insists that, in order to grasp this concept, one must place it in history. By doing so – by assuming the urban has a history – one of the key conjectures it builds upon (one that Cerdá also proposed) is that the urban and categories such as 'city', 'town' and so on, although casually synonymous or overlapping terms, may be prised apart for the sake of exploring the historical and conceptual specificity of this space-process. Here, I take a cue from Cerdá, who in fact based his entire theory of urbanization on the stark isolation of the urban (urbe) from any other 'outdated' and 'politically overdetermined' term. However, I also depart from him in this distinction: I will engage the urban more broadly as a historically situated spatio-political order in its own right – a modern spatiality that first became legible and reproducible in the course of the nineteenth century in Europe, but whose genealogy spans centuries-old figures and disparate world spaces. I argue that this space materialized as an anonymous, parallel project of restructuring the space of the emergent liberal nation-state: more than simply a reflection of this new state form or the product of the capitalist relations it fostered, the urban, I argue, should instead be seen as a primary instrument of both – at once means and ends. Drawing together ideas, truths, figures and fragments of knowledge from across history, the urban emerged in the nineteenth century as a cohesive, legible and reproducible way in which to imagine and organize space; institute modes of inhabitation; conceive of infrastructures of movement and control; instrumentalize domesticity; and reconstitute labour, public life, social practices, law and the status of the human – a new order of space to accommodate a host of new social relations.

At the heart of this work is a historical investigation of the relationship between circulation and power, a relationship that, today, has become generalized through the ongoing urbanization of the planet. Circulation, taken both as an ideal concept and as the administrative category of traffic and infrastructure, plays a central role in this work for two fundamental reasons: for one, from the mid nineteenth century onward, circulation became a fundamental principle made useful for the burgeoning knowledge and practices of 'urbanism'. If there is a history of the urban, it is a history of what circulates. It is a history of infrastructure. For every new development, every new urbanism invented, the means of its innovation is undoubtedly infrastructural. Urbanists, architects, planners, economists and politicians continue to place endless faith in circulation, materializing social value in the infinite networks and corridors of human connectivity. Circulation has been conditioning the experience of life in the West for at least 200 years, and infrastructure has come to appear as a kind of default apparatus by which societies around the world mediate their needs: it is the medium that resolves crises, as well as the source from which they invariably emanate. It is, we could say, the locus and boundary of society's imagination: we cannot imagine a world *not* determined by infrastructure – by the logic of circulation.

Yet circulation is more than just an ideological default of modern rationality. Beyond its use in modern urbanism discourse, as this book will argue, circulation also offers insight into the nexus between political form and spatial order that can be traced across history. By reading a history of circulation in relation to forms of political power, the book at once depicts the urban as a historically recent spatial order, while also allowing the political character of its otherwise domestic, infrastructural spaces to be examined as augmented, entangled technologies of modern power. In so doing, I hope to eschew both essentialist histories of the urban and art-historical portraits of this space, drawing instead from a history of spatial orders and technologies of political power.

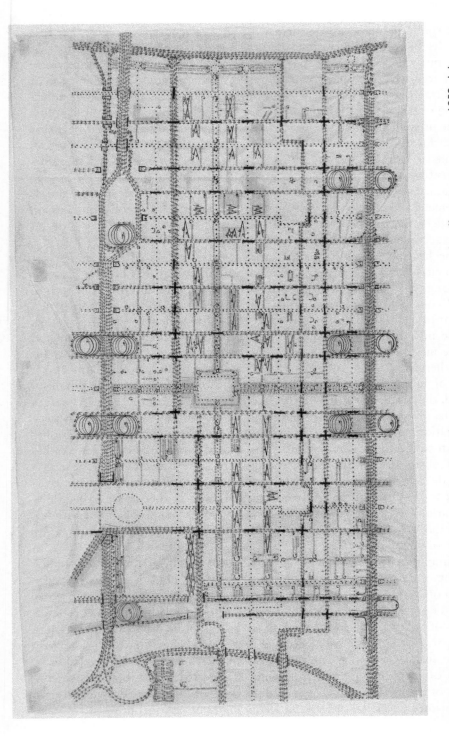

Figure 0.1 Louis Kahn, *Traffic Study*, project, Philadelphia, Pennsylvania, Plan of proposed traffic-movement patter, 1952. Ink, graphite, and cut-and-pasted papers on paper

I privilege the nineteenth century only as an entry point into a larger archaeology of political spaces, making use of cartographic knowledge, discourses of trade, political treatises, debates of natural philosophy, theoretical conjectures of cosmology, colonial administrative protocols, architectures and infrastructural technologies in order to map the notion of circulation in its changing relationship to both modern and premodern political forms and the ordering of the spaces of the world. The core of the book can be framed by three fundamental questions: When and how did circulation become epistemologically bound up with the knowledge and administration of the city? What relationships are fostered between circulation and urbanization? And, more broadly, what relationships can be traced between circulation and power? Within such an archaeology, what makes the urban unique, I argue, is that, unlike any previous spatial order, the boundary separating spatial order from modes of political subjectification and control disappears almost entirely: urban space is, in its ideal form, unmediated power – a characteristic that has only intensified today with the rise of cybernetic infrastructures and the general climate of crisis in which the urban continues to re-present itself (Adams, 2016: 181–90). Such a reading, however, remains obscured today by our tendency to treat the urban as a transhistorical background condition or rendered as a category made legible by purely empirical knowledge.

PORTRAITS OF THE URBAN

The urban today is at once unavoidable and yet curiously undoubted. Almost always taken as a given, the urban appears as a historical constant whose presence, more often than not, serves as a kind of inevitable or static background against which other problems are given visibility. If it is the object of enquiry, its examination tends to remain fixed by predominantly empirical analyses that give it consistency as a matter of the immediate present: through the mapping of the areas of its most rapid transformations, its categorization through perceived abnormalities or disclosure of its most extreme reach into the natural world, the urban nevertheless seems to elide questions about itself. Instead, it is rendered as a condition made visible only through its *effects*, a visibility that affirms broader assumptions that it is the inevitable outcome of a certain naturalized, transhistorical capacity of human cohabitation. When it is interrogated as a concept, it all too often remains a partial notion – a quasi-category that seems insufficient in itself and thus requires some supplementary conceptual framework for it to speak with any consequence. Indeed, there is a disturbingly tautological character found in much of urban theory today: the closer it gets to confronting its fundamental object (the urban), the more its collective response seems to be that what is missing is simply the right adjective to describe it. In this sense, what we call 'urban theory' tends to limit itself to staking out particular modes of analysis of a category that otherwise goes unexamined: 'urban' tends to be a loose signi-fier for a zone of academic research, typically having something to do with cities. Despite how much the urban may have become a part of everyday life today, and despite the many discourses that attempt to give meaning to this condition, we nevertheless lack a language with which to speak directly about the urban itself.

Likewise, as much as the world has become a domain ordered by networks of circulation, from the expansion of traditional infrastructures to global supply chain infrastructures to the layering of planetary computational and ICT net-works, the relationship between urbanization and circulation remains insufficiently examined. This, despite the fact that research into ideas proximate to circulation (e.g. the 'space of flows', logistics, mobility studies, network geog-raphies, etc.) has blossomed of late.[2] Circulation and urbanization, often loosely paired together in implicit association, each appear as evidence of the other: wherever infrastructures of circulation can be mapped also indicates the de facto sites of urbanization. As a result, the urban remains as self-evident a category as it is vague, and circulation orbits perhaps too closely to the urban to invite criti-cal reflection on the relationship between the two.

For architects, the urban – a term more often used in its adjective form – tends to signify the dynamic sociotechnical ecology in which a given project develops its sensibilities. At the same time, the urban has, in recent years, moved from context to object of architectural design, as architects are increasingly commis-sioned to plan districts, neighbourhoods, economic or cultural 'clusters' and even small cities. Despite this centrality to practice, the urban for architects has gone almost completely unquestioned and is better understood as a kind of condition 'out there', whose rules and technologies are often described in terms approxi-mating those of nature. On the other hand, in a recent turn in architectural scholarship to expand architectural knowledge beyond its traditional scalar boundaries, posing questions of territory, resource extraction and circulation, logistics, climate change, and indeed global or 'planetary urbanization',[3] we tend to find the same problems in which infrastructure uncritically stands in for the urban in the urgency of defining the problems of our present. The urban as a historically unique spatial order, nevertheless, rests safely beyond the boundary of most scholarly or practical examination.[4] What is more, circulation as a cat-egory of critical enquiry has remained nearly invisible outside (and perhaps because of) its positivist application as a technique of design[5] or its largely unquestioned appearance in architectural history, where it serves as a self-evident signature of modernism – an unquestioned historical condition of possibility.[6]

Geographers and sociologists have made the most progress towards an under-standing of the urban. Discourses in both urban geography and urban sociology have traditionally framed questions of the urban around socio-economic (and, most prominently, Marxian) analyses, situating the urban as a site ravaged by uneven development, struggle over resources, the terrain of capitalist accumula-tion, class antagonism and social inequality.[7] If there is a history of urbanization, it often appears in this literature tightly bound to the history of capitalism, as, for many in these fields, the former is taken as the materialization of the latter.[8] Henri Lefebvre's profound work, for example, particularly *The Production of Space* (1974) and *The Urban Revolution* (1971), has undoubtedly helped to underpin this tendency, which continues to influence a lot of contemporary work in urban geography and urban sociology (Lefebvre, 1991, 2003). Other, more recent, accounts of the urban have emerged that, on the one hand, describe it through a political ecological lens, bringing questions of nature, resources and infrastructure together with ontologies of power that circulate throughout its spaces.[9] On the other hand, an urgent body of work has emerged calling us to address the urban from the often marginalized frames of feminism, queer studies, critical race studies and postcolonial critiques (see, for example, Peak et al., 2018). Although all of this work continues to open up urgent new perspectives from which to engage urban space in the age of climate change, neo-liberalism and a resurgent fascism, its focus tends to reaffirm the urban as a kind of historical given. Research that has addressed the urban more directly, from Louis Wirth's early twentieth-century writing (Wirth, 1938) to Jean Gottmann's work on the 'megalopolis' (1990), to Henri Lefebvre's depiction of 'urban revolution' (2003), to Ed Soja's theoretical accounts of American urban sprawl (1998), to, more recently, Neil Brenner and Christian Schmid's theorization of 'planetary urbanization' (2013), has created parallel readings of the urban by situating it as a space determinate, in one way or another, of social organization. David Harvey's oft-used citation of sociologist Robert Park – 'if the city is the world which man created [. . .] indirectly, in making the city man has remade himself' (Park, 1967: 3, quoted in Harvey, 2008) – reflects both the academic lineage on which many urban geographers and sociologists build their theoretical frameworks and the enduring socio-spatial assumptions at its core. Although this has lent a tremendous foundational insight into the urban, it nevertheless seems to faithfully stop short of engaging the very object of enquiry itself. Despite various attempts to the contrary, nearly all such accounts retain a perception of the urban as a kind of pre-existing condition that must be assessed quasi empirically in order to develop any theoretical consistency. In nearly all cases, history appears useful only in illuminating tendencies that can be extrapolated into conjectures for the immediate future.

Because of both tendencies, the terms that anchor these various discourses remain largely descriptive and disappointingly fleeting, often grounded in a myopic overestimation of the veracity in the discoveries of the immediate present. This is in part because urban theorists have not yet changed the way they ask questions of the urban or urbanization. Decades-old frameworks of analysis persist in the way we seem more intent on asking *how* urbanization is changing, than in posing questions trained on understanding what has given rise to this space-process, or what it consists of. Thus, the basic object of study seems to be reappear with every new descriptive terminology produced: What is an 'urban agglomeration' if defined in terms of population density? How can we differentiate between an 'urban settlement' and a 'city', 'town' or any other denomination? On what grounds can we separate the 'urban' from the 'rural'? How can we differentiate between a 'city region', an 'urban region' or a 'megalopolis'? What is an 'urban territory'? In our present discursive framework, any attempt to produce firm definitions of even the most basic terms only ever appears to be based on a host of unquestioned assumptions, and thus proves to be largely provisional, driven by a desire to capture and name the latest empirical discoveries. Urban theory remains descriptive. To propose quantitative thresholds, demographic delimitations or other empirical (or even theoretical) sociological tools to explain the nature of something as persistently changing and immeasurable as the urban has shown itself to be a Sisyphean task. Even in Wirth's classic text, 'Urbanism as a Way of Life' (1938), where he sets out to define the urban (in contrast to the city), his very reliance on such sociological frames of analysis allows a somewhat circular argument to emerge. Similarly, many of Gottmann's ideas allow for the urban to appear as a completely self-regulating, self-governing, 'evolutionary' and, one might say, 'natural' system.[10]

This tendency continues into the contemporary literature of critical urban theory, which, in rejecting anything suggesting a universal theory, tends to shift the analysis towards an emphasis on the plural: the urban is heterogeneous, uneven, multifarious, unequal, undecidable; it is a multiplicity of spaces, actors, temporalities, a milieu of rhythmic and arrhythmic performances and events; the urban is relational (among the many texts that could be cited here, see, for example, McFarlane, 2011, and Amin and Thrift, 2002). Just as global capitalism is uneven in its modalities, effects and distributions across the world, so too are the spaces, experiences and infrastructures it produces, rendering the urban as unendingly multifarious and, thus, only characterizable in the local. And who could doubt such a characterization? The ease with which one can produce evidence to disprove any general claim about the urban perhaps explains the persuasion that this critique of urban theory has had recently (see, for example, Roy, 2015). Now, when one does attempt the controversy of a generalized urban theory, it is typically fronted with caveats and gestures towards complexity and difference, often arriving at apologetic frameworks so broad and all-encompassing as to beg the question: what is at stake?

Contemporary urban theory, we could say, suffers from a certain arresting quality: as soon as we try to confront the urban in its undeniable ubiquity across the surface of the Earth, we are immediately faced with its absence as such. With Heisenberg-like uncertainty, the urban is everywhere and nowhere; totalizing yet ungraspable. The vague presumptuousness with which we treat this category means that 'urban theory' *as such* can assert itself only as a means to propose diverse methodological frameworks through which further research on contemporary urban conditions may be undertaken. It is an arena in which schools and camps of all stripes compete for the most legitimate, inclusive terms by which to capture, describe and make visible contemporary urban phenomena. All of which presumes a well-established conceptual understanding of the very category in question. And, despite the meta-discursive allure of 'big questions' today, contemporary urban theory tends in practice to repeatedly retreat from such a task, electing instead to turn the debate into a relativized field of partisan opposition and intellectual hair-splitting (see, for example, Storper and Scott, 2016), hardening the core presupposition that urban theory has always made, namely that its relevance remains in its capacity to provide descriptive frameworks for contemporary phenomena.

Consequently, the historical, political and epistemological consistency of the urban – regardless of its infinitely variegated appearance – remains almost inaccessible to current debates. If a relationship between urban space and political form is attempted, it is often one imported from other, pre-existing discourses. Rather than excavating the concept itself, such critiques of the urban are all too often extruded around Marxian critiques of capitalism (the work of both Henri Lefebvre and David Harvey stands out as the most influential within this framework) or plugged into Foucauldian analyses of power (see, among others, Osborne and Rose, 1998, or Joyce, 2003), or tested through Deleuzian sociologies (McFarlane, 2011), in all cases affirming the discourse in question while leaving the urban, as an epistemological, political and historical category, unexamined. Once again, the urban is a vehicle for expressing sentiments that already exist. It is this discursive lapse that this book attempts to address.

As, today, we debate the veracity of distinctions such as 'rural' and 'urban' or as we confront the tenuous notions of limit and scale; as we contemplate new epistemic understandings of the city; as we theorize provocations such as the urbanization of the oceans or the status of nature in the face of endlessly merging so-called 'megacities'; as we lament the atrophy of the public realm and the incursion of governmental surveillance into private space; as we question the urban as a site of algorithmic administration and control; as we dissect the politics of domesticity, infrastructure and territory or gasp at the planetary reach of the urban systems they constitute, it is perhaps useful to critically examine the 'discoveries' of Cerdá, whose work, perhaps unintentionally, lends tremendous insight into all of these facets that we experience in the shifting, scaleless and endlessly penetrated spaces we inhabit today.

CIRCULATION AND URBANIZATION

This book begins examining the historical emergence of the urban by calling into question a certain consensus that cuts across various histories of the city in which a focus on the city of the nineteenth century seems to mark out an undeniable set of transformations in practices, forms of habitation, technologies, infrastructures and economies, all of which reflect key social, political and discursive shifts that this century (primarily in Europe and North America) may claim as its own. Ranging from a signifier for historical origins to a period in which foundational structures of state, society and capitalist economy concretized in the spaces of the modern city, the nineteenth century holds a certain representational place in our histories of the city, suggesting also that this century inaugurates a new historical condition whose coherence extends up to the present. My intention here is not to verify these histories or to expand upon them, nor to add more evidence to familiar narratives. Rather, I will argue that, precisely because of these frameworks, an examination of the very object these histories narrate becomes an improbable, if not impossible, task.

To this end, this book approaches the question of a historical emergence transversally: far from discovering an 'origin' of the urban, it will look to chart the co-production of a number of significant spatial, political, conceptual, social, legal and economic factors whose relationships could cohere against the epistemological horizon of nineteenth century Europe in the emergence of a spatial order new to the world. Yet, for this reason, it is impossible to credit any century with this emergence: the urban is a space, as I try to show, constituted by a patchwork of ideas, diagrams, truths and remnants composed by both ancient and contemporaneous histories alike. In that sense, 'emergence' implies a far longer process than can be compressed into the span of a single historical period or a single paradigmatic space (e.g. the 'modern city', Paris, 'the European city', etc.). Central to this approach is the concept of circulation, not only because it seems to play a fundamental role in providing the 'modern city', as it were, with a new *raison d'être*, but because it does so with a distinctly political valence, suggesting a shift in the relationship between power and space towards techniques of circulation.

Although circulation and power may have long shared a site in the space of the city, the relationship between the two was not one that was essential to it. Circulation must be seen, rather, as an idea adopted into the thinking of the city at a certain point in time. Thus, despite insisting that the emergence of the urban can be historically situated, it is not a historically autonomous configuration; the analysis this book makes will look at the urban as a spatial correlate of a form of power whose political configuration cohered over the course of the nineteenth century. That is to say, it will attempt to frame urbanization as a *particular expression of power* in a larger genealogical relationship of circulation, power and spatial order. In this way, the city can be purged of any transhistorical presuppositions or essentialisms that inevitably lead to the search for 'origins' and other false universals. The book instead poses the question that, if a bond between modern power and circulation can indeed be located within the urban, can such a coupling be found elsewhere in history, in spaces *outside* the city? What is the history of the bond between circulation and political power? What other figures of space did this relationship give rise to? How is it that the city would eventually become the key site in which this complex would take root?

The trajectory of this book begins amid the spatial developments of the nine-teenth century, before embarking on a more historical-conceptual examination of circulation. Chapters 1 and 2 offer an initial sketch of the urban as it appeared in the work of Ildefonso Cerdá. The first chapter looks to disentangle Cerdá from the place he holds both in the architectural canon and in his recent rediscovery by contemporary urbanists. Instead, it approaches his work by first examining the intellectual scaffold on which his project was built. By situating his theories of urbanization not only at the break of modern urbanism, but against the rise of liberal capitalism and its idealism in Enlightenment thought, it seeks to pre-empt the technical, spatial and political analysis of Cerdá's work, that follows in Chapter 2, asking first what kind of a project *urbanización* was.

Chapter 2 explores the spaces, policies and technologies of the *urbe* in detail, offering a reading of it as a concise diagram of the contemporaneous mechanisms of planning in Europe. Tracing the central role that circulation (*vialidad*) played in constituting the *urbe* allows us to dwell on the subtle, new relationships of power and subjectivity that are forged in the spaces and technologies the *urbe* suggests. From his copious writings, drawings, calculations and measurements, we see how this space reconstitutes power in the paternalistic provision of ser-vices, its decentralized, formless web of roads, rails and sewage pipes and in new machinic circuits of circulation and biological reproduction that it institutes.

Of course, the appearance of the urban in Cerdá's work certainly does not constitute an 'origin': its invention should instead be seen as an unconscious culmination of centuries of spatial, political and social experimentation in Europe and the colonial world that drew on figures, ideas and artefacts as diverse as maritime technologies, anatomical knowledge and hydrological mathematics to form a spatio-technical programme for nineteenth-century life in perpetual motion. To understand how these histories might possibly lend themselves to construction of the urban, the book looks to document the ways in which circu-lation as a concept was made useful for giving order to the physical world, as well as making legible forms of power that ruled over it. Chapter 3 traces how the emergence of circulation as a concept in sixteenth-century natural philosophy derived from a longstanding perception of the ancient world in which the circle gave visibility to divine, cosmological and natural orders. It traces this metamor-phosis, revealing how, in its concept form, circulation would prove to be one of the most important spatial principles from which a new sphere of earthly, *œco-nomic* and political power could be imagined.

Chapter 4 then takes up this history to examine how, into the seventeenth century, circulation permeated political and spatial thought, establishing itself as a concept central to the emerging knowledge and techniques of *territory* and to the discourses governing the maritime networks of trade in Europe's imperial spaces and colonial territories. Although both adopted divergent understandings of circulation through which their respective spaces could be imagined, their shared investment in the foundational 'truth' of this concept, as well as the intimate relationship it had with early modern forms of power, cannot be denied. This chapter focuses in particular on the history of territory, exposing the role that circulation played in its constitution, as both an idea and an objective. Within the space of territory, this chapter explores the emergence of a new knowledge and architecture mobilized to literally reconstruct the landscape of territory and to materialize its borders in fortified cities.

Chapter 5 picks up from this to look more specifically at the changing status of the city within this disciplined space of securitized, calculated movement that territory had prescribed. Nested and interconnected sites of coordinated productivity, cities also began revealing themselves as a practical and epistemological problem whose visibility would unwittingly foreground an urban knowledge to come.

Chapters 6 and 7 unfold over a consistent interrogation of the relationship between the city and territory. By returning to the debates and developments of nineteenth-century space that helped precipitate the emergence of the urban, Chapter 6 re-examines Baron Georges-Eugène Haussmann's canonical reconstruction of Paris from a rather unorthodox perspective. Against the broader history of circulation, what becomes clear is that Haussmann's novelty, almost entirely overlooked as such, extends from his treatment of the city as territory – the direct application of territorial techniques and knowledge to the city for the first time.

Finally, Chapter 7 returns to Cerdá from this perspective: if Haussmann had invented a method by which the city could 'become territorial', in following his lead, Cerdá's *urbe* would take this a step further. It would propose a radically new spatial order that redefined *both* the city *and* territory as an indistinguishable whole. The formation of the urban that emerged in the space between the two figures' work would be conditioned almost exclusively by the epistemologies of movement that, until the nineteenth century, had only found purchase in spaces and practices outside the city. From this vantage point, my analysis of the urban will offer some perhaps unexpected conclusions: namely, that the urban was discovered not in the spaces and architectural forms of the city, but rather in the knowledge, practices and experiences of *territory*[11] – a discovery that reveals further epistemological and technological threads that run between the urban and histories of maritime spaces, colonial technologies and utopian diagrams.

In total, this book will follow ways in which circulation both gave form to pre-existing political ideas and truths but also offered a model for new ones. In doing so, I aim to challenge a presumed linear causality and historical rigidity that have dominated much of the literature on the city, assuming the spatio-material world to be the product of rational human thought. Rather, this book attempts to show how a more slippery, non-linear, non-causal relationship between the two persists in a grey zone where rational projection and irrational (mis)interpretation are two names for the same phenomenon. Such an approach is used here to counter what I consider to be a certain consensus around the city, architecture and the spatial, material world in general. That most canonical histories of the modern, Western city begin in the nineteenth century not only is a means to cleave history into neatly defined periods or phases, but, in doing so, allows us to view the city, its architecture, infrastructure and the overall spatial order of which they are a part as historically passive. That is, we can presume the spatio-material organization of the world to be the output of human intellect and, thus, imagined as fixed configurations of matter that, at most, reflect a certain 'spirit' of a period, the idiosyncrasies of its key protagonists or, in its more ambitious register, the armature that serves the logic of capitalism.

The modern European city, as the story goes, is the reflection of an ascendant bourgeois society, the outcome of a new form of life made possible by novel technological advancements, animated by the forces of capitalist entrepreneurship or fostered under the auspices of the liberal nation-state. At the core of these histories, circulation appears as an unproblematic principle, sheared of its more difficult, politicized history, finding its roots instead in the modern innocence of a natural human capacity to communicate. Still today, we draw from the truths and presuppositions this historical form imposes, perpetuating a positivism that sees unlimited circulation as a freedom tethered to technological innovation. In this way, the mere fact of technological innovation that colours many histories of modernity helps grant the last two centuries a kind of historical autonomy, freeing their objects and ideas from the politically burdened historical trajectories upon which they enter modernity. Thus, bound up with uncovering the notion of the urban is also a set of critical reflections on spatial histories we have inherited.

When we interrogate the nature of political form in its relationship to the spaces of circulation, there appears to be more of an inconvenient continuity in the history of the Western city than some of its historians may be comfortable admitting. Indeed, the importance of circulation is not simply contained as a concept relevant to the city, but one that has persisted for centuries outside the realm of the city and beyond the strictly human ordering of space, as a metaphor and model connected with absolute power, whether divine, natural or political. This is even more pressing to recognize today precisely because any relationship between circulation and political power may seem, to many, accidental, oblique.

The nexus between political power, space and circulation indeed thrives behind the dauntingly naturalized, apolitical veil of urbanization: in the urban, things just happen. Urbanization has come to be viewed as a vague, unquestioned background of the human condition. Both itself and its more 'scientific' partner, urbanism, have bizarrely come to serve as the receptacle for all processes relating to the city that somehow remain beyond question. They persist as the inevitable horizon of human cohabitation, the blinding 'reality' that is only to be understood by 'learning from' its tendencies, monitoring its processes and mapping its effects. As we gaze bewilderedly into the utter 'nature' of urbanization, we seem helpless to do anything but reproduce it in all of the various 'urbanisms' that multiply in the gloss of new books and on the websites of corporate architectural offices.

In all accounts, there is a tremendous lack of understanding of the *political* dimension as well as the *historical* basis of urbanization – two categories bound together in the obscurity of dogmatic disregard: just as urbanization appears more often than not as an *apolitical* condition, so too does it manifest itself as an *ahistorical*, originless category inherent to the human condition. This book is an effort to open up a new understanding of the urban precisely along these lines: *as a historico-political category* – one that stretches from the constitution of subjectivity to the ordering of territory, from domesticity to statecraft, tracing the often hidden political structures that underpin the processes and spaces of urbanization. It will attempt to approach this subject outside any traditional discursive framework, viewing it instead as a scaleless meta-apparatus spanning from the body to the planetary in scale – a condition that makes it appear at once totalizing and elusive. Its ability to apply one, overarching logic to all scales of material organization of life is a result of its prescribing a form of apparently *depoliticized* power, no longer bound to a delimited space, but one that thrives precisely by *circulating* throughout a formless, interconnected total-ity. This paradoxical condition presents us with a form of politics, new to the modern world, that appears as its opposite: a network of anonymous infrastruc-tures and private property.

What I want to offer with this book is not so much a counter-history to the current understanding of urbanization, the city and urban space, but rather an assessment that cuts perpendicularly across our current histories, an approach that I hope will reveal opportunities for new discursive beginnings along the way. In that sense, I see this work as an opening towards a political and spatial com-prehension of the urban as a historically situated category – a material process and a spatio-political order – all of which cannot be grasped from the vantage point of a single disciplinary structure. I use the concept of circulation to do this, although there are, doubtless, many other ways to examine the urban.

Although my historical material is admittedly limited to 'Western' sources, the scope it sets should be seen as the testing of a particular hypothesis that could be brought to bear on other histories and vice versa. The scope I have chosen covers material spanning roughly between architecture and geography and is hung together by a persistent interrogation informed by various political histories and analyses of power. Although the book takes a deliberately broad view, its consis-tency is maintained by an insistence that a unique relationship between spatial order, political power and circulation can indeed be historicized. I have chosen to treat the material I examine less as case studies than as 'vignettes', as a means to allow the book more agility in composing its argument. The material that can shed light on a category such as the urban naturally comes from a vast range of sources that are just as likely to arise from treatises and theories as they are from concrete architectures, spaces, practices, perceptions and experiences; in other words, from both discursive and non-discursive sources.

To question urbanization in this way requires a specification of the interrela-tions between the various terms that accompany it, namely 'the urban' and 'urbanism'. Although I discuss the historical relationship between 'urbanization' and 'urbanism' in the first chapter, I place scant emphasis on the notion of 'urbanism' throughout the rest of the book, prioritizing instead 'the urban' and 'urbanization' – terms that I use somewhat interchangeably to denote a specific characteristic of what is at once a spatial category and a process. This is a deliberate choice: the idea here is that, despite the confidence with which we typically deploy the term 'urbanism' in contemporary discourses, I believe that we cannot begin to critically examine this practice in a meaningful way without first mapping out the spaces and processes that this term purports to address. Furthermore, to ask this, and to follow with questioning the urban (as opposed to the city), I must remark that the implied question, 'What is a city?', is neither taken for granted, nor addressed in this study, as this is a matter of a different type of history altogether (see, for example, Mumford, 1961).

Finally, by choosing events and ideas produced in the nineteenth century as both the point of departure and end point of the book, I have necessarily restricted myself to a span of history that may be called 'modernity' (both early and high). Certainly, questions will arise about this, especially as, by confining myself to this historical period, I am excluding discussions about urban and regional planning in the welfare state, the rise and fall of socialism and its history of urbanization, neoliberalism, globalization, Empire, climate change – topics to which the notions of circulation and urbanization certainly bear particular relevance. Even within the history I have chosen, I have left out other discussions, particularly around the 'circulation of ideas' that is so ideologically tied to signifiers such as 'the Enlightenment'. Nevertheless, although I discuss this history tangentially, clearly an excursus into what Armand Mattelart has called the 'invention of communication' (Mattelart, 1996) would be an obvious trajectory that could expose much more about the relationship between circulation and power. The decisions I have taken have been informed in part by a conviction I have that there is an all too dogmatic treatment in discourses and research today that equates 'the present' (as a site of research) with 'contemporary' (as relevance of research), specifically around topics such as urbanization (see Adams, 2014b). Such a perception allows us to detach ourselves and the material we are examining from any even cursory historical knowledge and typically leads us to the problems outlined above. Although a 'history of the present'[12] may be something of an academic truism by now, it is still worth underlining that the thoughts and ideas developed in the pages that follow have all been motivated by a critique rooted firmly in the contemporary world.

NOTES

1 Joan Busquets credits Cerdá's *Teoría* as a way to rationalize modern urban planning: see his Innovative Project, which has become a great urban reality, in Busquets and Corominas, 2009. On the comparison between Haussmann and Cerdá, see Bergdoll, 2000: 261–5.

2 On the notion of 'space of flows', see Castells, 1999, 2000, 2010. For a series of counter-arguments surrounding Castells' notion and its implications, see,

for example, Agnew, 2005; Painter, 2010; Steinberg, 2009. On the 'mobility turn' more broadly, see Cresswell, 2006, and Urry, 2007. More recently, critical research has developed around logistics and their inherent relationships to power, politics and control. On this literature, see Cowen, 2014; Neilson, 2012; Neilson and Rossiter, 2010; Toscano, 2014.

3   In addition to Neil Brenner's work, a project that has received quite widespread attention is 'The City of 7 Billion' by Joyce Hsiang and Bimal Mendis (Hsiang and Mendis, 2013–14).

4   Several anomalies in this tendency are worth mentioning here. Although not attempting to historicize this condition, the work of Albert Pope, in the mid 1990s, had already identified a gaping hole in architectural discourse around the post-war American urban condition (Pope, 1996). Another exception concerns the recent writings of Reinhold Martin that explicitly situate their enquiries around the urban against a selection of twentieth-century critical theory (see Martin, 2014, 2016).

5   Le Corbusier famously wrote that, 'in architecture and city planning, circulation is everything' (Le Corbusier, 1991 (1930): 128).

6   Adrian Forty's comment on the history of circulation in relation to architecture, whose use was found first in Viollet-le-duc's *Lectures*, remains a single example of tracing this notion through a disciplinary-specific concept history (see Forty, 2000: 87–101).

7   To name only a few of the best-known exponents of such work, see Manuel Castells' early work (Castells, 1979), a whole range of David Harvey's work (including Harvey, 1996, 2001, 2009), Neil Smith's prolific writings on gentrification and uneven development (Smith, 1990, 2005), and Andy Merrifield's work (Merrifield, 2014).

8   For more on this, see my short piece, Adams, 2014a.

9   See, for example, Erik Swyngedouwe's important work (Swyngedouwe, 2004, 2006) or that of his collaborator, Alex Loftus (2012). Others who have offered insightful depictions of the city by interrogating multiple urban natures are Maria Kaika (2004) and, of course, Matthew Gandy (2014).

10 See, for example, Gottmann's essay, 'How Large Can Cities Grow?' (Gottmann, 1990).

11 With this notion, I refer, among others, to the work of Stuart Elden around the historical construction of territory as a 'political technology' of the emergent European states. See his most comprehensive publication: Elden, 2013.

12 Although differing in scope, Paul Rabinow's unorthodox effort to write a socio-spatial 'history of the present' by examining twentieth-century urbanism in France and its colonial experiments in Morocco comes to mind (Rabinow, 1989).

To Fill the Earth:
The Invention of *Urbanización*

Ildefonso Cerdá occupies a peculiar position in the canon of European architectural and urban history. Once a figure known to many, scholarship on this Spanish engineer certainly does not afford him the centrality that others hold. His is a position that, we are told, confirms the topographies of the 'modern city', more than it defines them. Nor is Cerdá a figure obscured by the canon – one whose bringing-to-light in the present may help to either confirm the dominant narratives of the past or to disrupt their contours. What Cerdá's work offers may instead be a base on which a discourse on the relationships between urban space, infrastructure, architecture and power can be built – a nexus of processes, spaces and technologies that Cerdá compacted into the term *urbanización*.

Originally designated around 1861 as a neologism by Cerdá as the basis for his monumental *Teoría general de la urbanización* of 1867, the term 'urbanization' circulated throughout Europe alongside the great urban reconstruction projects, eventually adopting its younger French derivative, *urbanisme*, as a more generic term for the same. By 1884, the terms appeared in English, at which point distinct meanings emerged (Cerdá, 1999: 90–2). 'Urbanism' came to refer to the 'scientific' knowledge of the city, its growth, demographic make-up, resources, and so on, whereas 'urbanization' generally denoted the concrete fact of the processes of the city's growth over time. Despite their increasing centrality in popular and intellectual discourses today, urbanism and urbanization have become background terms. They are terms whose definition, meaning and history are simultaneously vague and unquestioned. Together, the terms seem to inscribe a receptacle of thought for all processes relating to the city that somehow remain beyond the realm of question. Yet they are not inactive; urbanism and urbanization have come to function as a set of universal constants – homogeneous containers inside which

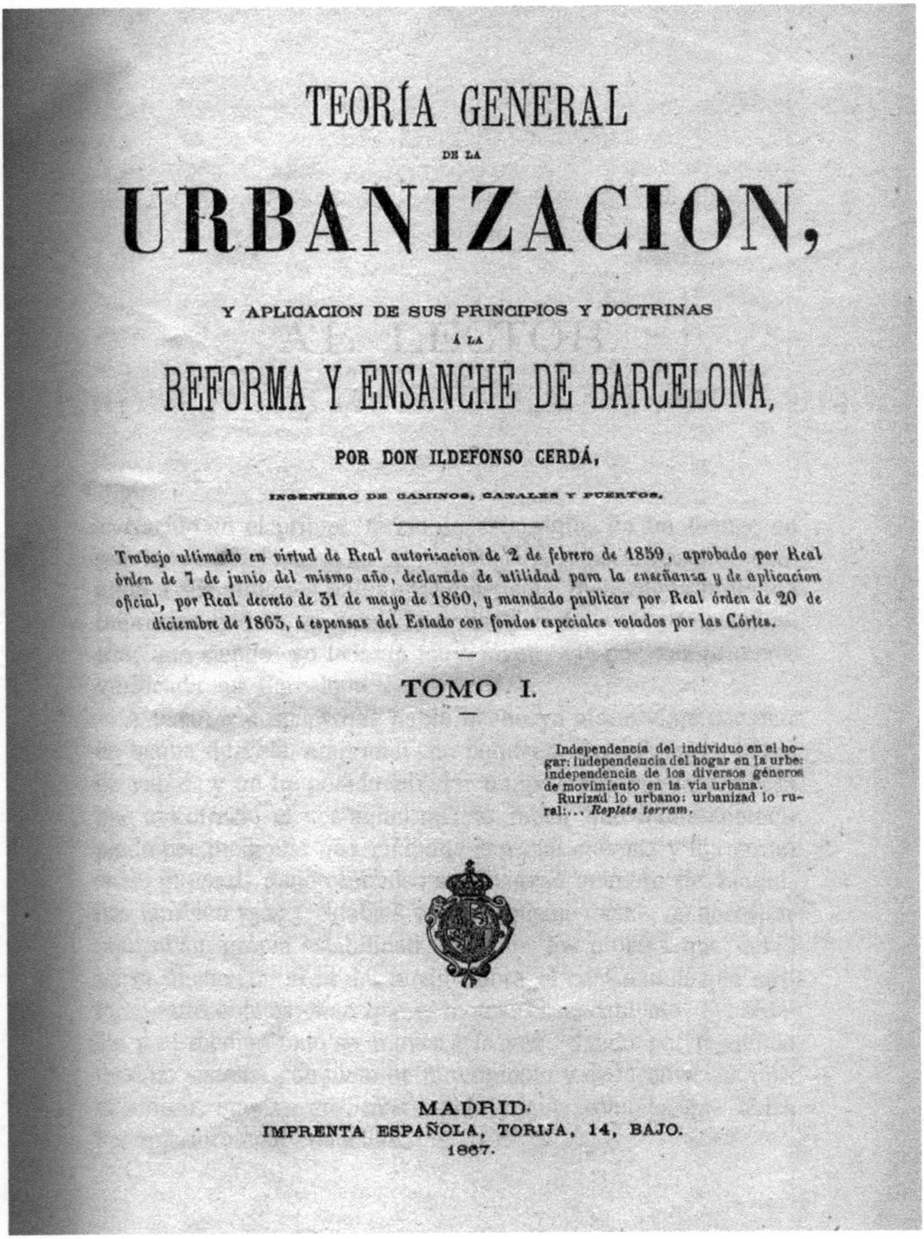

TEORÍA GENERAL

DE LA

URBANIZACION,

Y APLICACION DE SUS PRINCIPIOS Y DOCTRINAS

Á LA

REFORMA Y ENSANCHE DE BARCELONA,

POR DON ILDEFONSO CERDÁ,

INGENIERO DE CAMINOS, CANALES Y PUERTOS.

Trabajo ultimado en virtud de Real autorizacion de 2 de febrero de 1859, aprobado por Real órden de 7 de junio del mismo año, declarado de utilidad para la enseñanza y de aplicacion oficial, por Real decreto de 31 de mayo de 1860, y mandado publicar por Real órden de 20 de diciembre de 1863, á espensas del Estado con fondos especiales votados por las Córtes.

—

TOMO I.
—

Independencia del individuo en el hogar: independencia del hogar en la urbe: independencia de los diversos géneros de movimiento en la via urbana.
Rurizad lo urbano: urbanizad lo rural:... *Replete terram.*

MADRID·
IMPRENTA ESPAÑOLA, TORIJA, 14, BAJO.
1867.

Figure 1.1 Ildefonso Cerdá, Frontispiece of *Teoría general de la urbanización* (*General Theory of Urbanization*), 1867

human action is expected to gain effective purchase on the effects of the human condition; a background of nature against which the artifice of human inventiveness can reciprocally take shape: urbanization suggests a natural, human process, and urbanism suggests the techniques by which humans can intervene in it.

Yet, for the author of the *Teoría general de la urbanización*, the notion was anything but vague. Spanning two volumes totalling more than 1,500 pages, Cerdá's *Teoría* remains a vast body of theoretical speculation, which would supplement the project he is better known for, The Project for the Reform and Extension of Barcelona of 1859. Drawing together for the first time rigorous statistical and demographic assessments, historical study and, most importantly, theoretical conjecture, his *Teoría* would bring to bear all the scientific diligence the nineteenth-century world could muster to reconstitute the form and conception of contemporary modes of co-habitation completely. Unlike his contemporaries who were busy with the reconstruction of specific cities, Cerdá sought to create a general, universal 'science' of urbanization, one for which his project for Barcelona would serve as a mere prototype. The relationship between these two sides of his *oeuvre* remains one of the clearest and most profound in the history of modern urban thought – certainly throughout the nineteenth century – stretching from the design of sewerage fixtures to the ways in which the entire planet could be urbanized.

Despite all this, in most canonical accounts of the modern city – histories in which the terms urbanism and urbanization gain any kind of clarity – the figure of Baron Georges-Eugène Haussmann and his mid nineteenth-century reconstruction of Paris form the ideological and factual centre, passing over the immense work of his contemporary, Cerdá, as only a minor figure and reducing his work to his design of Barcelona's reform and extension. In his epic work, *Space, Time and Architecture*, Sigfried Giedion overlooks Cerdá altogether, while dedicating half of an entire part of the book, 'City Planning in the Nineteenth Century', to an examination of Haussmann's work, stating that '[n]o one arose with Haussmann's power to attempt a general attack upon the new problem of the city' (Giedion, 1982: 775). His omission of Cerdá's work provokes embarrassment, as many of Giedion's more speculative remarks about the future of the city mirror those written by Cerdá a century before. Unaware of even the fundamental achievements of the *Teoría*, Giedion clumsily praises the foresight of Le Corbusier for suggesting, in 1953, replacing the 'inadequate' terms village, city, metropolis, and so on, in favour of the more modern, universal *agglomération humaine* (ibid.: 858) – again, a call Cerdá made clearly in 1867. Leonardo Benevolo's comprehensive work on the history of the city, from his 1963 *Origins of Modern Town Planning* (*Le origini dell-urbanistica moderna*; see Benevolo, 1975) to *The History of the City* of 1975 (*Storia della Città*; see Benevolo, 1980) and his *European City* of 1993, gives a broad and insightful historiographical account of

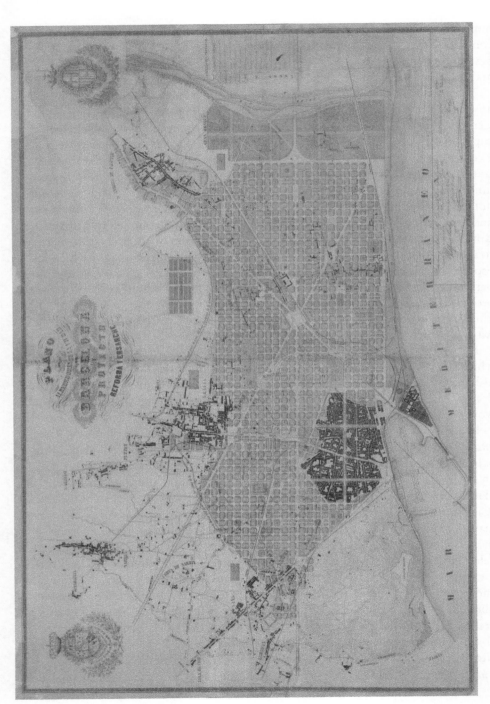

Figure 1.2 Ildefonso Cerdá, Plan of the surroundings of the city of Barcelona. Project of its Reform and Extension, 1859

Source: Arxiu Històric de la Ciutat de Barcelona. Reproduced with permission from l'Arxiu Municipal de Barcelona

the city. Yet he also tends to give Haussmann the privileged role in the creation of the modern paradigm, despite his awareness of Cerdá's work. Although his intentions were to expose a link between the political and the urban, his lack of detailed knowledge of Cerdá allows him to generalize the conditions of urbanization that arose from Haussmann, concluding that 'town-planning fell largely within the influence of the new European conservatism' (Benevolo, 1975: 110). If broadly true, this sentiment, however, enables a traditional leftist position that pits liberal reformism against royalist conservatism – a position that, at this point, offers little help in articulating a more profound relationship between the political and the urban. For both of the aforementioned authors, Haussmann's reconstruction of Paris is contrasted with many of the early nineteenth-century developments in London. Indeed, much of the works inaugurated by Haussmann were influenced by the various innovations already in place in London's sewerage systems and street design, and the insinuation that the model for modern urbanization was forged out of an amalgam of the two is hard to miss. Françoise Choay's compact volume, *The Modern City: Planning in the 19th Century*, reiterates this point, characterizing urbanization of the industrial era as strictly following one of two models: 'the open city, like London, which was free for unlimited expansion, and the closed city, like Paris, bounded by ancient walls' (Choay, 1969: 15). Despite her acute knowledge of Cerdá (Choay, 1997), and even opening with an account of his invention of the term *urbanización*, Choay too falls in line with the traditional narrative treating the specifics of Haussmann's work as a generalizable template of modernity.

Indeed, the canonical history of the modern city is a history of objects, rather than one of thought; outcomes and influences, rather than systems and power structures. That it oscillates between nineteenth-century Paris and London, suggesting concurrent forms of urbanization at work in Vienna, Barcelona, Brussels, Florence and others, should not surprise us. At times implicitly, at others, explicitly, historians and urbanists have largely accepted and continue to repeat the narrative that the history of modern urbanism began with the reconstruction of Paris at the hands of Haussmann, whether painted as villain or hero. Paris was perhaps Europe's most important city of the time, and, because Haussmann's work was so radical and indeed influential, other developments of urbanism tend to fall under his shadow; we are compelled to remember what influenced him and what was influenced by him. As a result, for the historians, urbanists and architects taking either term as an object of study, the history they describe tends to stress the spectacular, the oppressive and the romantic, reflecting the scandals and escapades of Haussmann and Napoleon III and drawing on the vast literature that emanated from Paris's painful transformation. In this way, such a generalized extrapolation of the project carried out by Haussmann into a modern, universal *urbanism* must therefore also account for its many contradictions, its innumerable peculiarities: Haussmann's project emerged, it must be remembered, out of an idiosyncratic political configuration[1] and benefitted from an erratic and complex economic model – contingencies that shaped his project through and through and that could hardly be made universal. This may either provoke urban historians to retreat from any attempt to theorize urbanization as a singular paradigm, emphasizing instead its contingent nature, or it permits them to generalize the atypical. Furthermore, such an ingrained history also produces claims about its present. As David Harvey noted, '[today's] global scale [of urbanization] makes it hard to grasp that what is happening is in principle similar to the transformations that Haussmann oversaw in Paris' (Harvey, 2008: 30). Although this may not be entirely untrue, and the work of Haussmann is indeed influential in the history of the modern city, this convenient simplification permits a gap to propagate unnoticed within it. It is in the recesses of this gap that the foundational, theoretical work of Ildefonso Cerdá lies in obscurity.

Part of the reason for this is that Cerdá's project, unlike Haussmann's, remained incomplete, and he eventually left Barcelona frustrated and was consigned to poverty. The reason for this can only be understood if we recognize that the enormity of his *oeuvre* is not composed of several individual projects, but rather consists of multiple facets and stages of a singular, unified work, the aim of which was to thoroughly transform the very idea of the city itself. This project began not with a theoretical sketch, but rather with a political plea. In 1851, as a prominent young civil engineer, Cerdá made what would be his first impassioned speech to Parliament, lambasting the state of Spanish cities and the infrastructural backwardness that had persisted in Spain as a result of political neglect. It was a speech that set the scene for Cerdá's lifelong critique of state politics that would underpin his subsequent work. Between 1855 and 1859, he drafted the plan for the Reform and Extension of Barcelona, on which he based his first theoretical work, *Teoría de la construcción de las ciudades* (*The Theory of the Construction of Cities*; Cerdá, 1991 (1859)). In 1861, after being commissioned to work on a plan for the reform of Madrid, he accompanied this project with a further theoretical treatise, *Teoría de la viabilidad urbana* (*Theory of Urban Viability*; 1991 (1861)).[2] By 1867, Cerdá dedicated himself to what would become his magnum opus: the four-volume *Teoría general de la urbanización*. Only the first two volumes were published, Volume I providing an extensive 'historical' foundation for the concept of urbanization, and Volume II, a painstakingly meticulous statistical analysis of the actual 'facts' of the urbanization of Barcelona – an effort Cerdá saw as mandatory to justify the theoretical with the empirical. Alongside his efforts to plan Barcelona, which he was commissioned to do, he saw that what was increasingly necessary was to provide a unitary theoretical and, thus, universal basis on which modern society as a whole could flourish. This progress would be accomplished by employing the virtues of technology and science to construct a new conception of the city in which democracy and urbanization would proceed, hand in hand, to emerge from the ruins of political absolutism into the interconnected space of liberal universalism. As we will see, this body of texts reveals the great foresight Cerdá had in thinking about urban space, bearing concepts far more profound than the aestheticized boulevards of Haussmann and predating theories from Howard's garden city, to experimentation in the development of linear cities, to various strategies of decentralization championed by Le Corbusier (1987 (1929)), to Ludwig Hilberseimer's 'Groszstadt-architecture' (2013) and his notion of the 'open city' (1960), to a type of thinking that would be later described as 'regional planning'. Even more recent tendencies such as landscape urbanism and urban agriculture can find their template in Cerdá's theoretical proposition of 'ruralized urbanization', which we will discuss in the pages that follow. As Françoise Choay argued, some of the most renowned theorists of urbanization, even in the case of progressive urbanists such as Tony Garnier (1989 (1918)), Le Corbusier or Constantinos Doxiadis, endorse projects that merely replicate some basic moves and patterns of problem-solving within a framework predefined by a clearly Cerdian conception of urbanization (Choay, 1997: chap. 6).

Only recently has Cerdá's work begun to gain recognition internationally. By the mid 1970s, after the fall of Franco's regime, Cerdá emerged from historical oblivion through the efforts of various Spanish and Catalan architectural journals to publish and expose his work. In 1976, the Colegio de Ingenieros de Caminos (College of Roadway Engineers) launched an exhibition of his work and life. Following this, an illuminating review of his work was carried out by the architectural journal *2C Construccion de la Ciudad*, which published a special issue in January 1977 dedicated to the work of Cerdá. In its most daring article, 'Perspectiva y Prospectiva desde Cerdá: Una Linea de Tendencia' ('Perspective and Prospective since Cerdá: A Trend Line'), Augusto Ortíz roots Cerdá at the beginning of a history that extends through Arturo Soria y Mata, Le Corbusier and Hilberseimer (Ortíz, 1977). Directly after this publication, the *Architectural Association Quarterly* published an issue featuring a review of Cerdá's work and life, exposing it to an anglophone audience for the first time. Urbanist Joan Busquets has dedicated much of his historical assessment of Barcelona to writing about Cerdá, placing his *Teoría* as the basis for modern urban planning (Busquets, 2006). Choay's seminal work of 1980, *La règle et le modèle* (see Choay, 1997), made an extensive examination of Cerdá's written work, placing it firmly and critically in a genealogy of Western thought on the city. Since then, the literature on Cerdá has expanded, in particular in Spain. Between 1993 and 1994, a major exposition entitled 'Cerdá: Urbs i Territori' was organized in Barcelona, following which Electa published an extensive anthology of Cerdá's writing edited by Arturo Soria y Puig, an expert on the figure. In 1999, this book was translated into English and remains the single most comprehensive collection of Cerdá's work in English to date. Most recently, Italian philosopher Andrea Cavalletti published his thesis entitled *La citta biopolitica*, which offered a critical account of Cerdá's plan for Barcelona following Foucault's work on security – a study revealing the strikingly contemporary relevance of Cerdá's conception of the urban to modern politics (Cavalletti, 2005).

Despite these developments, Cerdá's work continues to remain a marginal and rather reduced contribution to the established histories of the city. The recent unearthing of his vast work has produced largely uncritical, and at times completely positive, responses (with the exception of Choay and Cavalletti), in which Cerdá is cast as a socially conscious reformer concerned with equality and the working class, or as an advocate of architectural minimalism set in a geometrically rational urban grid. This is accentuated when he is compared with the conservative, imperial figure of Haussmann, seen as fighting for the interests of the bourgeoisie and bound up with the political excesses of an illegitimate empire. In such light, the uncritical embrace of Cerdá the reformer helps to perpetuate the perspective that urbanization is a 'natural' phenomenon that can only be tamed by enlightened, rational, socially conscious reform. Paradoxically, what is missed in the praise of Cerdá's 'humanitarian' efforts to distribute political justice and economic opportunity to all classes of society is the *political* nature of the space he proposed itself – the radical constitution of a new, universal space of economic production and biological reproduction that would replace both the city and territory altogether. As we shall see, Cerdá's project, unlike those of any of his contemporaries, aimed to be universally reproducible – a spatial machine embodying and specifying economic, legal, administrative and political frameworks through which to restructure the basis on which humanity is to organize itself: 'Rurizad lo urbano: urbanizad lo rural: . . . *Replete terram*'.[3]

Cerdá's texts are the central objects with which this chapter and the following are concerned. Although the physical extension and reform of Barcelona may be a model for urban design to this day, the actual outcome is a co-opted, reduced version of Cerdá's original plan, and much of the actual regulations over which he laboured so intensively were never implemented. Indeed, far more important than his work on Barcelona, and almost entirely overlooked by urban and architectural historians, is his theoretical work. This body of work stands as a unique contribution that puts in check the entire history of 'the modern city' and, more importantly, sheds a particularly trenchant light upon the urban as a category of modern and contemporary space and its subtle relationship with the political. This relationship is what this book looks to explore in detail. The purpose of this chapter is to trace the intellectual scaffold on which Cerdá's project was built so that, in the subsequent chapters, we may critically interrogate the spatial, technological and political implications it had for the ascendance of liberal capitalism and the construction of the nation-state.

Indeed, Cerdá's radical conceptualization of space remains one of the most prescient and far-reaching political projects of the modern era. The *Teoría*, together with the partial realization of the Reform and Extension of Barcelona, are built upon a sustained critique of the state that draws on the history of Enlightenment discourse to stage a call to rid the world of the remnants of political abstraction and the excesses of state power. In this sense, his work should be seen less as an affirmative modernism than as an effort to *complete* the project of Enlightenment itself, realizing its principal concerns for the first time in the production of a new, universal spatial order. The product of Cerdá's critique was the proposition of a radical, uniform projection of the domestic spheres of labour, reducing the composition of space to an ordered system of what I will call 'functional separation' – an organization defined by spaces of economic production and those of biological reproduction. This new differentiation, broadly standing in for former divisions between private and public realms, was meant to structure the entire composition not of the city, but of what he called the '*urbe*', a new logic of space, infrastructure and architecture spanning from the large-scale division between networks of circulation and spaces of rest down to the mechanisms that would pertain to the most intimate, inner constitution of subjectivity. Cerdá managed to radically fold the transformation of life itself into the emergence of the *urbe*, mirroring its divided nature across all its scales and inscribing a new *domestic* make-up on to the formal, the biological and what he called the 'transcendental' modes of a new urban experience. To accomplish this ambition, Cerdá set out to create a universal 'science' of urbanization, whose object – the *urbe* – he intended to make reproducible across the entire surface of the Earth. Yet, for all of his attempts to constitute a new form of knowledge, because of its structure and the complex of external bodies and forces that *urbanización* required, this 'science' bore the seeds of its own demise, dissolving into, on the one hand, an assemblage of norms and regulations and, on the other, a governmental mechanism aligned with the forces of capital. In other words, Cerdá's project ultimately called for the construction of a vast and anonymous machine of governance, the political decisions of which emanated under the cover of an ever-expansive, normative legal aggregate, the correlate of which was the materialization of a uniform grid of governmentally managed processes of production and reproduction. The space he imagined gains resolution not so much as a formal entity, but rather as a continuous, expansive space-process governed by this new administrative–legal totality.[4] Although Cerdá can be credited neither with fully realizing this project in Barcelona, nor for writing its first by-laws (which in many cases were indistinguishable from his theoretical proposals), his conviction of the political spirit of his time allowed him to construct a model ahead of its time, anticipating a simplified version of the legal, administrative and governmental apparatuses that would accompany a global paradigm of capitalist urbanization more than a century later.

The aim of this chapter is not to recover the work of Cerdá for the sake of 'rectifying' the history of the modern city or that of urbanism. Rather, its intention is to tie Cerdá's work to a deeper intellectual and political history in which the transformation of space is immanent. From this point of view, the examination of Cerdá's theories provides grounds on which to establish the contemporary relationships between politics and space that reside in the urban. As early as 1967, the words that rounded off Leonardo Benevolo's *Origins of Town Planning* remain pertinent today: 'the facts call for a new confrontation of the respective programs of town-planning and policies, to try to bridge the gulf that opened between them a hundred years ago. This is the task that faces us today' (Benevolo, 1975: 147).

SITUATING THE *TEORÍA*

There is no question that Cerdá's work belongs to the history of modernism in both its form and content. His writing exudes an urgency that could only speak in the name of the modern, and the ideas that he developed are fit for a secular, progress-obsessed liberalism echoed by architects, urbanists and social reformers of the twentieth century.

Published in 1867, the same year Marx would also publish *Das Kapital*, Cerdá's *Teoría general de la urbanización*, like *Das Kapital*, draws on a universalist idea of history in order to illuminate a revolution yet to come – a sentiment underlined by the outbreak of the Glorious Revolution just a year later. More comprehensive than any of his previous writings, the *Teoría*'s aim – to establish a universal model of space that would replace the city – is supported by an extensive history and conceptual justification of *urbanización*: it draws from its history in order to vindicate the invention of what Cerdá calls an 'urbanizing science'. Volume I is composed of four books: 'Origins of Urbanization', 'Development of Urbanization', 'Analytical Examination of the Actual State of Urbanization' and the 'Historico-Philosophical *Raison d'être* of Actual Urbanization'. The entire volume can be divided into two halves, the first two books establishing the prehistoric 'origins' of urbanization and the history of its 'natural' processes, and the third and fourth establishing an account of urbanization as a general, concrete theory based on its 'actual' existence. This division opens the symmetry between what we now refer to as *urbanization* on the one hand and *urbanism* on the other: natural process and normative science, past and future. The symmetry of this work is centred around a faith in technologies of mobility – a historical yardstick that Cerdá extends back in time to construct what he calls the 'philosophy of history of urbanization'. This philosophy of history describes five succinct epochs in human history, each marked by the development of a new mode of locomotion that, in turn, determines a new form of urbanization. The tone of the text expresses the coming of a new world and a new civilization of scientific invention and technological capacities that promise to unite humanity. With the birth of telecommunications and the railroad, Cerdá announces the arrival of universal human communication. Indeed, the principal process that has driven historical urbanization turns out to be unlimited circulation and universal communication, or *'vialidad'* (a neologism he invented, which we shall return to shortly).

Although this work embraces a fully forward-thinking sense unique to the modernist tradition, it also bears the marks of an older tradition, which is seen in Cerdá's argument in the way he addresses his audience and in the moral confidence of his claims. Indeed, perhaps more than to figures such as Le Corbusier, Milyutin or Hilberseimer, his work speaks with greater urgency to Hobbes, Rousseau and Kant. In this way, Cerdá's work should be seen not only in the context of modernism, but more as an attempt to *recover and complete the project of the Enlightenment* begun two centuries earlier. Throughout the entirety of his various *Teorías*, the Kantian influence over his thinking is hard to overlook: from his emphatic drive towards a universal conception of history, to a shared desire for the establishment of perpetual peace, to an unwavering belief in civilization governed by the rational force of law, even to certain notions of 'Nature' as caretaker of civil society. In fact, the notion of urbanization itself can stand as the realization of Kant's notion of cosmopolitan purpose – a drive that is innately inscribed within human beings' capacity for technological invention. But, in addition to following a line of Kantian thought, what becomes apparent is that Cerdá's work is also an *attack* on it. His *Teoría* is at once a theory for a future spatial order *and* a critique of the Enlightenment itself – a criticism based on the perceived failure of Enlightenment thought to advance its goals into the material formation of human cohabitation. Just as Kant had responded to the growing political crisis of the late eighteenth century with his subtly provocative 'Was ist Aufklärung?',[5] Cerdá's *Teoría* responded to the mid nineteenth century's own plight – a period in which a general crisis, felt most acutely in the city, had reached a tipping point – for which, he envisioned, a 'bloodless' revolution lay imminent. The city that Cerdá's generation across Europe had inherited was undergoing compounded crises due in large part to its incapacity to handle the rapid expansion of capitalism, the restructuring of labour and the massive influx of people from the countryside that this forced. This was acutely so in Cerdá's own Barcelona: if revolutionary activity is an indication of the general discontent brought on by the conditions of industrial capitalism, Barcelona was one of the most intense centres of what Cerdá would flatly categorize as crisis.[6] For him, the medieval walled city represented much more than obsolescence: in the face of an economically mobile society, with its technological advances in communication and locomotion, it was a major political impediment inside which the population suffered:

> This constitutes a state of constant strife reproduced daily, hourly, every minute, a struggle in which we are all involved, and one we all feel – everyone, because the circumstances of our cities are such that at every step they erect obstacles to everyone in everything, and these hamper the action of the individual, whatever his class or social position. (Cerdá, 1867: 13)

Yet this crisis could not be remedied through enlightened thought alone, and, indeed, as Cerdá gripes, none of the Enlightenment's philosophers had ever considered the material configuration of the city to be both the fundamental cause of such social ills as well as the site of its cure. 'The reason for all this', Cerdá asserts, 'is that nobody can yet have hit upon the true root and fundamental cause of that deep malaise which afflicts modern society' (ibid.: 11–12). More than a simple claim, with this remark Cerdá places himself and his task firmly in the line of Enlightenment thinkers from Hobbes to Rousseau (at whom this particular comment is directed) and up through Kant. For Cerdá, it was a simple misdirection of efforts: the technological, material and moral improvements of *the city*, together, were the true source of public happiness and wealth. So, just as Kant answered Rousseau's critique of society, so too would Cerdá, taking the task a step further. He poses:

> [I]s civilization the true cause of his physical decay, which produces the moral enervation deplored by Rousseau and those of his school? This question is worthy of careful examination. [...] We roundly deny that civilization, the child of man's innate sociability, the cause of his progress and improvement, and the general expression of his destiny on earth, could ever be an enemy of man nor, consequently, cause him the slightest physical, moral, or intellectual harm.

To which he unhesitatingly responds:

> If, instead of allowing his lively imagination to ramble through the fields of an unachievable theory, the Geneva philosopher had focused within himself, and examined and studied within the depth of his heart and his very dwelling the genuine cause of that deep disgust [...] arose from the privations and terrible conditions of his existence – to which he was condemned by the then-excessive concentration of Paris [...] which he attributed to such a different origin. And then, with his great talent, instead of a social contract, he would have dreamt up a system for organizing cities better, which without depriving the individual of society's legitimate enjoyments, would have allowed him to live with the independence and comfort that provident nature, which he praised so highly, tends to provide. (Cerdá, 1991 (1859): §§ 4–8)

In spite of this, Cerdá saw that, in his time, the culmination of the Enlightenment was imminent. 'Everything in this century is leading towards the disappearance of limits, towards a general merging, and everything tends towards peace' (Cerdá, 1991 (1859): § 1036). This was a result not of enlightened philosophy having found purchase in a mature society, but rather of the maturation of technology. Following Kant, Cerdá would build a theory of space whose material, technological consummation would finally realize the goals of the Enlightenment. As his theory of urbanization was based largely on the human capacity for mechanized locomotion, he saw the railway as the harbinger of the enlightened era approaching. He, like many other liberals of his time, placed endless faith in the development of technology, which he believed could, in itself, overcome outdated political divisions, joining humanity in the shared interest in the infrastructure of international exchange. '[T]he man of today, active, daring, entrepreneurial man [. . .] that man who in a few brief instants travels vast distances; the man who in just minutes transmits and circulates his news, his instructions, his commands right around the globe' (Cerdá, 1867: 595). Beyond this spirit of commerce that, like Kant, Cerdá championed, he also saw that such interconnecting technologies could join neighbouring states in a single, fraternal, cosmopolitan unity. In both cases, such unity would be capable of permanently neutralizing political conflict:

> Railways and electric telegraphs will harmonize language, weights, measures, and currency. They will destroy ancient hatreds between nations and secure the supremacy of universal peace, sweeping away that class antagonism which arises from the need for civilization and justice. They will give rise to the harmony needed between the different classes within society. (Cerdá, 1991 (1859): § 1435)

What, for Kant, would be fulfilled by the creation of a federative association of states – a 'universal state' 'whose sole intention is to eliminate war'[7] – would, for Cerdá, be achieved by the act of *total* urbanization. Both saw each configuration as the culmination founded on a universal arrangement in which relations between individuals would be bound by natural law. Only such configurations would civilize humanity, removing it from the burden of the state of nature completely and, thus, heralding the long-sought era of perpetual peace. For Cerdá, however, the creation of such laws would never suffice without the physical, concrete correlates to them. What would stand as the ultimate achievement of an enlightened human race for Kant – the 'right to the earth's surface' – remained at a moral, legal level. For Cerdá, such a goal could only manifest itself as a single, interconnected urban network spanning the entire globe. Urbanization, as Cerdá imagined it, adhering to the rational prescriptions of a unitary theory, would prove to be the only solution, for he deduced that, originally, 'urbanization and civilization sprang from the same principle – man's sociability' (Cerdá, 1867: 50). The aim of urbanization is to establish the actual infrastructural relations and communications among individuals. For him, human locomotion sat at its heart as the rudimentary cause of all urbanization; circulation was the fundamental core and historical force that drove the process itself. And it was with this technological prerequisite that Cerdá was able to neatly fold almost all of Kant's goals of the Enlightenment into the single project of *urbanización*.

> When railways have become commonplace, all European nations shall be one single city and all their families one, for their forms of government shall be one, their beliefs one, they shall speak one language, and their customs shall be similar. Then the revolution will be over and will have fulfilled itself, with neither victims to grieve, nor destruction to mourn. One power shall have replaced another. The creations of science shall have defeated the spirit of discord, and law alone will rule because it will be the expression of the

general will – and when laws are so based, they have no need for bayonets.
... However you view them, railways are the censors of vices, the generators
of enlightenment and, ultimately, the regulators of the social fortress.[8]

Like many of his liberal contemporaries, Cerdá viewed politics with suspicion.
He saw it as a corrupted category of human activity crafted alongside the absolutist state and distorted by its many injustices. Much of his work directly opposed
politics with a sense of moral objectivity, echoing a sentiment that had been instituted by eighteenth-century thought and underscored in particular by Kant in the
appendix to his 'Perpetual Peace'. What Kant accomplished here was at once to
separate morality from politics and to subsume the political under the moral.
Morality, as he writes, is 'a collection of absolutely binding laws by which our
actions *ought* to be governed' (Kant, 1991: 116; original emphasis), a group of
universal laws that constitute the 'theoretical' face of right. The other face of right,
the so-called 'applied' right, or politics, is a realm whose shrouded secrecy so easily
gives itself over to intrigue and deception. The integration of the two is possible
only by privileging the absolute, universal and *natural* laws of morality above the
'practical' execution of politics, because morality is the only realm capable of capturing a general principle of right. In this way, morality should, therefore, guide the
diurnal implementation of an enlightened politics. For Kant, it is the idea of
publicity, the carrier of public opinion, that bridges the two forms of right: 'All
maxims which *require* publicity if they are not to fail in their purpose can be reconciled both with right [i.e. moral laws] and with politics' (ibid.: 130; original
emphasis). In other words, *publicity*, as understood by the eighteenth-century
'enlightened' bourgeoisie, was the effective currency of the emergent 'public sphere'
and one that is capable of binding politics to natural right, forcing it to 'remain in
harmony with the aim of the public through making it satisfied with its condition'
(ibid.). In so many of Cerdá's writings, Kant's influence is indisputable, and this
makes all the more clear his frustration that the Enlightenment had lacked a proper
project equivalent to *urbanización*: 'For me, moral and material improvements,
taken in their broadest acceptation, can and should be considered the genuine
sources of public happiness and wealth. Without them, all institutions will fall into
discredit' (Cerdá, 1851: § 888). In another passage, he continues,

> [T]he solution to a portion of social, political, moral, health, and economic
> issues that the modern spirit of discussion and free examination has pro-
> moted, depends to a large extent on the manner of building a new city, or
> reforming, transforming, and extending those that past generations have
> bequeathed us, full of vices and defects which make life painful. (Cerdá, 1991
> (1861): 51–2)

Echoing Kant's discourse on morality, Cerdá mirrors the form of critique that
Kant made in his political writings while also paying tribute to the (political)

force of the public sphere. In these passages, the material world provides precisely an apolitical, *moral* site from which an otherwise political problem can be approached. By sublating a political critique within a physical diagnosis, Cerdá forces the political to be assessed in moral terms.

Yet what Cerdá presents in his writing is something other than a reinterpretation of the goals of the Enlightenment. For what appears in such thinking is an entire conception of history that emerged around Kant's 'Was ist Aufklärung?' In the first case, Cerdá is clearly conscious of his audience. Although soliciting politicians and administrators, his writings aim rather to be heard by and to indirectly mobilize another far more powerful ally, namely bourgeois society. His work, therefore, must not be seen solely as a set of persuasive engagements with the state's administrators, but rather as a contribution to the free discussions of an active, liberal 'public'. In this sense, his work takes root within a certain defined community: Cerdá's writing, like Kant's seminal essay, identifies a distinct 'we', marking his affiliation with a certain elite bourgeois society. Furthermore, clearer than this 'we' is the temporal framework of Cerdá's writing. His myriad condemning remarks on the 'vices' bequeathed to his generation by planners and politicians who belonged to the absolutist past point to a period from which Cerdá is attempting to radically break. For him, the central question is not how he stands in relation to some tradition of constructing the city in the past, but rather the conditions of his *present*. Only by breaking with the weight of a despised, anti-'progressive' tradition is he able to comprehend a notion of the present. Through such a Kantian perspective, Cerdá grasps what appears to him as a universal crisis, the source of which is the city. In this perspective, Cerdá is able to situate his present within its own temporal framework, which bears a unique past and future. In other words, by capturing the full singularity of the present moment, he is able to see the totality of the project that awaits him.

Michel Foucault has shown that, when Kant asked the question, 'what is Enlightenment' – when he 'discovered' the present as such – another question simultaneously emerged: 'What is Revolution?' (Foucault, 2010). Bound up with the notion of progress that the enlightened present inaugurates is the event that will fulfil its self-prescribed goals. Kant, like many others of his time, thus welcomed revolution as a *sign* of progress, despite its actual accomplishments or failures. Cerdá embraces revolution in the same way, yet is more emphatic about its imminence:

> It is certain, self-evident, palpable, utterly beyond dispute and acknowledged by everyone that human society has for some time been undergoing a profound but silent commotion whose effects must be a general upheaval of the established order, one of those cataclysms by which Providence allows mankind to halt briefly on its march towards self-perfection in order to resume its majestic advance with new strength and zest. (Cerdá, 1867: 11)

Indeed, the Revolution, as Foucault observed, was itself 'the completion and continuation of the very process of *Aufklärung*' (Foucault, 2010: 18). Furthermore, the cycle put into play by the process of Enlightenment, where progress is marked by the arrival of revolution, creates a history whose temporal trajectory becomes at once linear and cyclical. Revolution is 'a sort of event whose content is unimportant, but whose existence in the past constitutes a permanent virtuality, the guarantee for future history [. . .] and continuity of a movement towards progress' (ibid.: 19). In other words, what the Enlightenment gave birth to was a particular temporality – a way of thinking that inscribed the future in a critical analysis of the present; a prognostic form of thinking that arises once the present is detached from tradition.

If Cerdá's work is a critique *of* the Enlightenment, it is also one fully embedded within its aspirations, embracing its maxims and principles. It is no surprise, therefore, that Cerdá's writings adopt a temporality unique to the Enlightenment. In this sense, a particular attention is required to analyse the question of the past in Cerdá's *Teoría*. How, for example, do the 'origins of urbanization' that Cerdá claims to have discovered fit within the critique he clearly subscribes to? Unsurprisingly, the form that the *Teoría* most closely adheres to is the principal form of political critique also established in the tradition of Enlightenment thought: the utopian critique.[9]

The utopian critique, which was born in the obscurity of eighteenth-century secret societies and became a potent weapon against the state, is both the flip side of the Enlightenment and the product of the philosophies of history on which it is based. As a form of criticism, its political claims remained secretly couched within the various philosophies of history, and thus its ability to criticize the state depended on the moral innocence from which such narratives came. The integration of morality and politics that Kant achieved, and that Cerdá drew upon in his quest for the origin of urbanization, can be seen as the end of a process based on the *opposition* between the two – one that was initially set in motion by Thomas Hobbes and culminated with the realization of the Revolution in France. Whereas, for Hobbes, the conception of the absolutist state answered his central philosophical problem of lasting peace, for Cerdá (and for Kant), it would be precisely *because* of this apparatus that peace remained impossible to achieve as a lasting condition. This reversal resulted from an internal void that Hobbes placed at the heart of the state, namely a zone of neutrality the existence of which made possible the absolutist state – one that would eventually be the precondition for its downfall. For Hobbes, it was human nature's subjectively pure will to peace that remained the very element that paradoxically provided the conditions of possibility for civil war. Thus, left to its own devices, civil war would permanently accompany the human condition. For this reason, the only way to achieve peace was to transfer the moral commandment of universal peace from natural law to state law, thus justifying Hobbes's call for a 'Commonwealth'.

The uniqueness of Hobbes's state theory is a split he imparts that runs down the Commonwealth's centre, separating permanently public and private interests from one another, thus severing the state from its subjects. The protection provided to the subjects by such a gulf was a promise the price of which was their tireless obedience to the sovereign's will. This fissure at once rendered private interests politically irrelevant and, for that reason, created an opening in the space of the state that secretly remained absolutely free. 'The Law is the publique Conscience – private Consciences . . . are but private opinions' (Hobbes, 1986, quoted in Koselleck, 1988: 37). As Reinhart Koselleck writes, 'Hobbes's man is fractured, split into private and public halves: his actions are totally subject to the law of the land while his mind remains free, "in secret free"' (ibid.). This is the contradiction: the interior zone of political neutrality was guaranteed to be free insofar as it remained a secret, an interior realm of darkness where private censure provided sanctuary for a certain freedom to express itself in apolitical, moral judgement. The internal division of modern subjectivity would be the source of the genesis of mystery that would unfold in the interstices of society and the nascent states of eighteenth-century Europe. By excluding natural law morality from the state's concerns, it opened a space in which private opinions founded on moral judgement could circulate, providing scaffolding on which a growing moral indictment of the state could take shape. This would take on concrete meaning in 1690, when John Locke, in his *Essay Concerning Human Understanding*, would counter Hobbes by identifying three kinds of law: divine, civil and the law of opinion or reputation. This third law, introduced by Locke, provided a space for individual moral judgement where personal views of vice and virtue could become a public concern the character of which would take the form of the law (Locke, 1849 (1690)). This retort to Hobbes would undermine the clean distinction he had prescribed between public conscience and private opinions by allowing the latter to acquire the force of law, thus indirectly politicizing them. By the eighteenth century, with Kant, '[c]riticism, which had initially kept itself apart from the state so as to be able to function unimpededly, now, by virtue of its own authority, eradicated the boundary line it had once drawn' (Koselleck, 1988: 121), allowing itself to surface under the guise of the universal. It was precisely under this cover of the universal that the utopian critique was born, for '[t]o justify itself at all, the critique of the eighteenth century had to become Utopian' (ibid.: 10). Coloured by moralist self-assurance, the scattered yet empowered bourgeois elite, withdrawn into a network of private, obscure societies, gained a sense of power in the appropriation of Utopia. Increasingly, it was through utopian histories founded on the innocence of an imagined past that the iniquities of the state's official history could be revealed. Utopia, deployed as universal history, proved a very powerful resource in undermining the historical foundations on which the legitimacy of the absolutist state rested and would eventually assist in its downfall. Furthermore, by remaining autonomous from the concrete political reality of the state, it became clear that evoking a particular Utopia as a critique also prefigured a very particular outcome. Utopia, in this way, could be integrated into the planning of the bourgeois future (ibid.).

More than half a century into the nineteenth century, the temporal symmetry that structures Cerdá's *Teoría* nevertheless reveals itself as a signature of such a critique. By removing himself from the burden of tradition – and thus history – Cerdá is able to isolate his theory within an autonomous temporal framework the geometrical centre of which is his present. The privileging of the present affords Cerdá a degree of freedom, which he asserts in unfolding in equal proportions both past and future: 'The study and knowledge [*the past*] of an illness [*the present*] would be useless if they did not lead to recognition and application of the remedy [*the future*]' (Cerdá, 1867: 17). The city, for Cerdá, appears as a kind of *pharmakon*, both the cause of society's illness and its cure. This is the conceptual crux on which the *Teoría*'s utopian symmetry is able to stand. The assuredness of a theory untethered to an asymmetric tradition affords Cerdá the ability to construct what he confidently calls 'la filosofia de historia de la urbanización' (ibid.: 677), a likely reference to Condorcet's 'great epochs of history' (Condorcet, 1795), which seeks to characterize the history of urbanization as a linear, progressive process determined completely by each epoch's technological means of human locomotion. From here, he is able to project this 'history' on to a concrete future of urbanization the 'cause' of which is *vialidad*, a neologism he uses to signify an inherent propensity of the human being for unlimited circulation. Because all of history can be explained through urbanization, the present condition of the city stands as a historical perversion, the result of centuries of abuse committed in the name of the absolutist state – itself a deviation from a 'truer' history of human movement and dwelling. Cerdá's task is, therefore, to seek the 'origin' of urbanization outside history altogether, locating the first stage of urbanization in an invented stage of prehistoric human society. 'Urbanization', he writes, 'starts with the first man, whose patrimony matters little to our objective, for we know, as we have said elsewhere, that wherever man was, there was the first element or germ of urbanization' (Cerdá, 1867: 49). Its origin is in the need for shelter. Indeed, Cerdá is able to avoid the complexity of history by placing urbanization at the heart of 'humanity', as a product of a natural human instinct for sociability. '[W]ithin urbanization, man's intelligence and noble sentiments have found the necessary development to create the elements of civilization' (ibid.: 45). By drawing a line from an innate human instinct – an origin 'so noble, so ancient, so exalted' (ibid.: 41) – to the need to construct dwellings, Cerdá offers the genealogical preconditions for urbanization, the capacity of which leads necessarily to 'civilization' itself: '[Urbanization] led him to the state of society; it taught him culture; it civilized him. In a word, to the urbanization which was born with him, and grew with him, man owes everything he is, everything he can be in this world' (ibid.). Unsurprisingly, civilization for Cerdá does not come through the artificiality of political formation, but emerges instead in the natural, immanent fact of human cohabitation. This alternative history overflows with the virtues of a reality governed by nature's Providence, revealing that, throughout catastrophes and barbarian invasions, although civilizations may be destroyed and reborn, urbanization 'has always marched forward along the path of its perfection, on which the Almighty chose not to set limits as he had done for the waves of the Ocean' (ibid.: 49–50). By construing urbanization as an innate *social force*, and making it the precondition for civilization, Cerdá depicts it as a kind of secularized *katechon*,[10] the history of which cleverly displaces any historical power that achieved the same, whether it be the Holy Roman Empire, the Catholic Church, the modern state or simply the political. The founding 'constitution' – the *origin* – of urbanization (as with the Third Estate's constitution) is constructed around a fictional and ahistorical figure, the *noble savage*. This marks the utopian foundation of Cerdá's theory.

If the question of an 'origin' signals a latent utopianism in the *Teoría*, Cerdá's notion of 'ruralized urbanization' leaves no doubt. Ruralized urbanization is a concept, central to his work, that at once describes the 'original', 'historical' form of urbanization and defines a structure on which the prospective science of urbanization can in turn be based. This essentialist concept articulates itself on the single-family dwelling, linked to others by a network of paths, the connection of which to a pastoral nature is immanent in the configuration of the whole. It was an effort, like many of Cerdá's, to unite opposites and overcome 'obsolete' barriers. In this case, he casts the division between the rural and the urban as a remnant of the absolutist state and its oppressive, artificial limits: 'The word *términno* [limit], the only one we know, refers solely and exclusively to the administrative jurisdiction which was marked out many centuries ago, motivated by reasons quite different from those that should govern the staking out of a genuine field of action for each *urbe*' (Cerdá, 1867: 471). According to his philosophy of history, urban expansion across a rural landscape was the very essence of 'historical' or 'ruralized' urbanization, and would, therefore, return as a meta-principle aimed to reunite the rural with the urban in a kind of hybridized, expandable network of dwellings stretching endlessly across the surface of the Earth. It would designate a system of occupying land no longer bound to the outdated dichotomy of city and country: ruralized urbanization would be a model of *both* city and country – *both* culture and nature. 'Until now, enlightenment and civilization have displayed a resolute tendency to *urbanize* the countryside. The time has now come to think about *ruralizing* the major cities' (Cerdá, 1991 (1861): § 697; original emphasis). It would be a vehicle for perfecting the human species by delivering measured doses of nature to each individual, distributed family, thus also uniting Rousseau with Kant. As Françoise Choay comments, 'ruralized urbanization' 'is both effect and cause of progress, but it is also the point of departure for the fall from grace, the origin of a process of corruption which has henceforth perpetually undermined our built environment' (Choay, 1997: 251).

Cerdá's appeal to understand history is not to say the consistencies held in a sequence of chronologically situated events: 'history' even in its most reductive sense. Rather, 'history' appears as a selective series of transhistorical 'social practices', which together constitute an imaginary past. As Choay notes, 'Urbanization symbolizes each one of these constellations: it shows us its face, as it were, its most directly perceptible identity' (ibid.: 239). Urbanization, because founded on a set of universal human capacities, becomes, for Cerdá, a lens through which to view the progress of history. For this reason, the symmetry between past and present can be read rather as a utopian identity, where original past and teleological future are conceptually indistinguishable from one another. The present, in contrast, forms a kind of oppressive hinge around which the two oscillate in their attempt to recover the glorious past in the construction of a planned future. This is, perhaps, why so much of Cerdá's writing in the *Teoría* seems to slip from one temporal frame to another, often losing track of past and future, history and projection.

Reading the *Teoría* as a kind of fulfilment of the Enlightenment gains clarity only if we recognize its utopian form. By the nineteenth century, this form of critique had become at once less politically risky, as it had been in the eighteenth century, and far more pervasive within liberal society and state politics through its various practices and institutions of reform. Cerdá's use of this in itself is thus not surprising; what remains striking is the degree to which he carries the legacy of Utopia into an adamantly pragmatic programme for the planning of *urbanización*. What separates the *Teoría* from an eighteenth-century critique is that its lack of censure comes in equal proportion to its pretences in proposing a fully realizable and universal science. Its critique of the state no longer hidden, what remains obscured is rather its Enlightenment ambitions: that the fulfilment of urbanization provides an ideological *and* material narrative by which humanity can recover the *bon sauvage*, within a distinctly *urban* society, covers over this fact. The conversion of Utopia to a fully-fledged programme to reorganize the inhabited world would have implications beyond the mere principles and pretences of achieving such a project. Indeed, as it will be shown in what follows, if Cerdá's project proposed a kind of fulfilment of the Enlightenment, urbanization would invert the concept of the city, revealing a radically new, formless space in which neither public nor private spaces properly exist as such, and where an entirely new set of distinctions would arise instead. The fulfilment of the Enlightenment, it would seem, is the *making domestic* of the world.

NOTES

1 Although many historians attribute all of Paris's transformations to Haussmann, as his *Mémoires* flaunt, a somewhat overlooked part of this history is that the project was initiated with a plan sketched out by Louis Napoleon, many of whose attributes are contained in Haussmann's reconstruction. See Jordan, 1995.

2 Although meaning 'viability', '*viabilidad*' is a neologism invented by Cerdá derived from *via*, meaning 'way' or 'road'. *Viabilidad*, or *via*-bility, is distinct from, yet similar to, his more commonly used *vialidad*, which, loosely speaking, refers to circulation. This term will be examined in greater detail in following sections.

3 'Ruralise the urban, urbanise the rural: *Fill the earth*' appeared on the frontispiece of Cerdá, 1867.

4 A full account of Cerdá's efforts to rename the city the *urbe*, as well as a technical and spatial overview of this concept, will be given in the next chapter.

5 Kant's 'An Answer to the Question: "What is Enlightenment?"', in Kant, 1991: 54–60.

6 As Engels states about Barcelona, it 'has seen more barricade fighting than any other city in the world'. See Engels' 'The Bakuninists at Work', in Marx and Engels, 2001.

7 From 'Perpetual Peace: A Philosophical Sketch', in Kant, 1991: 129.

8 I. Cerdá, 1857, 'Proyecto de ferrocarril Granollers a las Minas de San Juan de las Abadesas', unpublished notes, pp. 4–5. Quoted in Cerdá, 1999: 63.

9 In using this term I draw on what Reinhart Koselleck has described as the 'indirect political critique'. See Koselleck, 1988.

10 *Katechon,* from the early Greek meaning literally that which holds or possesses, is more readily translatable as an entity with the capacity to withhold or restrain. Traditionally, Paul's use of *katechon* (2 Thessalonians 2:3–9) has been interpreted to refer to the Roman Empire or the Roman emperor himself, restraining the advance of the anti-Christ or *eschaton*, but can equally be attributed to the Catholic Church or the modern state. See, among others, Agamben, 2005, and Taubes, 2004.

$$\text{2}$$

Vialidad and the Anatomy of the Urban

It is one thing to map the intellectual legacy from which Cerdá's project drew its convictions; it is another to interrogate that project in the conditions of his contemporary world and the possibilities it afforded to collective imaginaries that Cerdá fed off. In the shadow of the Napoleonic wars, the continuing struggles between liberal bourgeois society, as well as its more radical offshoots, and the ruling monarch in Spain unleashed a series of wars and revolts that extended throughout the nineteenth century. Despite the turmoil, after the French Revolution, the nation-state in Europe had gained a certain inevitability, in part by setting in motion a new relationship between the state and society that would be felt everywhere, particularly in Spain. This relationship, or rather the aspiration to a kind of merging of the two, was, we might say, a corollary of eighteenth-century utopian planning.[1] With the new freedom of the learned societies who initiated the Revolution, an entirely new configuration of political relations would emerge, and the division between public and private life, marked by Hobbes's *Leviathan* and coloured by a century and a half of absolutist rule, would undergo a major transformation. If, following Kant's 'Was ist Aufklärung?', the distinction between the public and private spheres had begun to erode, by Cerdá's time, the dominant tendencies pointed not only to the disappearance of both (Habermas, 2010), but to the emergence of new spheres. Replacing them, as Hannah Arendt has shown, were categories neither strictly private nor public: 'the social' and 'the intimate' (Arendt, 1958).

A DOMESTIC WORLD TO COME

The rise of 'society', for Arendt, marked the emergence of the modern age (ibid.: 28). It is a sphere the birth of which was nurtured in the depths of necessity of the private family, and its claims were made in the name of its newly 'public' character. As Arendt writes, '[s]ociety is the form in which the fact of mutual dependence for the sake of life and nothing else assumes public significance and where the activities connected with sheer survival are permitted to appear in public' (ibid.: 46). In other words, society is what appears when all life processes are channelled into what had previously been the public realm. It is a figure with a degree of political power that would come in equal measure to its ability to appear apolitical. Forged in the private sphere, its political constitution would remain concealed under its moral, universal pretences, and thus the 'public' sphere that emerged out of it would be coloured principally by its self-assured sense of moral virtue.

The rise of the 'social' would set in motion a silent yet pervasive process that would transcend all existing political forms, from its liberal proponents to the reactionary royalists opposing it, transforming the terms by which politics and economics were understood and inverting the previously overt dominance of sovereign power over market matters. Its claims to provide a form of life in which neither domination nor sovereignty need exist also eliminates with it, at least in theory, the need for the state altogether. More importantly, it would create a new subject of government that was simultaneously also its object – a strange contortion that resulted from the imagined removal of the single, horizontal, *political* cut dividing public and private realms (conceptually separating the state and its subjects), and the subsequent interpenetration of the two (Schmitt, 2007). With this, bourgeois society would demand equal status with the state, requiring that the state's role be changed from one of sovereign protection to one of managerial administration.

Yet it was not simply the unification of these two spheres that the emergence of society accomplished. The notion that society was founded upon moral universals meant that it was to enclose everyone in a totalizing condition of collective participation: in its promise to provide humanity with its 'civilized' correlate, society also implicitly demanded the unvaried commitment of each individual to its moral premise. As Koselleck writes, '[m]oral totality deprives all who do not subject themselves to it of their right to exist' (1988: 152). This totality would unfold in what Arendt describes as 'the image of a family whose everyday affairs have to be taken care of by a gigantic, nation-wide administration of housekeeping' (1958: 28). And it would be to this new order that Cerdá's theory of urbanization would most closely correspond.

'CONTENT AND CONTAINER': THE URBE

For this emergent order, the task as Cerdá sees it is to abandon the category of the city and to create a new form of existence based on an organized system of human cohabitation and circulation. Echoing the universality of a world conceived under the social, Cerdá's initial task is to find a name for a space congenial to such a totality. 'The first thing that occurred to me was the need to give a name to this vast swirling *mare-magnum* of persons, of things, of interests of every sort, of a thousand diverse elements' (Cerdá, 1867: 29), a condition in which the apparent independence of these innumerable elements belies the singular unity they share as a complex of pre-existing social and economic relationships. He embarks on an etymological study to identify a contemporary term accurately describing the 'great beehives which are commonly called cities' (ibid.: 28), doing away with the outdated, politically burdened term *ciudad* ('city'). *Ciudad* is a term rooted in the Latin *civis* and the broader concept of *civitas*, terms that express the Roman legal and political status of citizenship in relation to a particular city – a civic community related to a particular town or city. *Civitas*, like the Greek *polis*, thus denotes a political form of life consecrated by shared rights and duties and made possible in the collective habitation of a city – a term that endows the city with a symbolic capacity the meaning and form of which follow the concept. *Civitas* can be distinguished from the Roman *urbs*, which refers to the material agglomeration of buildings, things and infrastructure that resulted from the necessities of managing the domestic sphere[2] (similar to the *oikos*, in the case of the Greek city-state – the space of domestic, economic management that stands outside the political community of the *polis*).[3]

Working his way through the Middle Ages, Cerdá concludes that *ciudad* and all its derivatives are 'strictly speaking, no more today than an expression of what [they] were in other eras, and not what they are today' (ibid.: 479). He describes the city as a figure established in the distant past: 'In ancient days [. . .] the *city* [*ciudad*] represented the first administrative, political, and social hierarchy. The *city* [*ciudad*] was the centre of civil and political administration of an extended region or area that included various townships, towns, villages, and hamlets' (ibid.: 476; original emphasis). In this way, Cerdá couples the term *ciudad*, as a *political* entity, with a scalar hierarchy of authority, relating each subsequent designation to the various spaces and territories it controls. Not only the *ciudad*: indeed, the town, place, village, burgh, ranch and homestead are also politically (over)determined designations for human settlement. For Cerdá, in the 'public's judgement' of nineteenth-century European life, such distinctions and oppositions were to now be rendered meaningless. And, because they were meaningless, the new name for cities – one that would necessarily remain universal, generic – would prefigure their structural transformation.

Cerdá turns to the Latin root *urbs* upon which to base his new term. Yet, in order to fully abandon *ciudad* as a term too tightly bound to political forms of life, he must prove the etymological veracity of *urbs* over that of *civis*. He reasons that the distinction between *urbs* and *civitas* is actually a false one, and that the two really have, over the course of history, come to mean one and the same. Superimposing a moral meaning over a political term, Cerdá argues that *civis*, far from denoting a political status, signifies rather 'a moral sense referring to man' (ibid.: 4). Accordingly, at one point in history, '*urbanus* and *urbanitas*, urban and urbanity, came to have a moral acceptation, analogous if not identical to *civilis* and *civilitas*' (ibid.: 505–6; original emphasis). In other words, the problem appears to be that, 'over the course of time, the content and container must have become mixed up and considered as a single entity' (ibid.: 485). By rendering the two terms identical, in a move mirroring liberalism's flattening of state into society, he was able to argue that *urbs* is the more correct and genuine root for the name of the spatial order fit for modern life. Stripping any vestige of political meaning from the modern city, for Cerdá, became simply a matter of etymology: because 'the city' for Cerdá was in fact reducible to 'the material part of the grouping of buildings' (ibid.: 505), *urbs* most effectively identified the root ambition of his project. Thus, he proposed to replace the word *ciudad* with the term '*urbe*':

> For what the word *urbe* does [. . .] is to express simply and generically a group of buildings with no specific relationship to its size, which is of almost total indifference for the application of the fundamental principles of urbanization, nor to its hierarchy, since urbanizing science can recognize none. (Ibid.: 30–1)

The *urbe* is universal: it pre-exists and is presupposed by the historically and politically overdetermined 'city'. Its singularity stands in contrast to the apparent ambivalence of meaning Cerdá identified in the term *civis*, denoting *both* 'content' and 'container'. Overlooking the dialectic meaning at the heart of the term *civis* – the fact that it is precisely the political status that precedes and gives meaning to the material form of the city, thus rendering clear the distinction between itself and the apolitical sphere of domestic life restricted to *urbs* – Cerdá's reductive analysis allowed him to invert the hierarchical relationship between the two terms, subsuming *civitas* into *urbs* by imagining that their distinction from one another is a kind of historical lapse. His notion of 'content' and 'container' belies a revealing intention that he had in naming the *urbe*: by choosing a universal, 'timeless' term, he effectively nullified the distinction between 'content' and its 'container'. That is to say, in reducing the city to its bare, material immanence of cohabitation and movement, dismissing the political forms and relationships that constitute it, he defines the *urbe* as a completely depoliticized entity; the *urbe* is in fact *without* political form and, therefore, transcends any such category and the history to which it is bound. The 'container', as it were, is displaced by the fact of an assemblage of buildings and the infrastructures connecting them – the 'content'. In a word, the *urbe* is the *condition*, rather than form, of cohabitation and exchange for society.

If the figure of 'society' was the new object/subject of the budding nineteenth-century nation-state in Europe, then its epistemological and administrative correlate, as Foucault has shown, is the population (Foucault, 2009). This category of both scientific and governmental consistency figures heavily throughout Cerdá's work, and, unlike his contemporaries, who drew upon statistical descriptions of the population in planning cities, Cerdá was the first to have completely conceived his *urbe* around the category of population.[4] Tellingly, before finally arriving at the term *urbe*, Cerdá considered using the name '*población*' (Cerdá, 1867: 480), a term that in Spanish means at once 'population' and 'town'. Together with the individual, the population would form the second of two poles that constituted both the subject of the *urbe*'s calculations and the object of its spatial management. Demographics and statistics, for Cerdá, would offer radically new material for the city's representation, and the notion of a singular, quantifiably knowable population drove Cerdá's entire thinking. 'Successful planning requires that, in each case, the circumstances of the locality, its centres of life, the needs of general *vialidad* and the number, habits and customs of the population should be studied' (Cerdá, 1991 (1861): § 688).[5] Indeed, one of the prime tasks of the *urbe* would be to mathematically distribute the population and its necessary services across the territory.

THE NETWORK OF WAYS

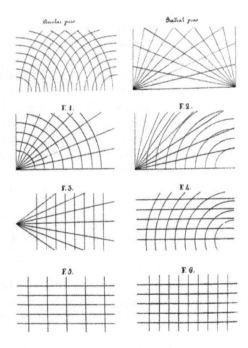

Figure 2.1   Ildefonso Cerdá, Composite diagrams of various configurations of networks of ways, 1861

Source: Cerdá, 1991 (1861)

With the 'cause' of urbanization founded in *vialidad*, and the population as its main subject/object, Cerdá rationalizes an appropriate form in which to design the *urbe*, which he calls the 'network of ways'. He considers both radial and orthogonal grids in depth, as well as several variations thereof. In the end, he decides in favour of the square grid, noting that the pure radial system is applicable only for systems of 'artificial' domination and subordination, systems in which 'the administration is everything, and the populace are its mere instruments' (ibid., § 675). Moving from urban form to population studies to the needs and concerns of the individual, Cerdá declares that, '[j]ustice demands that the interests of each and every one to be attended to and respected with all possible equality' (ibid., § 688), and that the square grid is, therefore, justice itself. Considering equality in all manners and from all perspectives, from justice to the provision of services, to land value, to, of course, access and *vialidad*, Cerdá reasons that the square grid is the only distribution and form of a 'network of ways' that will suffice for the needs of the *urbe*. But, more than merely a matter of equality, the square grid has another fundamental capacity, which is to allow for perpetual expansion. Cerdá reasons this claim with reference to his notion of 'ruralized urbanization':[6] because he views cities as artefacts that have artificially separated the 'rural' from the 'urban', in turn giving rise to the general crisis in which it finds itself in the mid nineteenth century, by recovering 'ruralized urbanization', the city will overcome itself in a limitless outward growth:

> From this spreading of the population derives another moral, material, political and social benefit [. . .] namely, the benefit of *ruralizing* our major towns. [. . .] This ruralization, with the moral and material perfection of civilized man [. . .] shall easily be achieved by the adoption of the *square grid* system. It is essential that no artificial limits be set on the enlargement of towns. [. . .] By not limiting the space where a town may be laid out, grow, and extend with the assistance of the square grid system, spontaneous dispersal will naturally ensue, and consequently the ruralization which, beyond improving conditions for social man, will provide the resources for any paternal and protective administration. (Ibid., § 697; original emphasis)

'Ruralized urbanization' could naturalize society, according to Cerdá's philosophy of history, while also destroying all political boundaries that constituted the 'contained', walled *ciudad*. The use of a square grid presents itself as a kind of scaffold of civilization, but, by allowing ruralized urbanization to take its course, it will also provide the physical correlate of a new form of government – one whose dominion is the population for which it provides a kind of 'paternal' administration (Cerdá, 1859b: § 8). In contrast to this, Cerdá sees what he calls 'deplorable magnificence' in the excesses of the baroque urban plazas and squares that continue to be built by his contemporaries. He finds the iniquity of this condition in the trade-off between the splendour of design and the utility and comfort of necessity. It is the mentality of contemporary city design, he claims, that permits lavish, grandiose and 'artificial' urban forms in which the natural flows of *vialidad* are hindered and the family dwelling's conditions lead to poor health (Cerdá, 1867: 801). By privileging the poles of domesticity and economy, he recognizes that, 'in our present day urbanization, they [plazas] would have no logical reason to exist, since strictly they offer no benefit for the leisure of the inhabitants, provide no greater space for urban movement, and they are not even used as a market anywhere' (ibid.: 175). Departing from the symbolic, Cerdá would opt to functionally distribute the plaza by atomizing it throughout the *urbe*'s grid, designating plazas at each street intersection and inside the space of each city block. If need be, he would even allow an entire city block to be converted into a plaza, as long as it would not spill out of the block's boundaries, disrupting the network of ways. Lacking any formal centre, for the *urbe* the notion of a 'centre' translated instead as anywhere the most intense manifestations of *vialidad* emerge naturally; for this reason, a centre could not be prescribed in plan, and any attempt to do so would be merely a formal gesture. Nevertheless, as the port and the railway station were 'gateways' connecting the single *urbe* to the great universal *vialidad*, it made the most sense that, in Cerdá's understanding of centrality, these hubs of infrastructure could constitute the most natural 'centres'.

Beyond his critique of baroque mannerisms or his scorn for centralized urban systems lay a critique of form itself. Form, for Cerdá, was the meaningless remnant of a corrupt mode of repressive politics. The indulgence in something as 'useless' as form represented an embodiment of injustice itself. The formal design of the grid was a minimal investment in a 'form' that would absorb all others in its cool rationality. The grid would be exceeded by the natural processes that its formal singularity cultivates. And, because expandable, the grid was a form that dissolved in itself: if form is the deplorable representation of the 'container', the grid was the form most suited for the 'content' in its revolution against it. 'For urbanization, form is nothing; adequate and perfect satisfaction of human needs is everything' (ibid.: 50).

Of course, this is not to say that Cerdá succeeded in annihilating the 'container' altogether. In place of the subjective, political signification he found in the *ciudad*, the 'science' of urbanization, the pursuit of human perfection and, of course, the 'great universal *vialidad*' all constitute a kind of new, essentialist *raison d'être* for the *urbe*. Although he wanted to rename and reinvent the city as '*urbe*' in order to strip it and all subsequent designations of their political signification (the 'container'), by discovering the 'true' essence of the *urbe* in *vialidad*, he, as it were, discovered its 'repressed container', one that, in a Kantian sense, emerges from within the human being. In this way, Cerdá too managed to unknowingly conflate the container with its content, simply rewriting the terms of its new engagement. But, in so doing, what Cerdá would accomplish with the *urbe* would seek to replace the city entirely with a continuous social space reducible to the constant flux between movement and respite – between the 'network of ways' and the individual family dwelling. This transformation would be accomplished by designing the *urbe* against a hard-line determinacy of absolute circulation – the principle of *vialidad*. In a causal manner, he would conceive of this new space from the overall network of urban *vias* ('ways', or streets) to its blocks occupying the spaces left over between the *vias*, and on down to the intimate reconstruction of domesticity itself.

VIAS

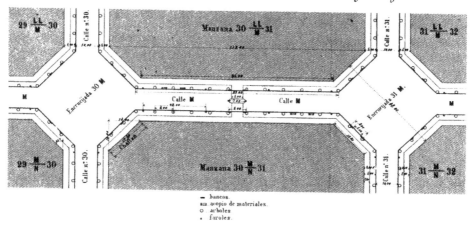

Figure 2.2 Ildefonso Cerdá, Disposition, dimensions and nomenclature of streets, blocks and crossings, 1863

Source: *Necesidades de la circulación y de los vecinos de las calles con respect a la via pública urbana y manera de satisfacerlas (Needs of traffic and of the Street Residents in Relation to the Public Urban Way, and Manner of Satisfying Them)*

At the heart of the network of ways was its elemental unit, the *via*, which would invite the same theoretical intensity that Cerdá applied to the network itself. After all, the concept of the *via* was a reflection of the overall concept of the *urbe*. He made a distinction between the *via*, or 'way', and the *calle*, or street: 'We have to remember that the street [*calle*] is composed of ways and buildings, the box formed by the ground and the collateral walls. [. . .] The way for transit and the houses for dwelling must, therefore, come together in order to form a street [*calle*]' (ibid.: 534). Cerdá's concept of the *via* would be founded on the 'box' made by the adjoining buildings that framed the street. But, beyond the concrete fact of their configuration, Cerdá's *via* would seek to conceptually unify the two elements. With the boundary between the rural and the urban having been 'artificially' preserved by the politics of the state in the form of the 'city', so too had the street (*calle*) been sundered from its 'natural' conviviality with the dwellings and buildings that occupy its flanks. From its 'history', '[i]n addition to being a public way, the street [*calle*] is an appendage and a most indispensable accessory to the house which rises at its side' (Cerdá, 1991 (1861): § 1861). The idea that the street was an essential 'appendage' of the private dwelling was one he developed as part of his theory of urbanization, which is to say along the parameters springing from the 'origin' of urbanization itself. The street, according to Cerdá, was initially a private access way. In its original sense, it is not simply that which facilitates public access, but, 'more immediately, more primitively, and more primarily, to provide entrances and exits, air, light, and views to the residents of those houses which delimit the street on either side' (Cerdá, 1867: 320).

His conception of the *via* is one that at once reduces it to mere utilitarian terms (i.e. the *calle* alone), while simultaneously expanding its surface of utility to dispense the very sustenance of life to the population. The *via* becomes a channel of substance, both material and phenomenological, that sustains the biological lives of the urban inhabitants. It is, like all components of the *urbe*, a technology. Not surprisingly, this principle would return to give justification to the actual economic planning for the construction of an *urbe* in his so-called 'economic base' of urbanization,[7] where the funding for any street was to be taken on by the property owners of adjacent buildings and limited to the length of street equal to that which abuts each owner's property. Finally, he distinguished several classes of *via* that corresponded to specific scalar types of movement that the *urbe* would engender: 'The first [*vias*] are transcendental because they are derivations or a continuation of the great universal *vialidad*; the second are urban because they are at the immediate service of the *urbe* as a collective whole; and finally the others are individual, intended to satisfy the needs of the individual and the family' (ibid.: 345–6).

LINKS

Having established the overall form of the network of ways as the square grid, and the concept of its most elemental unit, the *via*, Cerdá created a system by which the grid in abstraction could be practically realized as a totality of interconnected street sections, or 'links'. With what he called a 'graph', he laid out the hierarchy of individual categories that would need to be systematically coordinated in order to construct a complete 'network of ways'. Starting with the 'grid of ways', it considered both the 'horizontal' and 'vertical' layouts, denoting roughly plan and section, respectively. Most important was the coordination of the two, which he achieved through a system by which to both measure and set limits for street gradients, based not on site specificity, but rather on generic parameters to optimize conditions of *vialidad*. Following the 'grid of ways' was the 'cross section' of the street, setting limits and parameters for its width, number and designation of carriageways, pedestrian ways, drainage channels, building easements, as well as specifying variable street widths as a mathematical function of their distance from the city's centre.

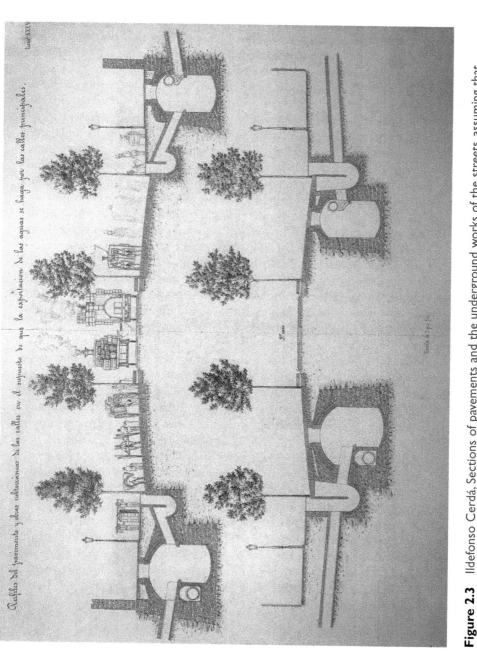

Figure 2.3 Ildefonso Cerdá, Sections of pavements and the underground works of the streets, assuming that export of the waters would be done through the principal streets, 1855

Source: Cerdá, 1991 (1855): Plate XXXVI. Reproduced with permission from l'Arxiu Municipal de Barcelona

Most important for the design of the 'cross section' was the separation of ways contained within a single section of street: 'A town's good conditions of *vialidad* are not achieved by having many roads, but by taking care that the ones it does possess have the breadth needed to contain not a single way, as has happened until now, but a genuine system of ways arranged according to current needs' (Cerdá, 1991 (1859): § 1213). The street must be divided and arranged according to lanes for specific, independent modes of transportation. Further, he would specify the category of 'ground', which provided restrictions and specifications for the types of pavement appropriate for these various traffic types, as well as formulas for the distribution of trees across the length of each street type. He would designate architectural categories to restrict lateral encroachments and projections from blocking the sky from the streets, all in the name of preserving the optimal conditions for circulation. Cerdá scrutinized porticos, awnings, even eaves and roof overhangs, considering them to be outdated and harmful to the general state of *vialidad*. 'Any balcony, any gallery, in a word, any class of projection beyond the general wall of a facade or over the alignment of the street is an abuse which should be proscribed because it constitutes an easement upon the public way' (ibid.: § 1002). The segregation of 'overground' and 'underground' would be the site of particularly intense thought and design of the links, constituting for Cerdá the principal categories in which public health would be affected. 'Overground' specifications would be made that permitted the maximum exposure to sunlight and circulation of air, reaching the maximum number of dwellings, while also satisfying the physiological needs of pedestrians in the street; 'underground' designated the system of public sewerage and water supply.

Cerdá dedicated a great deal of effort to the latter, designing a complete, interconnected sewerage system, with everything from underground street drainage networks to entire hydro-pneumatic systems, all of which were fully integrated into the layout of the street links. *Vialidad* applied just as much to the movement of people, capital and things overground as it did to the fluids of biological necessity underground. It was here that Cerdá imagined both the solids, liquids and gasses that sustained life, as well as those that were harmful to it, would flow incessantly. Because this followed the principle of *vialidad*, he designated this pipework within the category of *vias*, just as he had done for the channels of human circulation above ground. As a whole, the exhaustive 'graph' considered and described the totality of the street – an entity the design and purpose of which would be unencumbered circulation both above and below ground, a coordinated technology aimed at realizing the *vialidad* of people and goods, as well as that of the waste products and resources of life.

NODES

As the first law of *vialidad* is continuity of movement (Cerdá, 1991 (1861): § 811), it follows that the design of *encrucijadas*, or 'crossroads', of *vias* (what he would later call *nudos*, or 'nodes') – the famous chamfered street corners of Barcelona – would need considerable attention in order that no single traffic flow disturbs another. In the same manner as he set out the parameters for the links, Cerdá dedicated an equally thorough effort to specifying those by which nodes would be designed. As critical points in the overall network of ways, he framed the conception of the node around the ambition of 'universal connectiveness', where, for traffic movement along any given street, 'neither the passing pedestrians nor the vehicles should ever, from the start point to the end point, suffer any interruption along their way' (ibid.: § 802).

Recalling Cerdá's hierarchy of different *vias* (individual, urban and transcendental), the notion of *vialidad* becomes perhaps clearest in his thinking on the node: *vialidad* is the means by which the individual family can be incorporated in the universality of limitless movement – a fluid hierarchy of ways that, as it suggests, connects the family with the technological 'transcendence' of capital. It is from this aspiration that Cerdá worked out the geometry and surface area of the chamfered nodes. He did so, in usual form, by scrupulously 'graphing' in detail all of the possible formations of nodes, together with the traffic patterns that are generated, following the basic principle of *vialidad* so that no individual should ever have to forfeit his or her own freedom of movement to another's. As with his conception of the street, the node, too, had a historico-philosophical foundation, in which he recalls a barbarous time when the design of buildings was pitted against the circulation of the street by necessity:

> Since that era in which the progressive though slow development of traffic made itself felt quite strongly, an open battle has been observed between traffic and building. [. . .] This battle has lasted until the present day, and persists in part, even though [. . .] between traffic and buildings there exists an indestructible solidarity. (Cerdá, 1991 (1863): § 85)

This 'battle' resulted in bottlenecks and choked crossings, presenting traffic with innumerable obstacles.

In a particularly well-known drawing published in a leaflet in 1863 depicting an array of *encrucijadas*, Cerdá in fact conflates this history with his own design, reflecting the seamlessness of his utopian historicity. From the first (upper left-hand image) to the last (lower right) drawing, this image depicts the node in its genealogical evolution, beginning with the 'historical' condition of obstruction and continuing through a progression where Cerdá, seemingly without recognizing it, inserted his own array of possible configurations of nodes for the future *urbe*. Somewhere between historical speculation and pragmatic reasoning, Cerdá portrays both buildings and infrastructure as caricatures locked in 'battle', which, over time, through the virtuous 'conquest' of *vialidad*, reveals the precursor to the chamfered street corner as the natural outcome: 'So it was that, while property amused itself building its aristocratic lookouts, democratic *vialidad*, which no

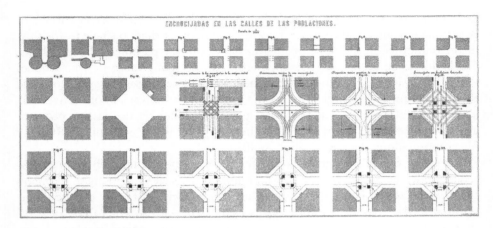

Figure 2.4   Ildefonso Cerdá, Crossroads in the city streets, 1863

Source: Cerdá, 1991 (1863)

longer fitted into the old intersections, eroded away the sharp corners to create a cylindrical tube shape from the street level' (ibid.: § 92).

As with his historical justification, Cerdá projected the concept of the chamfer through a series of calculations in order to arrive at an ideal configuration. In so doing, the node, the ample dimensions of which allowed for both horse-drawn and pedestrian traffic to pass without disturbing one another, revealed spaces left over from the multiple lanes of traffic. In these islands, Cerdá began to design multiple configurations of mini plazas and pedestrian 'refuges', which he viewed as communication zones between the different footways. On these various configurations Cerdá designated various configurations of kiosks and stands that would, in some cases, attend to the domestic needs of nearby residents; in others, they would provide the sites to house municipal administration and street workers, storehouses for maintenance tools, posts for local police and first aid, and letter boxes, telegraph stations and even designated places for street performers. He would even go so far as to recommend a clock be placed at every intersection as a means of promoting unyielding efficiency. 'Time is money, and clocks are necessary to be aware of time wasted and time well spent' (ibid.: § 40). In all cases, the various nodes, each with their specified purpose and allocations for services and security, would be evenly distributed throughout the grid by a calculation based on the population and its various traffic flows. In this way, he was able to subsume the notion of a public plaza under the terms of *vialidad*, while also giving it a sense of utility. Furthermore, in addition to merely specifying a logical distribution of built elements throughout the city, Cerdá went on to specify the way in which they are all to function within and along the ways, distinguishing between the various types of movement and the needs each type requires. He even realized a means by which to integrate the old city with the new extension in the concept of the node, in what he called 'articulation plazas' (Cerdá, 1991 (1861): § 834) – nodes that would institute 'the regularity of the modern in the very heart of the ancient' (ibid.: § 836).

Between the graphing of the links and the nodes, Cerdá presented a system by which to organize the main principles that would, for him, constitute the *urbe*. It considered and described all of its layout, hierarchies and relationships, integrating the minutest details into its general configuration and calculating each of its elements as a function of *vialidad*. 'Everything in this animated picture presented by the movement and life of the *urbes*, everything has a character or different type and nature' (Cerdá, 1867: 609). Providing a location or placement schema for every single type of built element in or along the street, the 'graph' is the biopolitical equivalent of a Linnean system, as it not only proposes to describe everything that belongs to the urban realm, but also subjects it to a series of universal rules, prescriptions and restrictions. In short, it provides the infrastructural basis on which a single, generalized framework could be made for constructing an *urbe* anywhere. This represents an epistemologically new mode of spatial organization in its perspective as a science of technical specifications, if not simply in the scale and level of detail in which Cerdá fixed such prescriptions.

THE INTERVIA

If the need to regularize the *urbe* was played out in Cerdá's rigorous graphing of the vast 'network of ways', it would arise as a paradox that the spaces 'left over' by this network – the city blocks – would constitute the sites requiring far more scrupulous calculation, 'scientific' consideration and regulatory normalization: to supersede the concept of the city would undoubtedly mean the redefinition of the concept of the city block, or *manzana*, as it is commonly called in Spanish. Indeed, consistent with his thinking, Cerdá's first task when confronted with the *manzana* was to seek a new name for it. As he had given clear priority to the network of ways (thanks to his concept of *vialidad*), he would view the city block as the residual space that resulted from the designation of the network – a 'void' 'isolated' by it. Hence, the name '*intervia*'. From a space 'left over', this element, for Cerdá, would come to take on the greatest importance, forming what he came to recognize as the fundamental unit of the *urbe* itself (Cerdá, 1991 (1861): §§ 127, 847).

His utopian reasoning led him to etymologically speculate that *manzana* had originally been spelled *mansana*, coming from the Latin *manere*, meaning 'to remain', and bearing other derivatives, *manso, mansio, onis*, meaning dwelling or house – an idea that helped to bolster the duality of movement and rest at the heart of his theory of urbanization. From here, he recovered the term *insulae* from Roman history, the root of which, *isla*, likens the city block to an island, isolated from others by the water that surrounds it (ibid.: 364–5). Despite his eventually abandoning this root as a proper name for the city block, the notion of *isolation* nevertheless would remain crucial to his understanding and designation of the concept of dwelling, in contrast to circulation associated with *vialidad*. As its name, '*inter-via*', suggests, the relationship between the block and its adjacent *vias*, or streets, was determined by the circumscription of the former by the latter (ibid., vol II: 691).

Although Cerdá initially considered the *intervia* to be a secondary, almost incidental, element, he came to realize that it in fact played a far more crucial role, constituting the site on which two critical areas of scientific concern for him coincided: the concern for continuous *vialidad* and the hygienist concern for public health. As the source of both general ills and the evils of society, the *intervia* would, for Cerdá, prove to be, at the same time, the source of its cure. This element of the *urbe* was the space in which Cerdá's immense statistical analysis of the population would find its architectural counterpart, as well as the technology through which a distributed and coordinated system for preserving human life could unfold. The *intervia*, if scientifically conceived, would transform domestic architecture into an interconnected biological system, placing life at the centre of the process of urbanization. Rather than the individual dwelling, it was the *intervia* that had proved to be the fundamental unit of the *urbe*, precisely because of its capacity as a *system* to sustain human life.

According to hygienist theories to which Cerdá subscribed, the principal factors that could affect mortality rates in urban areas were density, isolation, access to nature (gardens), sunlight and, first and foremost, air and respiration. Such thinking, influenced by French hygienist studies of his time – in particular that of Michel Lévy – led Cerdá to consider the *urbe* itself to be a kind of biological machine with a network of ways that would have to simultaneously administer the circulation of both the removal of contaminated air and the supply of fresh air. For this reason, Cerdá calculated the space of a dwelling not in square metres, as is typical, but rather in *cubic* metres, even adjusting his calculations by subtracting the volume of furniture. Cerdá considered contaminated air as a problem not only of the external, cramped conditions of the medieval city his generation had inherited, but also from within the human being itself, who, after inhaling, must then exhale contaminated air. He says, 'at night, the atmosphere we are obliged to breathe is nothing other than the breath of death' (Cerdá, 1991 (1859): § 187). Considering a person's exhalation to be the 'breath of death' (which he oddly associates with the night) – that the most basic rhythms of life are themselves toxic – reveals the extent to which a certain biological frame of mind had determined a new terrain of thought. By extension, the dwelling, for Cerdá, was both the site of life's rest and repose and also precisely the opposite: the primary source of toxins and disease. Thus, Cerdá posited that dwellings must also contain reservoirs of 'urban health', or gardens (Cerdá, 1991 (1861): § 902) – 'air tanks from which each of the houses is supplied' (ibid.: § 909) – in order to counter the deadly toxins emanating from within. Such areas, in combination with the broad *vias* he specified, would work in unison to carry away contaminated air (miasmas), replacing it with fresh. Strangely enough, however, he felt compelled to justify the necessity for a garden accompanying each dwelling not through biological rhetoric alone, but with reference to a utopian 'state of nature' in which individual dwellings once existed in isolation from one another. The garden was to be considered the 'sphere of action of family relations with nature' (ibid.: § 908). Indeed, given his philosophy of history, Cerdá identified the essential and most original function of the *intervia* as 'neither more nor less than the field of operation of family life and functions, that is to say, that area of land which may be considered appropriate for domestic purposes and to meet the needs of daily consumption' (Cerdá, 1867: 694).

The epidemics that Cerdá himself had witnessed during that period undoubtedly presented a new kind of biological terror with the potential to irrupt within the urban population and spread throughout it. Such epidemics were compounded by class privilege, where the rich could take leave of the city during bouts of disease, inscribing an image of disease on to the lower classes. Because of this 'threat from within', it became clear to Cerdá that the occurrence of epidemics was directly proportional to population density. Such biological crises were pivotal in Cerdá's thinking from the very beginning of his design for the Extension and Reform of Barcelona in 1855 and underpinned almost all of his theoretical work. Concerns for public health led him to pursue his vast statistical analyses that he engaged in in the 1860s and were also reflected in his design of the *intervia*. In no small way, statistics found its site of application in the *intervia*. Almost entirely from the viewpoint of public health, he would distribute in a purely mathematical manner the 'fills and voids' (by which he meant houses and gardens, respectively) 'by determining how much space the houses should occupy and what area would be suitable for their respective gardens' (Cerdá, 1991 (1855): § 111). Cerdá calculated this in the following formulation:

> If the gardens are considered as a means of providing copious light to the whole neighborhood, their minimum width must be equal to the maximum height of the surrounding buildings. If viewed from the perspective of ventilation, or as air tanks intended to supply and renew the air of the houses, they will have to contain an area equal to that which the houses occupy. [. . .] Thus, by way of conclusion, we can establish that the minimum area devoted to a garden can be represented by a square whose side will be the cube root of the product of the length multiplied by the depth and by the height of the bordering house or houses. (Cerdá, 1991 (1861): § 912)

Carrying forward this principle of isolation, Cerdá first proposed, in 1855, an urbanization composed of detached houses, which attempted to spread the

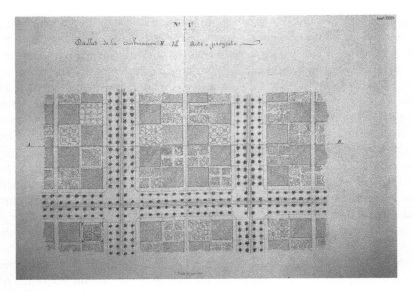

Figure 2.5 Ildefonso Cerdá, Details of the combination M. from the preliminary project for the extension of Barcelona, 1855

Source: Memoria del ante-proyecto del ensanche de Barcelona, Plate XXXIV. Reproduced with permission from l'Arxiu Municipal de Barcelona

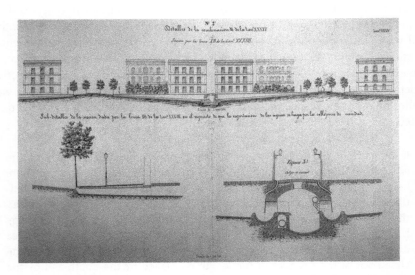

Figure 2.6 Ildefonso Cerdá, Details and sub-details for combination M. of the section cut by line AB in Plate XXXIIII [sic] assuming that the export of waters will be done by way of the neighbourhood alleyways, 1855

Source: Memoria del ante-proyecto del ensanche de Barcelona, Plate XXXV. Reproduced with permission from l'Arxiu Municipal de Barcelona

population out to a minimum density. At this point in his thinking, '[j]oining more than two houses to each other, and especially, completely closing off the space of an *intervia*, are monstrosities, incompatible with the culture of our century' (Cerdá, 1991 (1855): § 115).

Finally, by identifying the competing interests at play in the layout of the *intervia* (between the state, the municipal council, property owners and speculators, and tenants), he attempted to design it such that it could resolve any potential conflicts between them, balancing density and comfort, public health and taxation, profit and justice, and so on. In the end, these various interests, he reasoned, were reducible to interests either of economics or of public health – a conceptual distinction that reverberated throughout the *urbe*. These two concerns gave concrete form to Cerdá's design of the *intervia*. He concluded, after rigorous calculations (Cerdá, 1991 (1859): § 1497), that the ideal *intervia* that could mediate all these various interests should be between 110 and 120 metres a side. Integrating his statistical surveys into its plan, he sought in the *intervia* to achieve a model that would distribute the population across the territory, maximizing *vialidad* and the degree of isolation between dwellings simultaneously. Yet this could also be achieved in reverse: as hygienist theories of the time recommended a population density of 250 people per hectare, Cerdá inverted this figure to indicate an ideal unit of square metres of *urbe* per inhabitant, set at 40 (Cerdá, 1991 (1859): § 1500).[8] In other words, the *urbe* itself becomes a regularized substance, a service like any other to be distributed among the population. Finally, calculating street width, depth of the site, length of facade of each building, number of inhabitants per dwelling and his 40 square metres of *urbe* per inhabitant, and marrying these figures with those of the node, he arrived at the final form and dimensions of the *intervia*, at 113 metres per side, with its corners chamfered at 45° (ibid.: §§ 1498–1502). Additionally, the orientation of the *intervia* would need to be such that it maximized the exposure to sunlight, the 'life-enhancing' force. Ensuring adequate ventilation and countering the potential monotony of the grid, the *intervias* had to remain open, that is, with only two of the four sides occupied by buildings.

With such a configuration, as Soria y Puig and others have argued, Cerdá was able to create a 'language' through a combination of the various *intervias* and nodes (Cerdá, 1999: 281–90). Yet establishing a spatial language per se would engender a meaning for each set of *intervias*, which clearly was not Cerdá's intention. Instead, he strove to endow the grid with a kind of relative indeterminacy – a system that could accommodate *any* possibility and combination of the various *intervias* as long as they accorded with the primary geometries of the *urbe*. The architectural resolution of his *urbe*, as well as the determination of its programme, points of centrality, and so on, was relatively unimportant as long as the principle of *vialidad*, the 'cause' or urbanization, was upheld uniformly throughout. At the root of Cerdá's grid was a minimal condition of possibility for the urban, a minimal framework of rules that provided the overall geometric and hygienic functioning of his system and the distribution of its elementary parts. The grid was 'the most favorable to the traffic, expansion, good administration and governance of any great city' (Cerdá, 1991 (1861): § 707). Beyond the mere establishment of the grid itself or the circulation patterns its nodes prescribed, there was a large degree of indeterminacy built into his *urbe* from the perspective of the network of ways. 'In our view it is beyond all doubt that in drawing up the plan of a new city, the only thing that can be foreseen in its layout is the siting and importance of the major ways for ordinary and perfected [i.e. railway] traffic.' With confidence, Cerdá claims that any attempt to further determine the centres of urban activity in advance 'would be an attempt on the freedom and independence of the citizens' (ibid.: § 727).

Whereas this minimal condition of regulation pertained to the network of ways, it was the exact opposite for the *intervia* – the negative counterpart to the 'network of ways', the disposition and technologies of which were based on the permanent imposition of and *overdetermination* by municipal and state regulation. The *intervia*, for Cerdá, was the site in which the unification of the rural with the urban would take place, the locus of 'ruralized urbanization' and an 'instrument of general health for the whole population' (ibid.: § 1495). For this reason, despite (or because of) his liberal affinities, the *intervia* would also be the site for nearly unlimited administrative intervention in the name of public health. Proposing a 'Council for Health and Construction' (Cerdá, 1859b: § 57), Cerdá called for a body whose task was to balance public and private interests and to ensure that the construction of housing went hand in hand with the construction of and connection to the massive sewerage system below the network of ways, denoting an increasingly central interface between governmental and private realms. Additionally, he proposed that such an authority should oversee the overall construction of housing in accordance with an extensive set of by-laws, prosecuting those who 'trade in unhealthy housing'. He went on to outline his criteria for municipal intervention, placing first the head of the family who 'rules within the domestic [and ostensibly isolated] home', and '[t]he authority intervenes when families make contact, directs and regulates their relationship, and harmonizes their respective rights and interests' (ibid.: § 15). In other words, Cerdá articulates that the degree of isolation that exists between houses is inversely proportional to the degree of necessary intervention by municipal government. He clarifies this: 'the intervention of the authority becomes greater and more necessary because relationships, which create a portion of the interests and new rights affecting an indefinable number of individuals, increase' (ibid.: § 26). One can extrapolate from this that governmental authorities must intervene from the moment the urban is constituted. This apparent contradiction would drive a chasm into an otherwise uniform space, dividing the *urbe* down the middle and creating a space the unity of which, as we will see, is perhaps better described as a *bipolarity*.

ISOLATION

The success of the *intervia* in accomplishing any of its ambitions rested on its ability to remain at once isolated from the streets that circumscribe it while also integrating itself within the very same network for the circulation of air and supply of light and for its plumbing below ground. Cerdá invested heavily in working through this contradiction by conceptualizing a kind of buffer zone that would surround each *intervia* to achieve this delicate transition. With somewhat comical seriousness, it was a task accomplished by designing a pavement with ample width along with a perimeter fence that, together, would surround and thus protect the *intervia* from the incessant *vialidad* of movement that Cerdá imagined animating his *urbe*:

> But since the life of man, whatever his occupation or manner of living, is a constant alteration between stasis and movement, between rest and agitation, it is essential that alongside the very spaces intended for staying in, there should be *vias* constantly at his disposal to offer him passage to wherever he may attempt to go. And since the *vias* . . . do not always offer convenient and expeditious transit from the point of rest to the great *vialidad*, therefore, around the *intervias* unfolds another zone of roadways to be especially and inseparably at the service of the *intervias*. [. . .] In addition to transmitting movement between the *vias* . . . and the *intervias*, the path around the *intervias* has a further extremely important purpose which we must note, namely, to increase isolation. (Cerdá, 1867: 368–9)

In his effort to effectively depoliticize the city, Cerdá's *urbe* can be seen to annul what is perhaps its most political of spatial distinctions – that between public[9] and private worlds – replacing it with a single, universal space of *non-distinction*. This same ambition can be read across scales as well: the city and territory are to be smoothed out through a programme of 'ruralized urbanization'; the ontological distinction between 'interior' and 'exterior' that the state made absolute is obliterated in the international unification across boundaries that urbanization would help achieve, and so on. What we find, however, is that the dissolution of centuries-old boundaries and distinctions that Cerdá sought does not leave a seamlessly confluent spatial whole; far from it. Indeed, within Cerdá's work, we can see a whole new set of boundaries simultaneously being erected and distributed at a much finer grain throughout the elements and technologies of the *urbe*. In fact, the great emphasis Cerdá places on indeterminacy in the organization of the *urbe* as a whole (i.e. through its minimalism, non-centric orientation and apparent lack of limits), is compensated for by an *overdeterminacy* invested in a new set of membranes and thresholds that arise within this space, defining a new, more infinitesimal register of 'exterior' and 'interior' that appears, like everything else in the *urbe*, uniformly distributed across its domestic space: dwelling versus movement; urban versus rural, supply versus exhaust, economic transcendence versus biological necessity, and so on. In a broad sense, the new family of divisions split the *urbe*'s otherwise uniform, apolitical space down the middle, separating it into two distributed *functional* spaces: *spaces of human production and those of its reproduction*.

Despite Cerdá's attempts to unify space, his essentialist conception of the *urbe* belies this fundamental opposition that constitutes and conditions the *urbe* and seems only to be strengthened by each attempt to unify its constituent parts. This division can be seen within the plan of the *urbe* itself, composed of its two most basic elements: *vias* and *intervias*. Neither fully public nor private, each of these spaces – the space of *vialidad* and the space of dwelling – represents a new life function within the formless, domestic expanse of the *urbe*. It is as if the former category of 'public', which occupied the interface between subjectivity and sovereignty, is banished from the city forever, allowing its space to be reconstituted by the demands of a homogeneous conception of domesticity. Such a domestic, purportedly apolitical society, violently opening itself up to the vast exteriority of the world must then suddenly take shelter in a new rational and technological order, whose spaces functionally organize life into a set of regularized processes.

On the one hand, society in the *urbe* is now free to inhabit 'public' space, a space now moulded entirely by the historical force of *vialidad*, the imprint of which is visible throughout the totality of the 'network of ways' and in all of its details. As a space of movement, exchange, communication, the 'public' denotes a realm of freedom – the awakening of the world to itself and the harkening to a new sense of economic and biological purpose. Private, domestic life is now free to *circulate* and, in so doing, as Cerdá assures us, the life of the population can be enhanced. Through *vialidad*, life can achieve a 'transcendent' state of universal connectivity: 'Urban life everywhere and all of its elements, given the admirable and portentous mechanisms of the great life of humanity, always receives from it much more than it can transmit' (ibid.: 338).

Yet this expansive energy of life is a process understood within a bio-economic framework and, for this reason, it comes at a cost. Thus, on the other hand, as life is enhanced through its 'transcendent' circulation, it must constantly seek its earthly, biological replenishment in the 'private' spaces of the dwelling – in the space of the *intervia*. The *intervia*, as opposed to the network of ways, is the remnant of the domestic, private sphere, the space that traditionally remained outside the state's purview (Arendt, 1958: chap. 2). In the absence of this distinction that the *urbe* heralded, the 'private' sphere of dwelling becomes a function of the 'public' and vice versa, the two bound together in a circular economy. It is the space that, devoid of its own internal secrecy, becomes an organ of the *urbe* in which life must reproduce itself. It is where life both seeks its nourishment and where it must dispose of its toxins. In other words, the *intervia* is where life must be managed biologically, and this is why it is also the primary site of a new form of governmental intervention legible across Cerdá's work. The disappearance of the politically significant boundary between street and household would be replaced by a new, thickened interface whose terms define a new opposition between governmental administration and the isolated family, and whose relationship is now experienced *within the private dwelling*. The paired overlay of the network of ways and the network of serviced infrastructure below ground would allow the ancient political border between public and private (or state and subject) to be at once overcome and reproduced, transcribed in terms of biopolitical governmentality. For the private individual, the 'private' sphere was now determined more in relation to the infrastructure of services entering and exiting the home, allowing the individual to remain isolated without the interference of another, and the 'public' would be demarcated by the regulated action of individual movement, circulation and exchange – of the 'transcendental' experience of *vialidad*. Cerdá's notion of the 'field of action' (or the productive garden allocated to each dwelling) gains resolution as the physical correlate to *vialidad* in the space of circulation: more so than the individual garden allotted to each family, the 'field of action' is a kind of provision of 'nature' that functionally maintains the strength of the family in its productive capacity and in its ability to further isolate the dwelling from the toxic collectivity of life in the former *ciudad*. It is what feeds the individual and, thus, what provides sustenance for the population as a biological-statistical whole.

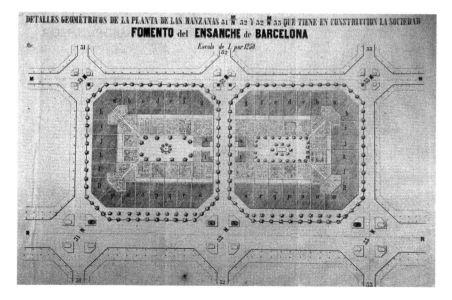

Figure 2.7 Ildefonso Cerdá, Geometric details of the plan of blocks 31 M/N 32 and 32 M/N 33 that society has under construction, 1863

Source: *Fomento del ensanche de Barcelona (Promotion of the Expansion of Barcelona)*

That Cerdá went to such great lengths to separate and isolate these two realms from one another should come as no surprise. The threshold between movement and rest, between circulation and nourishment, between capitalism and public health or, more broadly, the threshold between life's *production* and its *reproduction* was the fundamental division that structured the entire theory of the *urbe*. For Cerdá, the importance of this division could not be underestimated: 'At first sight, this change of movements, reduced simply to exiting or entering the house, may appear insignificant. Nonetheless, it constitutes a feature of the greatest import if we consider the incalculable repetition of entrances and exits, and their various methods and forms of occurrence' (ibid.: 631). In a certain paranoid fashion, Cerdá even described openings of buildings to the street as the source of 'a thousand perils and hazards' (ibid.: 624), emphasizing the danger that is the threshold between 'public' (movement) and 'private' (dwelling) realms. Ultimately, this drove him to propose buildings lacking any ornamentation and with openings that are recessed into the facades. Far more than a practicality, this division – this *functional separation* – stands as the lynchpin that would need scrupulous mediation for the success of the *urbe* as a total system. This was in part because, in order to achieve the purity of the space of *vialidad*, the spaces of dwelling had to yield to the network of ways. Cerdá's proposal to place clocks in every node (which he deemed a 'necessity') was an effort not only to assist in the coordination of labour in the 'public' sphere, but also to symbolically mark the new functional specificity of the network of ways as the space of capitalist production: the clock identifies the purpose and defines the limits of this space: both machine and sign, to paraphrase Maurizio Lazzarato (2014).

More importantly, the nature of this relationship implied a danger, as the space of *vialidad* was permanently in contact with countless individual dwellings, each of which housed the potential for biological ruination. Thus, this separation between the two had to be fully regulated – an administered threshold that required scrupulous thought, first through design and then through governmental oversight. Cerdá, as before, would attempt to resolve the opposition between the two realms (the *intervia* and the *via*) and cover over the volatility of this relationship by uniting them in a kind of 'historically' determined dialectic whole.

> Buildings and *vialidad* are two related and indissoluble ideas, and one cannot exist without the other. In fact, it is not even possible to conceive of *vialidad* without the building as its starting and ending point in the same way that we cannot conceive of the building without *vialidad* as its means of action, of movement, of manifestation of human life. [...] The house is the beginning and end of *vialidad*. (Cerdá, 1991 (1861): § 842)

He argued that the coexistence of the two realms sprang from an original relationship between the individual dwelling and its private access way. In its more contemporary appearance, this element 'serves simultaneously as a way and as a courtyard providing light and views' (Cerdá, 1867, Vol. II: 685). At once public and private, this zone, he reasoned, would have to extend precisely to the centre-line of each street, dividing the street down the middle and segmenting it into adjacent parcels down its length, each section doubling as both public street and private accessory of the house.

> If, then, in considering the intervias, we are unable to ignore this essential appendage, an integral complement to its being, if the two strictly form a single whole, it is just that we give to this whole a denomination [. . .] of *inter-ejes* ('inter-axes'), since these are its determining limits. (Ibid.)

The footways and their articulated fences Cerdá proposed should serve as a purely *functional* barrier within the *inter-ejes* that isolates the realm of human production from that of reproduction and arbitrates their relationship.

Constructing a space entirely around the single distinction between spaces of production and reproduction results in another, more bizarre effect: the *urbe*, in contrast to the traditional city, appears to have a certain fractal quality. In a curious revelation he made while conceptualizing the footway, Cerdá discovered that, beyond the fundamental element of an *urbe*, the *intervia*, along with each domestic unit it contains, was in fact *an elementary urbe itself*:

> So what does this all mean? It means no more nor less than this: in each of these spaces isolated by the urban ways, there exists a small world, a small *urbe* or elementary *urbe*, if you like, which, taken both as a whole and in all its details, bears the most admirable analogy and even similarity to a great *urbe* which, all things considered, is no more than a harmoniously composed grouping of such elementary *urbes*, linked to each other by the great system of urban ways. In fact, this footway along which we pass is nothing other than a genuine ring-way, similar to that which we have found around the great *urbe*, a way in which, in its special layout and development around the space which it circumscribes, puts itself in contact with the urban system of ways and through this, with the great universal *vialidad*. (Ibid.: 363–4)

The scalar flexibility that Cerdá realizes here reveals the *urbe*'s true opposition to the city and is evident in this passage where he exposes the conceptual non-distinction between a 'great *urbe*' and a single *intervia* – a transition he makes without recourse to simple analogy, as, with the *urbe* (as opposed to the *ciudad*), Cerdá is referring more to an array of functional elements within a machinic set of relations that exist *independently* of scale. In this way, scale becomes loosened from perception and representation, indicating a totally new structure and dis-position of human cohabitation seemingly not bound to political order, but fixed instead to a kind of biological-economic system. In addition to scale, the overall indeterminacy that becomes ingrained in the *urbe* seems to underscore the notion of a non-representational, apolitical order, the resolution of which was to be determined by a population made visible in its motion.

In this way, although *vialidad* clearly determines the *urbe*, endowing it with its *raison d'être*, the *intervia* remains its fundamental unit: it is an *urbe* in miniature. The opposition between the two is resolved in this dialectic whole, and the relationship between *vialidad* and dwellings becomes clear: 'Dwellings are the ultimate terminal point, yet at one and the same time, they [. . .] are the first starting point of the great universal *vialidad*' (ibid.: 337–8). Channelled through the hierarchy of *vias* ('transcendental', 'urban', 'individual' ways), *vialidad* is the agency through which the achievement of an earthly form of transcendence circulates, departing from and terminating in the private, isolated dwelling. In its secularized form, 'transcendence' no longer describes an act of passage from one world to another, nor does it articulate the sovereign relation to subjectivity. Rather, it articulates a means of connecting the individual with the immanence bound up in the sentient link between the single dwelling and the totality of an *urbanized society*. *Vialidad* is the essence of a mystical power by which the individual paradoxically remains isolated in order to achieve the collectivity of such 'transcendence'. Through *vialidad*, Cerdá envisioned a world civilized by and united in the freedom of unencumbered circulation – in a word, an urbanized world without an exterior.

The 'battle' that Cerdá depicted between buildings and *vias* ended in the *urbe*. As did the classical, political distinction between public and private. Because the *urbe* derives its claims from the domestic sphere – the private realm of production and reproduction, it will, therefore, redefine in spatial and formal terms the very essence and *raison d'être* of the new 'public' sphere accordingly. In its reappearance, the 'public' becomes a hybrid space of circulation and exchange – an infrastructural appendage of the 'private' realm of dwelling and vice versa. The task or 'function' of the 'public' sphere consists in providing substance to the spiritual health and vigour of domestic life *as a whole*, a category the expression of which becomes tangible in terms of 'population'.[10] For this reason, Cerdá reimagines a form of transcendence that is expressed in human *vialidad* and comes close to a direct experience of the very life force promised in capitalist production itself – an experience achievable through the act of unencumbered movement, exchange and communication: *total* urbanization. This is why he can claim that 'form is nothing', that satisfaction of human necessity is all that matters as the paradoxical aim of humanity must be the collective experience of individual comfort and freedom. Perfection will now be found in a humanity captured in a state of permanent flux, movement and communication. The multiple enclosures of the ancient city Cerdá sought to eradicate will now be replaced by a total freedom of movement within a single, universally enclosed, global *urbe*.

In his attempt to remove the 'container', imagining a new kind of space of habitation free from the political signification of the *ciudad*, Cerdá nevertheless replaces one with another, constructing his *urbe* using terms defined by *vialidad* on the one hand – the product of human sociability – and against the dark horizon of public health crises on the other. The conflation of such an apparently apolitical construct with the moral constitution of humanity is typical of nineteenth-century liberalism and only masks the fact that, in the process, the political is paradoxically transcribed more deeply on to the everyday processes of life under *urbanización*.

Although completely different in character, the new administrative divisions, regulations, checks and limitations constitute the anonymous face of modern biopolitics, a system perfectly mirrored in Cerdá's techno-spatial model of *urbanización*. No longer a strict, horizontal cut, separating sovereign power from its subjectivity, the division, now fractured a thousand ways, replicates itself at all scales, extending from the divided individual (the *dividual*) to the whole of society, a distribution reflected in the fractal organization of Cerdá's *urbe*. Whereas Arendt asserts that this line has become completely blurred with the rise of society (Arendt, 1958: 38), Cerdá shows us that indeed it can be traced, at least in part, through the spatial configuration of the *urbe*. Hobbes's inscription of an inner division of 'man', separating human subjectivity into public and private halves, far from receding in the *urbe*, would now be replicated in a new split, dividing the subject of urbanization in terms of economic productivity on the one hand (bourgeois, property owner, entrepreneur) and biological species ('human being') on the other (Habermas, 2010: 55). Cleaved down the middle, the subject of urbanization was at once two equally irreconcilable entities that nevertheless reinforced and naturalized one another through the gendered relationship they forged between productive male labour power and its isolated, unwaged reproduction in the feminized space of the *intervia*. Circumscribing each *intervia*, flanking every dwelling within it, and segregating the individual modes of transportation across the breadth of each *via*, the isolation that Cerdá fastidiously prescribes courses throughout the entire *urbe*, replicating and enabling this new human division to become the dominant diagram of modern urban life.

The emphasis Cerdá placed on freedom as one of the primary achievements of the *urbe* is directly related to its inverse, that is to say, the simultaneous enclosing of all of society into a new urban order that systematizes (and thus *politicizes*) life's natural cycles of reproduction while naturalizing the capitalist exploitation of life, thus appropriating and enslaving some lives in precisely the same degree to which it opens others to new experiences of (very specific kinds of) freedom. This is why freedom in the space of circulation is not experienced, for example, in the free transfer between the 'private' dwelling and the 'public' realm of the street, but rather as a kind of *compromise* on behalf of the 'private' space of the dwelling to guarantee its complete withdrawal from the 'public' space of *vialidad*: liberty narrowly defined as freedom *from* obstruction. Approached differently, freedom can be seen as the guaranteed *isolation* of spaces of reproduction from those of production. The sense of freedom Cerdá advocates is a distinctly negative liberty,[11] a notion rooted in the nineteenth century's conception of the new 'public' sphere of society. When the two formerly distinct spheres of public and private collapse into one 'social' body, the new set of divisions that emerge as its structural correlate is concerned not with sovereign signification, but rather with capitalist functionality: the *administered specialization of life's functionality in a universally domestic order.*

IMMUNIZATION

The rise of society, forged as a single domestic continuum as Arendt asserts, despite its effort to do away with political subjugation, nonetheless must impose upon itself a new, albeit elusive, apparatus of power. Caught in a perpetual cycle of transcendence and necessity, circulation and dwelling, expansion and withdrawal, its biopolitical composition gains clarity in terms that Roberto Esposito has called the *immunitary paradigm*:

> Rather than being superimposed or juxtaposed in an external form that subjects one to the domination of the other, in the immunitary paradigm, *bíos* and *nomos*, life and politics, emerge as the two constituent elements of a single, indivisible whole that assumes meaning from their interrelation. Not simply the relation that joins life to power, *immunity is the power to preserve life.* (Esposito, 2008: 454–6; my emphasis)

Indeed, more than guaranteeing a general division between processes of production (labour, exchange, communication) and those of life's reproduction (health, sustenance, species reproduction), freedom in Cerdá's terms may also be read as the promise that the processes of life's *preservation*, in order to function, will remain spatially, technologically and governmentally isolated from those of its *enhancement*. Cerdá's *urbe* can be understood as an apparatus that manages life constituted by the dialectic unity of preservation and enhancement.

This exchange can be seen most poignantly in the internal division of *vialidad* itself. Let us recall that Cerdá's notion of *vialidad* accounted not only for the free movement of people throughout the network of ways, but also covered the flows of toxic and life-preserving fluids below ground, plugging directly into each dwelling. Above ground, the interface between *vialidad* and the *intervia* consists of a carefully designed, initial (and in this way, pre-regulated) construction of the *urbe* and its constituent elements. Below ground, however, *vialidad* engages the dwellings of the *intervia* in a direct relationship of permanent monitoring and regulation. Because it provides the means by which the population can sustain and reproduce itself, unlike its counterpart above ground, it is the form of *vialidad* that is intimately bound to the province of human dwelling, the space that both consumes substances necessary for life and exhausts those toxic to it. Whereas freedom above ground is proportional to the ease of circulation, below ground, as in the *intervia*, freedom (if not nonexistent) is limited by perpetual governmental oversight and administrative interventions, corresponding more in a Hobbesian sense to life's protection from itself – to its preservation. In other words, regulation in the network of ways above ground is a function of the design of the *urbe* and thus naturalizes itself through its use, whereas underground, regulation is perpetual, *essential* – a division that mirrors the repressive character of the gendered isolation and obscurity of reproductive labour from the more open practices of productive labour. In the terrain of biopolitics that conditioned Cerdá's thinking, the greatest threat to society is perceived to be the biological threats residing within a population, within the *urbe*. Thus, the space of the *intervia* – which Cerdá took to be both the source of biological crises as well as their remedy – is the space of constant regulation requiring an apparatus composed of techniques and infrastructures of domesticity that doubled as the site of close governmental administration. In total, the minimally determinate, neutral grid of circulation is compensated by the overdetermined system of *vialidad* underground. The two sides of *vialidad* cohere in a unified whole, the aim of which is, respectively, to minimize conflict and interference while optimizing the health of the population: enabling the 'free' circulation of capital while maximizing the conditions for labour's reproduction. 'Transcendence', it appears, is the flip side of immunization.

The question is: what is the relationship between the two? Let us recall that Cerdá's idea of transcendence is that which occurs in a space defined precisely by the absence of obstruction – liberty by negation – and is a phenomenon experienced by the single circulating subject if and only if this person remains isolated from the 'collectivity' of other bodies circulating. In other words, the notion of universal transcendence encapsulated in the term '*vialidad*' is possible only by assembling a 'collectivity' insofar as the individuals who constitute it remain isolated from one another. This process is grounded in the fact that its point of departure and its end point are both the individual unit of *private property*. As Cerdá attests, this notion of 'transcendence' – of life's enhancement – is not possible without the reciprocal retreat of life to an administered state of care. The constant exchange between one state and its opposite seems to bind the two realms in a zero-sum game. Whereas one side of this cycle produces freedom through the expansion of a life force (again, in a negative sense), the other side violently injects a negative form of the biological protection of life, terminating its expansive capacity.

This reciprocal exchange between preservation and enhancement can be explained as a process of life's *immunization*. As Esposito explains, 'the potential risk of a world in common – and for this reason exposed to an unlimited indistinction – is neutralized by [. . .] the relation of everyone with himself or herself in the form of personal identity' (ibid.: 66), a mechanism of self-recognition that is projected on to the institution of private property. Following John Locke's argument for the latter (where private property springs from the necessary extension of the property 'Nature' bestowed on each person in the mastery over his or her body (Locke, 1821)), Esposito reveals a logic of self-preservation bound up in the modern conception of private property:

> Once the proprietary logic is wedded to a solid underpinning such as belonging to one's own body, it can now expand into communal space. This is not directly negated, but is incorporated and recut in a division that turns it into its opposite, in a multiplicity of things that have in common only the fact of being all one's own to the degree they have been appropriated by their respective owners. (Esposito, 2008: 66)

This logic is flawlessly reproduced less in Cerdá's description of the individual dwelling (as the dwelling is the absolute *withdrawal* from communal space) than in his notion of 'transcendence' that he associates with *vialidad*. Its paradoxical nature becomes clear: *vialidad* experienced within the network of ways, with its individualized lanes of traffic, the specially designed 'nodes' and its general removal of all conflict *is in fact a product of private property*. In other words, it is the logic that extends the mechanism of self-preservation bound up in private property into the 'public' sphere, transcribing it as the basis for a common mode of being – the 'universality' of *vialidad*. The negative sense of liberty that pervades the *urbe* is precisely the making-communal of that which springs from the isolated body, telescoping the Lockean concept of private property from the *dividual* to dwelling to the entire *urbe* itself. When liberty is understood this way, spilling out of the private dwelling into the communal space,

> the subtractive or simply the negative sense is already destined to characterize it ever more dominantly. When this entropic process is joined to the self-preserving strategies of modern society, the overturning of ancient liberties [*libertates*] into its immune opposite will be complete. [. . .] Without losing its typically polyvalent lexicon, immunity progressively transfers its own semantic center of gravity from the sense of 'privilege' to that of 'security'. (Ibid.: 72)

Arendt recognized this long ago: 'Society, when it first entered the public realm, assumed the disguise of an organization of property-owners who, instead of claiming access to the public realm because of their wealth, demanded protection from it for the accumulation of more wealth' (1958: 68). The conception of liberty as freedom from obstructions, as espoused by Cerdá, limits it to the relationship between the isolated subject and his or her will to autonomously circulate. Fused to the private dwelling as both the beginning and end point of the 'transcendent' *vialidad*, the freedom permeating throughout the *urbe* turns out to be its opposite: it is the prerequisite for the preservation of life.

FROM SCIENCE TO DOCTRINE: TEORÍA AS SOCIAL CONTRACT

Through the bipolar notion of *vialidad* (and with the entire *urbe* itself), Cerdá reveals a fundamental paradox at the heart of his project, one that would plague liberalism in general: the conflation of the biological necessity of the species with the promise of social and political liberation. As Arendt pointed out, '[n]ecessity and life are so intimately related and connected that life itself is threatened where necessity is altogether eliminated. For the elimination of necessity, far from resulting automatically in the establishment of freedom, only blurs the distinguishing line between freedom and necessity' (ibid.: 71). The *urbe* provides a concrete template on which this character of liberal politics can be mapped and reproduced in space. In its frenetic attempts to foreclose any possibility of political subjugation altogether, Cerdá's *urbe* (as with liberalism) must submit to a higher order that guarantees its smooth security. With one hand liberties are constructed and, with the other, they are taken away, and the idea of liberty unravels into its opposites of law, obligation and regulation. As Cerdá himself attests, '[t]his is why it has been said that liberty is the slavery of the law' (Cerdá, 1859b: § 11). After all, it was Cerdá's ultimate intention to propose what no government had done until his day:

> to reduce to a single code all those provisions which may lead to the building of a city and its maintenance under conditions favorable to public order, to good administrative and economic management, to general, family, and even individual welfare, to public and private health, to the comfort of each and every person. (Ibid.: § 13)

Cerdá's writings convey a conviction he had that law was a universal source of truth, and the notion of equality for him was the prime sense in which justice could be fulfilled. This can be read in his belaboured studies of the grid in which he chose the square grid because of its inherent 'egalitarianism'. But far more than this simple identity of the square grid with justice, 'equality' for Cerdá reflects an idealization of a universally distributed system of law by which all of society should abide. This conviction, unlike those of the philosophers of the Enlightenment, had to be realized in material form. Thus, Cerdá saw no difference between law and *vialidad*, or justice and an evenly distributed network of infrastructure. And this is why he, unlike any of his contemporaries, recognized that such a system would require its own self-contained set of protocols, regulations – its own jurisdiction. With the writing of by-laws in 1859 (despite their never having been adopted by the city of Barcelona), Cerdá proposed nothing less than a total, universal doctrine of urbanization – one containing 'a beginning, an end and the *raison d'être* of each and every one of their provisions, which must be within the grasp of everybody' (ibid.: § 8). More than simply denoting the technicalities of building and organizing the city fit for contemporary life, the concept of urbanization, for Cerdá,

> is the totality of knowledge, principles, doctrines, and rules, directed towards teaching in what way any grouping of buildings should be arranged so that it meets its purpose, which boils down to that of its dwellers being able to live conveniently and provide each other with reciprocal services, thus contributing to the general welfare. (Cerdá, 1867: 31)

Yet, in addition to the ordinances for a single given *urbe*, lamenting the limitation of municipal ordinances of his day, Cerdá proposed a new reach of urban by-laws that should extend beyond the spaces of a given *urbe*, regularizing the surrounding un-urbanized countryside as well. Indeed, for the science of urbanization to work, Cerdá had to propose a kind of 'supra-municipal' set of ordinances that would require the intervention of state authority in relation to municipal authority; a kind of state–municipal governmental axis to be constituted with regard to the process of urbanization itself.

> The government, responsible for supervising the health and the interests of all would be doing a great good for society and be preparing its genuine physical, moral and political regeneration by forming and elevating to laws of state some urban and rural building ordinances matching the knowledge of hygienists, economists and experts. (Cerdá, 1991 (1855): § 69)

With this move, the enactment of by-laws would in some cases be equivalent to that of state laws, and vice versa, blurring the boundary between the two, precisely because urbanization was a space-process intended to occupy territories that correspond to both. For, as with everything Cerdá had set out to accomplish, he never lost sight of the fact that urbanization denoted a process that transcends the spatial extents of a given *urbe* itself.

The *urbe* was a concept that had surpassed the city precisely because it is a concept bound to a process in excess of itself. Unlike the city, the *urbe* is only ever a momentary physical appearance of the otherwise invisible process of urbanization. As such, the powers that sanction it had also to exceed previously defined spatial limitations.

The *Teoría*, alongside the by-laws Cerdá prescribed, would together specify an entire urban constitution that effectively reconstitutes the notion of sovereignty itself. No longer a clearly visible singularity, sovereignty now described something that would circulate between the governmental body administering the *urbe* and the autonomy of the individual subjects circulating within it. It would emerge in the entirety of the laws and powers that constituted a new horizontal plane of municipal and state administrations and its infrastructural relations they created with urbanized society. Sovereignty, in this proposal, was now the convergence of a physical model and a legal edifice by which an urbanized society was meant to achieve a universal and *global* state of administered peace. Its self-enclosed nature hinted on the one hand at a system devoid of gaps and, on the other, at a new kind of sovereignty *in absentia* – a displaced sovereignty appearing as a kind of machine that now runs by itself (Schmitt, 2005: 48).

The fractal nature of the *urbe* – the slippery way in which a single concept can be equally applied to almost every component, phenomenon, entity and process within the *urbe* – both facilitates the universalization of Cerdá's theory, as a means to *explain everything*, and simultaneously allows for everything to fall under the remit of urban administration: air, light, fluid, disease, crime, insurgency, the rural, even 'nature' itself. Such thinking goes hand in hand with the desire Cerdá had to subject every contingency to a controllable, calculable metric of infrastructural regulation. For this reason, the governmental administration as characterized by Cerdá is no longer a fully sovereign body. At times, it is limited to the entrepreneurial game of property exchange and service management; at others, a more nuanced purpose seems to be called for by Cerdá – one that bears the brunt of implementing the ideological charge driving his entire work: the moral duty and (nearly theological) imperative *to urbanize*. The administration was to act as a caretaker who intervenes only to resolve problems, uphold the law and, more broadly, to manage perpetual circulation.

Sovereignty, displaced into the structure of law and administration, becomes at once opaque and spatially ubiquitous. The effect of such a doctrine, as Cerdá tells us, is that it 'will be obeyed more *spontaneously* and more *rationally* and the task of government will be easier and more paternal' (Cerdá, 1859b: § 8; my emphasis). Thus, across the homogeneity of a *domestic* society, such governance can extend limitlessly, as its presence is missed by those under its machinic sway. The legal character of Cerdá's *urbe* both 'spontaneously' renders and absorbs decision-making, while also making redundant the need for traditional forms of sovereignty. Like the minimal grid of ways, he wanted to limit the administration of it to a body equally minimal in its intervention. In fact, Cerdá would limit the role of the administration from even constructing the network of ways: 'Thus it emerges, naturally and necessarily that [. . .] the neighboring property owners impose on the street all the easements most essential to the house and without which the house cannot exist, they must pay for it' (Cerdá, 1991 (1861): § 1234). Yet just like the vast infrastructural systems his grid concealed underground, it would be the totalizing set of by-laws that would characterize a new, invisible, anonymous role for sovereignty to assume in an urban world.

That the *Teoría general de la urbanización* reads like a nineteenth-century social contract hardly comes as a surprise. Like the case with his Enlightenment predecessors, such a contract is the logical outcome of the moralist critique of political domination, even in light of the nineteenth century's liberalization. Cerdá's gripe with Rousseau, it will be recalled, was not in the form or intentions of his own *Social Contract*, but rather with the fact that Rousseau had missed the role that the city played in his rejection of society: that a social contract of sorts could be materialized in a new *urban* order, in an *urban* social contract. In a near Hobbesian passage, Cerdá exposes this new role, describing the capacity of the *urbe* as a body of political sovereignty – a kind of modern, administrative Leviathan that grants security at the cost of a part of individual freedom:[12]

> No one is a greater friend than we of unbridled freedom in isolated or rural building, in what we might call its natural state – please allow us this phrase – and which, like man in his natural state, is also completely free. But just as man, upon entering the social state, sacrifices a part of that freedom in exchange for the immense and inestimable advantages which society provides for him ... (Ibid.: § 844)

Freedom, thus, is not a matter of returning 'man' to a state of nature, but rather administering nature to man's social existence: a move blocked by the privations of an otherwise unjust state. Following a Rousseauian logic, where the 'general will' is recast in terms of a general 'well-being' (the protection/ enhancement coupling of *vialidad*), the municipal administration would take on the role of managing the 'particular will', conducting the multiple interests at play in the space of the *intervia*. In other words, the 'general will' for Cerdá would be provided, by analogy, through a general framework for organizing the *urbe* – through a *general theory of urbanization*. Sovereignty, placed in the hands of the population, would appear to be equivalent to the sum of individual will-power fulfilled in the homogeneous lattice of streets and ways and made possible by the 'paternal' administration's supervision over particular necessities. The liberty of individual sovereignty would be enjoyed only upon entering into a 'contract' of sorts – only if the population *urbanizes* itself – and thus its terms are limited by the regulatory structure of the *urbe*. As with Cerdá's extensive attention to the regulatory structure of *urbanización*, it follows that the only way such a system could operate would be by applying a kind of totalizing system of ordinances and by-laws: a minimal governmental structure, held up by a maximal legal infrastructure.

As such, the *urbe* was never aimed to be a kind of static, physical embodiment of such a social contract. Instead, as Cerdá described it, the *urbe* is to be a *'means and instrument* specific and appropriate to the advances of modern civilization' (ibid.: § 1117; my emphasis). That is to say, the *urbe*, for Cerdá, is not only intended to be adequate for the needs of modern society, but would additionally serve as an apparatus necessary for such a transformation process. It is a system framed by the poles of social justice, scientific advancement, private property and economic enterprise. From a philosophical standpoint, the former two go hand in hand, forming, as it were, the teleological ambition of urbanization: 'Science', Cerdá writes, 'has the sacred duty of placing itself alongside the administration and leading and assisting its efforts in its march towards social perfection' (ibid.: § 1319). As for the latter pair, entrepreneurial gain is cast as the natural outcome of the pursuit of (private) shelter.

> We were always aware, as an incontrovertible axiom, that since urban reform [urbanization] was the satisfaction of a need [for shelter, or private property], it should, of necessity, produce utilities and advantages and benefits, from which profits could and should be extracted in order to carry it out. (Ibid.: § 1320)

With this logical, rhetorical and conceptual pairing of ideas, we have perhaps the first, clearest constitution of what would become the liberal capitalist notion of the city, defined not as an entity, but rather as a *process*: urbanization must produce profits in order to solve social ills and to align itself with the path of human 'progress'. Capitalism for urbanization then becomes a kind of historical force giving credence to the liberal pairing of freedom with private property – an entity naturalized as an essential 'need' to be satisfied. The formless *urbe* can only be understood as a process whose measure of moral achievement is proportional to its ability to sprawl.

The utopian rhetoric Cerdá employed would play a crucial role in binding urbanism to forms of governance, permanently opening itself up to depoliticized, reformist progress, while simultaneously hardening it as an insatiable process inscribed in the mechanics of capitalism. In this way, one side always confirms the other: each 'reform' of urbanism affirms evermore the basic conception of urbanization as a 'natural' process tamed only by the deeds of scientific, humanist knowledge. Remarkably, this model has, in one form or another, reproduced itself worldwide as the coordination of agencies and resources called upon to perpetually expand, develop and enlarge cities in the name of 'urbanization'.

The scope of Cerdá's work should not be restricted just to the realm of local governments or municipal authorities: what he aspired to accomplish is nothing less than the transformation of the entirety of society, fulfilling ambitions prescribed by his Enlightenment predecessors. Nor can one look at Cerdá's work as something bound up with and limited to urban space. And it is this fact that makes his work so relevant today: one has to view it as a kind of idealism that has actually taken hold over the course of the past two centuries of 'actually existing' urbanization. The recentring (or decentring) of the political that his work invoked can be said to have been largely fulfilled, precisely through the introduction of institutions wielding administrative powers and backed by a legal edifice characteristic of liberalism. Yet just as the 'science' of urbanization – the form of knowledge Cerdá so diligently theorized – rapidly eroded into a 'single code' of ordinances, so too would urbanization over the course of the twentieth century exceed any such idealisms, degrading to a set of regulations governed by the unending imperative to expand its formless, beige grid of habitation and circulation across the surface of the globe.

NOTES

1 On the notion of utopian planning, see Chapter 1 of this book.

2 See, for example, the discussion on this distinction in Aureli (2011).

3 On the notion of *oikos* and its distinction from *polis*, see Chapter 1 in Agamben (2011).

4 It is, of course, false to assert that the population had not been considered a central concern for architects and city administrators before Cerdá. Indeed, from as early as Giovanni Botero's *A Treatise Concerning the Causes of the Magnificency and Greatness of Cities* of 1588, through the treatises of *Polizeiwissenschaft* of the seventeenth century, and their direct impact upon the layout and design of the city, to the efforts in particular by Edwin Chadwick to map the health conditions of the working classes for all of England in the early nineteenth century, as a way to address urban design from a public health perspective, the population has increasingly gained gravity. Nevertheless, Cerdá provides the clearest example of a mode of thinking about the design of the city in which the figure of the population is inscribed in every element of it.

5 Note here the intimate relationship at the heart of *vialidad* between unlimited circulation and a kind of measure of health. This definition still holds in the general use of '*vialidad*' today.

6 For more on this notion, see Chapter 1 of this book.

7 A concept we will return to later in this chapter. See also Cerdá (1999: 373–405).

8 Cerdá had not yet invented the term '*urbe*' when writing this publication and was still using '*poblacion*' to designate his new urban space. The reference to 40 square metres per inhabitant comes from Michel Lévy's *Treatise on Public and Private Hygiene* of 1844. For more sources that Cerdá drew from, see the bibliography he provides in his *Teoría de la construcción de las ciudades* (1991 (1859): §12).

9 'Public' here is used in both the Hobbesian sense and in its more ancient meaning in connection with the *polis*: to denote the sphere of the political, sovereign decision and a space of political activity, respectively.

10 'Population' here refers to Foucault's articulation of this category in relation to governmentality (see Foucault, 2009).

11 See, for example, Isaiah Berlin's lecture entitled 'Two Concepts of Liberty' (in Berlin, 1969). Roberto Esposito, in his *Bíos: Biopolitics and Philosophy*, elaborates on the notion of freedom understood in its more ancient terms (*libertates*): 'the concept of liberty, in its germinal nucleus, alludes to a connective power that grows and develops according to its own internal law, and to an expansion or to a deployment that unites its members in a shared dimension' (2008: 70).

12 Indeed, as has been shown, Cerdá often has more in common with Hobbes and his social contract than with Rousseau's.

3

An Archaeology of Circulation

That Cerdá placed circulation – *vialidad* – at the core of his theory of urbanization in an age in which biological concepts had themselves been circulating across disciplines is hardly surprising. What appears more unexpected is how Cerdá used this concept of *vialidad* as a political weapon with which to break open the anachronistic walled city and to materialize what he saw as a virtuous world of free and unlimited movement. In equal measures, this new world of *urbanización* would no longer have room for 'politics', just as it would have no further use for the burdensome 'city', insofar as the one was the product of the other. Although Cerdá seems to have unwittingly uncovered a potent relationship between spatial organization and political form bound up in *vialidad*, this relationship, however, was no discovery of the nineteenth century. Rather, it was one born alongside the modern state itself, and it could be argued that Cerdá, like many others of his time, captured a certain reality, temporarily bathed in the light of positivity, that had been centuries in the making. Perhaps equally blinded by the new, historians have seemed to follow suit. Although the majority of writings on urbanism tend to begin and end with an emphasis on the advances in technology and the epistemic introduction of the biological sciences into the thinking of the city, they fall short of a more profound analysis of this by investing the nineteenth century with a kind of historical autonomy. By emphasizing infrastructure, communication, the 'systemic' nature of the city, its functionally determined parts and its larger conception as a biological organism, the discourse – still intoxicated by the signifier 'modernism' – artificially sunders the more ancient concerns from which their nineteenth-century manifestations sprang. Although perhaps less convenient for historians, these concerns can shed light on precisely what this account of the nineteenth century loses: the metaphysical and political basis of the categories so important to it: *movement, energy, circulation.*

This chapter assembles a genealogy of circulation that traces its sixteenth-century emergence from its roots in more ancient representations, ideas and epistemologies offered by the figure of the circle to its modern inflections extending into the mid nineteenth century. It will look specifically at ways in which circulation (and the metaphor of the circle, previously) consistently provided a bridge between conceptions and perceptions of power – whether divine, natural or political – and interpretations and implementations of spatial order. It may seem a rather tenuous, even forced, task to direct our analysis of a nineteenth-century phenomenon at the ancient and early modern roots of a concept imbricated with its emergence. However, in doing so, we will be able to show not only how circulation has been a consistent concern for the establishment and maintenance of power in the West, but also that questions of circulation have also consistently identified a crucial juncture *between power and space*. In this way, by examining the political histories of circulation prior to their nineteenth-century integration into spatio-technical programmes of urbanization, we will open up a richer frame of analysis that will disclose the urban as a spatial logic with a lineage that may owe as much to the city as it does to colonial, maritime or territorial technologies.

Cerdá's *Teoría* may have been the first work that explicitly theorized the concept of circulation as the fundamental condition of the city, and thus of *urbanización* that would replace it, but it was certainly not the first work to bring circulation to bear on the organization and administration of the city. Indeed, from the work of Vitruvius, to that of Leon Battista Alberti, to the persuasions of Giovanni Botero, to the reign of Jean-Baptiste Colbert's administration over Paris, the free movement of people, goods, water and air through the city has provided a means to assess its form and guide its administration: circulation as a civic concern has long been synonymous with a measure of commodiousness, convenience and good sanitation. Nor, as we will see in the coming chapters, is Cerdá's the first text to have taken circulation as a key agent for the reorganization of space and power. Emanating from the natural sciences, astronomy, geography, cartography and trade, circulation would also consolidate over the seventeenth century into a model that made itself available not only to these disciplines in themselves, but also, for the first time, would present itself to power as a domain of human control: with the arrival of the doctrine of *raison d'état* in this same period, circulation as a category would find itself increasingly central to political calculations, folding a set of objectives and strategies of early modern state power into the movement of its subjects, merchandise, money and bullion. Circulation, in other words, would make itself available to the calculations and prognoses of the absolute state.

From the late sixteenth century and into the seventeenth, the introduction of circulation into natural philosophy provided the foundations for a new economic analysis at the same time that it came to explain anatomical function. In each case, the awareness of circulation introduced a model that gave both organization to, and principles for assessing, the motion of objects within (a typically closed, finite) space. Indeed, the city too would find itself as an arena to be measured by the category of circulation during this period, with the ways in which it was thought about and constructed being altered.

Michel Foucault has suggested that such a paradigmatic shift of the city took place in the eighteenth century, where the city became analogous with a biological notion of the 'milieu' (see Lecture 1 (11 January 1978) in Foucault, 2009: 1–27). In suggesting this, he leaves the colonial cities and settlements of the Americas out of his analysis – an omission that remains unexplored in such terms and will be taken up in the chapters that follow. Yet, even in the European context, little work has been done to account for this shift within the materiality and management of the city. Typically, the history of this period portrays the efforts of architects and urban administrations as subordinate to either the new economic demands of mercantilist and colonial trade, or aligned with the culturo-historical category of the 'baroque'. In either case, both historical accounts foreclose the possibility of analysing a form of knowledge specific to the city itself in its alignment with a new epistemological horizon. Too often, on the one hand, such economic determinism helps to reinforce certain narratives of enlightenment that preside over and vindicate nineteenth- and twentieth-century liberalism, while, on the other hand, the standard art-historical periodization schemes of the city and its architecture tend to analytically quarantine its material from the networks of power that produced it. Moreover, by focusing on its secondary role in developing an early modern economic system, we fail to understand how circulation *as a concept of space* can be brought to bear on the construction of an equally early modern political form, namely *government* (here, I refer primarily to Giorgio Agamben's account of government, 2011).

The invention of 'circulation' has no singular reference. For this reason, it is just as possible to view it as an early economic concept as it is one springing from anatomy. It is also impossible to imagine 'circulation' as a phenomenon outside the sixteenth- and seventeenth-century category of *motu* – motion, a category central to the discoveries of the period that occupied the minds of Kepler, Galileo, Descartes and Newton. Thus, rather than attempting to identify a disciplinary point of 'origin' of the idea, this chapter will suggest that the category as understood from the late sixteenth century until the nineteenth century has its root rather in the broader notions of circularity, circumference, concentricity – notions that, since the (re)discovery of the circularity of the Earth, drew upon new interpretations from the centuries old 'metaphor of the circle'.[1]

This new consciousness, reflecting upon the observations of heavenly, orbital motion, in turn projected a sense of universality onto earthly, corporal objects in motion. This chapter will build a genealogy of circulation by first establishing how the ideas of circular and cyclical movement, which had existed since antiquity, were inflected by the discovery of the circularity of the world and its heliocentric motion through the heavens, looking at the ramifications that reverberated between macrocosm and microcosm. It will then examine the diffusion and transformation of these ideas against the emergence of 'circulation' as a concept, tracing the ways in which it was taken up broadly by the natural sciences, anatomy, theories of trade, theories of the state and, contemporaneously, as a nascent principle of the administration of the city. We will look at how, as a concept, circulation would become most useful as a principle for organizing space and the objects that moved through it – in other words, in the materialization of an economic order. If, in the mid seventeenth century, the introduction of economic circulation and exchange depended upon dislodging the concept of wealth as a fixed entity, rendering it mobile and transferrable, it did so on two conditions: insofar as the actual concrete infrastructures in which wealth could circulate were in place and insofar as a certain logic had already made itself available to the elites of society who controlled these networks. Likewise, the reverse should prove to be true as well: within the administrative knowledge and planning of the state, there appeared an analytic category that made itself useful to this administration and thus became fundamental to the analysis of state power: *traffic*. In this way, the circulation of money – and thus of a state's wealth or power – can be materialized and registered by the circulation of all kinds of traffic in and between cities within its territory. Just as William Harvey's 'discovery' of the circulation of blood provided a pre-existing notion of circulation with a physical, demonstrative model, so too does the circulation of traffic within the body of the state lend a kind of physical evidence of the same *vital* phenomenon occurring within the 'Body Politique'. Indeed, the city provided the ideal ground on which both macrocosm and microcosm, sovereignty and administration, transcendent foundations and immanent concerns could, and indeed had to, coexist: the city as a unified body, the mirror image of divine composition – a microcosm on Earth reflecting the macrocosm above – was simultaneously nourished by the circulation of a new, immanent form of power signalled by objects and people in perpetual motion. A once divine construction, the city became the site in which the pulsing circulation of goods, people, resources and money would now render its power vital, visible.

CIRCULATION, CIRCULARITY, CIRCUMFERENCE, CIRCUMNAVIGATION

It is impossible to imagine the prolific appearance of the circle in the Renaissance as anything but a recovery of the symbol of a certain perfection that had persisted in the logic and metaphors that touched all of European life throughout antiquity. And for good reasons. An object of geometry, it appears ubiquitously throughout the natural world as the mark of the work of a providential force. Leaving its traces in the trunks of trees and stems of plants, in the spherical perfection of tears (Nicolson, 1960), binding necessity and the truth of emotion to the consistency of the universe, the circle inscribes and unites the world in its divine rotations through which the heavens project the daily, seasonal and yearly times of light and dark, imposing a regularity that in turn sets the activities of the earthly world in motion. 'The role of astrology in characterizing long periods of human history as ages under zodiacal symbols attests to the intertwining of astronomical and human sequences' (Lowry, 1974: 432). Indeed, some of the first pictorial representations of the cyclical, circular principles governing astronomical and earthly phenomena alike, as S. Todd Lowry points out, had to account for the complex relationships between nightly, monthly, seasonal and annual occurrences. All were bound together in the rotating motions of the cosmos (ibid.). Yet, far earlier than the Zodiac, the first devices employing circular, rotating parts, and even the wheel itself, were seen as a kind of evidence of a continuity between the patterns of the heavens and the rhythms of human activity. By the Hellenic period, the wheel had lent its cyclical motion to Greek poetry and philosophy as a *rota fortunae*, a 'wheel of fortune' or an allegorical device that would persist through the Middle Ages. For David M. Robinson, the first to use this metaphor was Pindar, who saw it as a symbol of the cyclical soul wandering from higher existence to lower and back again (Robinson, 1946: 207).

The symbol of the wheel, with its cyclical pattern, signifies fortune, connecting the affairs of human life with divine will. Sophocles wrote: 'Like a wheel, fortune turns in a circle' (Pearson, 1917, quoted in Robinson, 1946: 208) – a metaphor he would employ several times to relate the waxing and waning of the moon to fate, luck or chance. For this reason, the symbol of the wheel, according to Robinson, would itself circulate, appearing first over the entrances of gaming parlours and, later, on Greek coins. Indeed, even the ancient city itself was a figure governed by the circle: As Arendt noted, '[t]he word *polis* originally connoted something like a "ring-wall," and it seems the Latin *urbs* also expressed the notion of a "circle" and was derived from the same root of *orbis*' (1958: 64; for a further discussion on this, see Onians, 1951: 444, n. 1). Into the early Roman Empire, cycles, wheels and orbs all came to express the same binding principle of circular patterns of the heavens relating to human destiny, affecting thought from Sophocles to Herodotus to the Pythagorean thought of Hippodamus to Philo. By the last century BCE, the circle as a metaphor had made its appearance in Western thought.

To go from the metaphorical use of the circle as a guiding principle of both earthly objects and divine providence to advancing a notion of a *system* of objects passing in circular, cyclical phases or patterns requires the use of a kind of analytical thought. It is in this that an early ancestor of the notion of circulation appears, departing from its basis in the metaphor of the circle. Philo makes the transition between the divine metaphor of the circle and a systematic, recurrent process when he observed the transformations within the cycle of life: 'God willed that nature should run a course that brings it back to its starting point, endowing the species with immortality, and making them sharers of eternal existence' (Clagett, 2001: 137–8). Indeed, for 'circulation' to be observed there is first a requirement for the identification of an entity that 'circulates' – a common conceptual denominator. As early as the sixth century BCE, the Ionian philosophers, for example, were able to deduce meteorological phenomena, including the water cycle, by doing just this. Displaying a systematic logic, they were able to trace water's passage from liquid (in the sea) to gas through its evaporation, to its return to the earth as rain, snow and ice, finally returning again to the sea through the flows of rivers and springs – observations that would later be theorized by Aristotle in his *Meteorologica*. Reading Aristotle's *De Caelo* and *De Generatione et Corruptione*, Walter Pagel notes that circular motion appeared to Aristotle as 'the only motion which is continuous, it is a very great marvel for it is made up of contraries which are present together, namely motion and rest' (Pagel, 1951: 28). For Aristotle and his followers,[2] circular motion was perfect: it had no contrary motion to it. In fact, the *Mechanica* can itself be read as an attempt to characterize all of mechanics in terms of circular motion (Winter, 2007: viii). With Ptolemy, the circle, both as a geometrical form and as a principle of movement, would gain its first proof as a sign of divine perfection in the shape and concentric rotation of the planets and in their circular masquerade around the Earth. Yet such heavenly rotation was well known to classical Greek thought.

Plato's *Timaeus* discloses the philosopher's perception of the world as a singular proof of the god's hand in fashioning it as a spherical whole 'composed of all wholes' (*Timaeus* 33 in Plato, 1997: 1238), who gave to it but one of the seven motions as a sign of its perfection and wholeness: that of spinning.

> Applying this entire train of reasoning to the god that was yet to be, the eternal god made it smooth and even all over, equal from the center, a whole and complete body itself, but also made up of complete bodies. In its center he set a soul, which he extended throughout the whole body, and with which he then covered the body outside. And he set it to turn in a circle, a single solitary universe, whose very excellence enables it to keep its own company without requiring anything else. (*Timaeus* 34 in Plato, 1997: 1238–9)

What was observed in all cases was a common circular motion that seemed to describe the very processes that constitute nature. Such discoveries would continue to occupy classical thought for centuries, a basis on which knowledge would unite the relationship between heavenly order and earthly bodies.

In the second half of the fifteenth century, under the patronage of Cosimo de' Medici, Marsilio Ficino inaugurated a new tradition of Platonism with the publication of *Institutiones platonicae* and the translation of Plato's entire work into Latin (Benevolo, 1978b: 211–12). This introduction of classical thought into the blossoming world of the fifteenth century effectively folded the principles of classical philosophy (not limited to Plato's) into the practice and thought of Christianity. This re-emergence of Platonic thought within the Christian world saw a revival of the metaphor of the circle as a sign of works of God. The Neoplatonist turn also brought about an emancipation of artists from the medieval category of 'artisan', endowing the material construction of the world with a kind of divine duty. This led to an expansion of the aesthetic sphere and imbued it with a new autonomy of form that echoed a sense of truth, harmony and spirituality, providing experiments within the arts and architecture with a kind of 'theoretical' basis (ibid.: 212), from Brunelleschi's Rotunda degli Angeli to Alberti's S. Sebastiano to Leonardo's Bramante's Tempietto, to Palladio's church at Maser. As is well known in the history of Renaissance art and architecture, the circle appears as a principle in its works. Rudolf Wittkower's seminal study of the Renaissance's centrally planned churches brings to light the inherent continuity of the circular and polygonal forms advocated by Alberti as an attempt to 'return to the venerable forms of temples of the ancients' (Wittkower, 1971: 5). It does not escape Wittkower's analysis that Alberti had a distinct preference for the circular plan as a reflection of nature's providence: 'For nature aspires to absolute perfection, she is the best and divine teacher of all things' (ibid.). The Vitruvian figure projected Vitruvius's original claim of perfection in the proportions of the human body into the work of the *quattrocento*, vivifying a popular proof that nature's perfection has been conferred upon the human world itself – a *cosmografia del minor mundo* (Tarlow, 2010: 70).

The circle in the Neoplatonic spirit of the early Renaissance, perhaps more than in times past, became a figure for philosophical, mathematical, religious,

Figure 3.1   Robert Fludd, Detail of frontispiece of *Utriusque cosmi maioris scilicet et minoris metaphysica physica atqve technical historia*, 1617

artistic and scientific thought. The predominant ambition to reflect the perfection of cosmic circularity in either metaphor or in architectural form (or both) was certainly the outcome of a Christian-infused interpretation of classical texts that coloured the Renaissance. Yet the basic relationship between the macrocosm and the microcosm had been pursued since antiquity. Heraclitus of Ephesus associated divine intervention in the life and spirit with the 'spiritous vapors of air'. This was verified by Hippocratic medicine and it was possible to show an anatomical connection between the workings of the lungs and the heart, revealing that this spirit was indeed inhaled (Lowry, 1974: 435).[3] Ptolemy later would make this connection explicit in the *Tetrabiblos*, in which he described the relationship between the cyclical appearance of astral configurations and human health, emotions and events. The fate of human affairs was revealed within the realm of zodiacal constellations whose angelic power presided over them. This structure provided the foundations for the medieval construction of *Melothesia* – representations of the body inscribed in a ring of zodiac signs, each one corresponding to the particular section of the body over which its power governs.

Yet, although the perfection of the circle had been a subject of classical philosophy, its re-emergence in the Renaissance seemed to coincide with a kind of enthusiasm that went beyond its initial role in Greek and Islamic thought. Marjorie Nicolson demonstrates this in her book *The Breaking of the Circle* with regard to Elizabethan cosmology and poetry, which, she writes, was 'most often interpreted in terms of the circle'. She argues that Elizabethans believed the circle, which was found in the perfect spherical form of the planets, in the Earth and was visible in the round head of the human was 'more than analogy to them; it was truth. God had made all things in the universe, the world, and the body of man as nearly circular as grosser natures would allow' (Nicolson, 1950, quoted in Mintz et al., 1952: 98).

SECULAR DISPLACEMENTS OF THE CIRCLE

The relationship between microcosm and macrocosm had already provided a long-standing tradition in the history of Western culture in which the circulating and the cyclical conferred a sense of celestial providence upon the objects under its sway. Although the reflection of divine motions, forms and structures in earthly phenomena yields a kind of fractal relationship demonstrating the overwhelming continuum of truth that binds the fleshly, finite mortal animal to eternal and infinite divinity, there is another way to interpret the microcosm–macrocosm pairing. This is best expressed in the medieval concept of God as 'a circle whose center is everywhere and whose circumference is nowhere'.[4] This description has a somewhat cloudy origin in Hermes Trismegistus's *Liber XXIV philosophorum*, where, in posing the question, What is God?, he replies: *Deus est sphaera infinita, cuius centrum est ubique, circumferentia nusquam.* The widespread dissemination of this maxim can be credited to the theologian Alain of Lille (*c.*1128–1203), in his

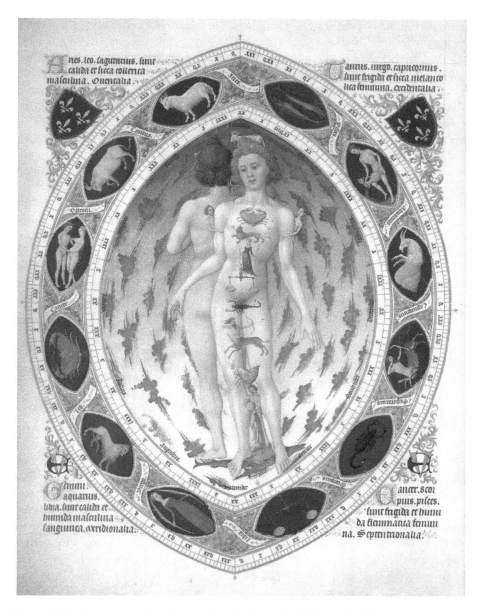

Figure 3.2 Limbourge brothers, Melothesia, 1413–1416 (*Très Riches Heures du Duc de Berry*)

Regulae de sacra theologia. Alain's interpretation of the formula remains significant in that he substitutes 'intelligible' for Hermes's 'infinite', which he opposes to the corporeal: 'In the corporeal sphere the center, because of its smallness, can hardly be said to be anywhere; the circumference however is taken to be in many places. But in the intelligible sphere, the center is everywhere, the circum-ference nowhere' (Migne, 1855: 627, quoted in and translated by Small, 1983: 91). As Robin Small explains, this transposition from the 'infinite' to the 'intel-ligible' marks a Neoplatonic turn in which the human appears as a finite point in comparison with the infinity of God's domain. In contrast to the metaphorical relationship typical of the microcosm–macrocosm conception, his relationship between the individual and God reveals what is indeed an *opposition* between the two rather than a continuum: 'in the corporeal sphere, the center is immobile, the circumference mobile. However, in the intelligible sphere it is God, the "unmoved mover", who brings about the movement of all else' (ibid.). What Alain intends to show by this opposition is not only the disjunction between the corporeal and the intelligible, but actually the distinction between the two spheres to which mankind is bound – the divine and the natural.

This clear distinction between the natural system and the infinite realm of intelligibility would carry forward for two centuries until Nicholas Cusanus's *De docta ignorantia* [*Learned Ignorance*] of 1440 introduced a bizarre collapse of this dualism into a singular identity: because only God was able to master perfect geometry, it is thus impossible, according to Cusanus, to construct or observe a true sphere or circle anywhere in the universe, and therefore any such imperfect body found in nature will never have an absolute centre, including the universe itself. In light of this, the world is an infinity of 'apparent' centres embodied by every individual – a kind of 'immovable centre'. 'In consequence, there will be a *machina mundi* whose center, so to speak, is everywhere, whose circumference is nowhere, for God is the circumference and center and he is everywhere and nowhere' (Cusanus, 1954: 111, quoted in Small, 1983: 95). Over a century and a half later, Giordano Bruno would echo this conception in his *Della causa, prin-cipio e uno,* by describing not the world, but the universe as that which has its centre everywhere and its circumference nowhere. The circle, for Bruno, was the 'symbol and pattern of all life and action in the cosmos' (Pagel, 1951: 31). This trajectory would soon be punctured by Pascal's more expansive use of the maxim in his *Pensées*, replacing the universe with 'Nature', understood as the infinite object of human reason. As Small explains, Pascal's attempt here is to reveal the limits of 'natural reason', in which human life is bound between the finite and the infinite by the expansive, yet limited, imagination – the circumference of which will always be less than that of Nature's infinity. As such, Nature's boundaries will, for Pascal, always remain unimaginable, unattainable (ibid.: 96–7).

The secularization of God, described as a circle whose centre is everywhere and whose circumference is nowhere, consists of the gradual collapse of the dis-tance between the macrocosm and the microcosm, as they progressively fold one into the other. The result of this validates a new kind of relativism of individual centrality, where the centre that, in God, was everywhere is discovered to coincide with the infinity of human knowledge contained within the totality of individu-als. 'All points were definable from any given center, thus producing a reticular

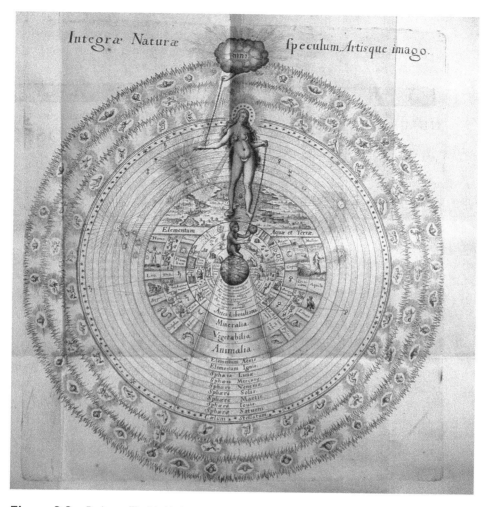

Figure 3.3   Robert Fludd, *Utriusque cosmi maioris scilicet et minoris metaphysica physica atqve technical historia, 1617 (The Mirror of the Whole of Nature and the Image of Art, 1617)*

grid of interaction subject to an infinity of points from which correlations could be made' (Lowry, 1974: 441). By the seventeenth century, the figure of a sphere whose centre is everywhere and whose circumference nowhere comes to describe at once God *and* the material universe, the heavens *and* nature – an image that gains a geometric differentiation no longer as a circle per se, but as a kind of 'spider-web' structure consisting of a multitude of fixed points bound together in a new pursuit of reason, rationality and cognition. 'Just as God was conceived as a universal point, so human understanding became an abstract center from which the essence of things could be summarized' (ibid.: 442). Seventeenth-century human reason sought for the first time to fill the infinite and the universal that had previously been the domain of God's solitary centrality in the cosmos.

Now located within human reason, each 'point' acts as an equivalent centre – an identical source of natural reason – displacing the singular source of meaning into the multiplicity of human knowledge. As a result, '[t]he notion of a unique "true world" thus disappears – and with it the contrast between true world and a merely apparent world' (Small, 1983: 100). The ontological collapse of the macrocosm into the microcosm would render, as Nietzsche would later lament, a frustrated state in which early modern Western culture finds itself caught. The pursuit of rational knowledge of the *finiteness of things* is now doomed to the same impossibility as humanity's capacity to reach the infinite, condemning human knowledge to pursue a kind of 'scientific', 'mechanic' interpretation of the world in which all appreciation and comprehension of it rests solely on its ability to be 'counted, calculated and expressed in formulas' (Nietzsche, 2001: 239 (§ 373)). Joseph Raphson would capture this in the annex of his *Analysis Aequationum Universalis* of 1702:

> Neither can Human Philosophy theoretically compose the smallest mouse or the simplest plan, nor can human praxis build them, much less the whole universe. These are problems worthy of the Primordial Wisdom and Power which produces these things. As for us, they offer us only a progress in *aeternum* of our knowledge both of the things themselves and of the perpetually geometrizing God. (Raphson, 1702: 95, quoted in Koyré, 1994: 205)

The assumption that macrocosmic universality coincides with the microcosm of human cognition would in part open up a world the wholeness of which is now given over to an infinitely grand and abstract space – a space that, nevertheless, must be accounted for as a *thing* with properties that present themselves as quantities available to the calculations and measurements of this new scientific perception. It is from this new world or, better, *universe*, that the individual-as-centre – the microcosm whose intellect and passions give it access to the macrocosm of human reason – will provide a reciprocal framework for the birth of the modern 'subject'. For, within this new universal perception, order will be seen to consist of measures as abstract as the Euclidian, 'geometrized' space within which it is made. Furthermore, by giving the reading of the microcosm–macrocosm duality an intellectual form, the notion of *circularity* defined by such a concept changes significantly: circularity here no longer confirms the divine continuum between God and the closed, circular systems in which objects move, but it now provides a geometrical model based on a circle as a circumference definable by the infinite rays that extend outward from its centre. In this way, each individual 'centre' can coexist intellectually with the (divine) totality of

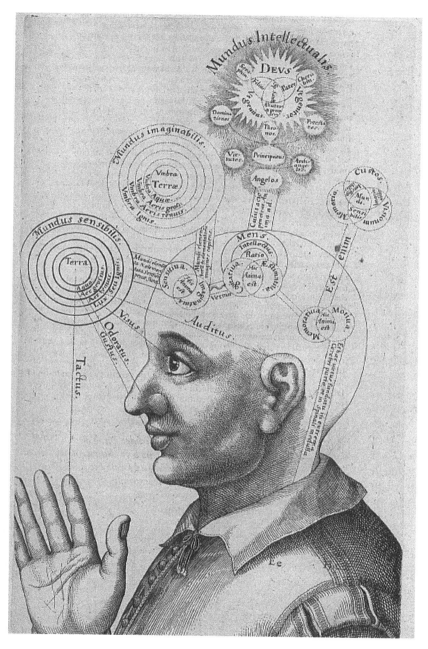

Figure 3.4 Robert Fludd, *De praeternaturali utriusque mundi historia* (*The Preternatural History of Both Worlds*), 1621

humankind's knowledge in the cyclical movement between the fixed, corporeal being and the limitlessness of the mental sphere. In this vastness of a new, measurable universe, it is no longer a matter of observing systems and objects of circulation as evidence of divine work. Such phenomena now present themselves to humankind's intellect to be grasped, calculated, explained and predicted. Truth, dislodged from a singular centre, now begins to freely circulate.

Sir Thomas Browne (1605–82) embodied this new consciousness perhaps better than most. 'There is no man alone, because every man is a Microcosm and carries the whole World about him' (Browne, 1928–31, quoted in Huntley, 1953: 358). For Browne, it made no sense to separate theological commitments from scientific pursuits in either anatomy or astronomy. Indeed, it was precisely through the theological use of the circle provided by Hermes that Browne was able, like others before him, to unite the two sciences – microcosm and macrocosm – in a theologico-scientific whole. Connected, the two sciences, revolutionized by William Harvey and Nicolaus Copernicus, respectively, both drew on the same circular concept, whose validity was, for Browne, confirmed not by empirical observation, but by the strength of its long trajectory from Plato to Hermes Trismegistus (ibid.: 357). Through the metaphor of the circle, Browne realized that time itself was circular, just as was the rotation of the heavenly spheres in their orbits around the Sun: 'the lives, not only of men, but of Commonwealths, and the whole world, run not upon an *Helix* that still enlargeth, but on a Circle' (Browne: xvii, quoted in ibid.: 362). The metaphor of the circle within a circle appeared everywhere to Browne, confirming the theological continuity between the finest elements of nature and the most grand understandings of God himself. As Huntley explains,

> [w]e have already seen how the smallest circle is the womb, that truest microcosm, and how Harvey discovered a circle inside that. Proceeding now from the smallest to the largest, we pass from the world of the womb, through this globe of geography, at last into the timeless spirit of God – through three stages of epistemology: sense, philosophy, and divinity. (Ibid.: 363–4)

For Browne, humankind, through the intellect, was placed at the nexus between material and divine spheres and, so, was able to perceive both. 'That mass of Flesh that circumscribes me, limits not my mind' (Browne: xi, quoted in ibid.: 363).

FROM METAPHOR TO CONCEPT: THE EMERGENCE OF 'CIRCULATIO'

Much scientific exploration of the sixteenth and seventeenth centuries in Europe drew from a similar relationship between microcosm and macrocosm, conceived as a synthetic whole observable by the new, centred, rational subject. During this epistemological transition, the concept of circulation would emerge as an extension and translation of the realm of observation and measurement, lending itself increasingly, as we shall see, as a principle to deploy in the organization of human affairs. Now that the distinction between microcosm and macrocosm, coinciding in the individual subject, had become consequently unclear, so too became the act of distinguishing between what in the past had been absolute in its separation: the labour of humankind from the works of God. From the seventeenth century onward, human intervention in the natural world would increasingly present itself *as* the natural world. And, just as the systems of circulation observable in nature had long provided evidence of their divine origin, the edifice of the modern world would be constructed by more sophisticated systems of objects, thoughts, materials and beings evermore bound up in perpetual circulation, only to be retroactively observed as the work of a divine, invisible hand. The ancient role that the circle had played as the signature of divine truth in the phenomena of the natural world would be heightened in the seventeenth century as it acquired a new status as a principle of human order.

Of course, as a principle of human order, the observations and measurements penetrating a world governed by circular movement would have to present such systems in a single operative model. To reproduce such circular systems in the microcosmos of human life, one needs a universal model. That, of course, was the concept at the heart of our investigation that, until 1593, had yet to enter into scholarly discourse: '*circulatio*', the term introduced by the natural philosopher Andrea Cesalpino in his *Quaestiones peripatetica*:

> Nature has given proof of great dexterity in creating lungs in terrestrial and gills in water animals – for the purpose of moderating blood temperature. [. . .] It is thus that the lung tempers the blood by mere air contact. That such 'circulation' [*circulatio*] does operate from the right to the left ventricle through the lung is borne out by the following anatomical facts. (Cespalpino, 1593, quoted in Pagel, 1951: 25)

By the end of the sixteenth century, this concept of *circulatio* had become a common term in natural philosophy (Pagel, 1950: 621), which no doubt accounts for Giordano Bruno's controversial claim that blood moves in a circular motion:

> The spiritual life-force is effused from the heart into the whole of the body and (flows back) from the latter to the heart, as it were from the centre to the periphery and from the periphery to the centre, following the pattern of a circle. [. . .] The material part of all these spirits is a fluid which cannot move on its own account, but by means of its innate spirit. Hence there is no circular or sphaerical motion outside the body, for the blood, which in the animal moves in a circle in order to distribute its motor, the spirit, lies immovable outside the body, is inert and decays, no longer deserving the name of blood. (Bruno, 1891, quoted in Pagel, 1950: 621)

In each case, the association between *circulatio* (and, indeed, circular movement in general) and an underlying sense of perfection was clear. For Caesalpino, *circulatio* designated not only a continuous movement of the blood through the body, but also the chemical process of distillation (*destillatio*) whereby blood is cyclically heated to a vapour by the heart and cooled down by the air in the lungs – a process by which blood was said to be chemically purified, and thus 'perfected'. Bruno's claim that blood 'follows the pattern of a circle' conforms to his overall belief in the perfection of the circle as the 'fundamental symbol and pattern of all life and action in the cosmos' (Pagel, 1951: 31). The combination of these two forms of perfection would provoke William Harvey's definitive research where he would demonstrate the circulation of blood for the first time, publishing his findings in his monumental *De motu cordis et sanguinis* of 1628.

For Harvey, the purpose of the circulation of the blood was also its perfection, and, similarly to Caesalpino before him, he initially took it to be a kind of distillation process, inspired by Aristotle's meteorological analyses. Like Bruno and so many others before him, he framed this process within the figure of the circle:

> I began to think whether there might not be a motion as it were in a circle. Now this I afterwards found to be true; [. . .] Which motion we may be allowed to call circular, in the same ways as Aristotle says that the air and the rain emulate the circular motion of the superior bodies; for the moist earth, warmed by the sun evaporates; the vapours drawn upwards are condensed, and descending in the form of rain moisten the earth again; and by this arrangement are generations of living things produced; and in like manner too are tempests and meteors engendered by the circular motion, and by the approach and recession of the sun. And so in all likelihood, does it come to pass in the body, through the motion of the blood; the various parts are nourished, cherished, quickened by the warmer more perfect vapours spirituous, and, as I may say, alimentive blood; which, on the contrary, in contact with these parts becomes cooled, coagulated, and, so to speak, effete; whence it returns to its sovereign, the heart, as if to its source, or to the inmost home of the body, there to recover its state of excellences or perfection. Here it resumes its due fluidity and receives an infusion of natural heat – powerful, fervid, a kind of treasury of life, and is impregnated with spirits, and it might be said with balsam; and thence it is again dispersed, and all this depends on the motion and the action of the heart. The heart, consequently, is the beginning of life; the sun of the microcosm, even as the sun in his turn might well be designated as the heart of the world; for it is the heart by whose virtue and pulse the blood is moved, perfected, made apt to nourish, and is preserved from corruption and coagulation; it is the household divinity which, discharging its function, nourishes, cherishes, quickens the whole body, and is indeed the foundation of life, the sources of all action. (Harvey, 1847: 46–7)

EXERCITATIO,
ANATOMICA DE
MOTV CORDIS ET SAN-
GVINIS IN ANIMALI-
BVS,
GVILIELMI HARVEI ANGLI,
Medici Regii, & Professoris Anatomiæ in Col-
legio Medicorum Londinensi.

FRANCOFVRTI,
Sumptibus GVILIELMI FITZERI.

ANNO M. DC. XXVIII.

Figure 3.5   William Harvey, Frontispiece of *De motu cordis*, 1628

As we have seen before, the circular motion of the blood is seen as the fleshy process presiding over the microcosm of the human body – a reflection of the perfection of the circular motions of the heavenly bodies that is not only referenced here by Harvey with Aristotle's meteorology, but that certainly was a common conjecture in his education at Padua, where, at the time, Galileo held a professorship. Indeed, Harvey owned not only his works, but also those of Copernicus, Kepler and many others in his personal library, and the relationship he established here did not go unnoticed: Baldwin Hamey, a contemporary of Harvey, would conclude Harvey's life with the following epigram:

> That according to the opinion of Copernicus as to the motion of the earth and of Harvey as to the movement of the blood we are here –
>
> *Tunc agit atque agimus nos rota nosque rotam*;
>
> Then are we all in a wheel and a wheel in us all. (Huntley, 1953: 359–60)

Johannes Walaeus, one of Harvey's key supporters and a principal agent of the dissemination of Harvey's work, would echo Harvey's beliefs with regard to the circulation of the blood in a report translated into all European languages and Chinese: 'Blood circulates for the sake of its perfection. By virtue of its continuous movement it is attenuated' (Walaeus, 1673, quoted in Pagel, 1951: 24).

What makes all of this stand out is not simply the fact that the metaphor of the circle had found its archetype in the circulation of the blood, nor the confirmation this discovery lent to the long-standing microcosm–macrocosm relationship. In fact, Harvey's 'discovery' was itself incomplete. Although he surpassed the previous Galenic and Aristotelian notions of the heart's function, discovering the powerful systole as the principal source of the blood's movement, he could not reveal how the blood would pass from the arterial to the venous system – a discovery that would be made in 1661 by Marcello Malpighi, who famously revealed the workings of the capillary system (Lowry, 1974: 438–9). In this sense, Harvey's 'discovery' of the circulation of blood remained largely framed within a classical description of this process. Instead, what seems more significant was the *discovery of the concept itself*, providing seventeenth-century thought with a new epistemological basis. The implications of this would unfold over the course of this century, giving the metaphor of the circle a thoroughly new dimension: circulation, by itself, would now denote a process in excess of the circular motion it describes. Equally universal, it was a concept that was *both* metaphor *and* process, *both* divine *and* material, *both* truth *and* praxis. For this reason, as we will see, by the middle of the seventeenth century the proliferation of the use of circulation as a concept across many forms of thought would draw from Harvey's model, while continuing to follow a roughly classical model, offering a new metaphor that would remain imprecise, thus having a certain discursive versatility. It is as if the demonstration and naming of the process translated the validity of the metaphor of the circle into new terms, giving new life to a notion that for centuries had been a foundational truth of Western epistemologies. Thus, the 'discovery' of circulation would offer forth a new, mechanical principle now useful to the ordering and management of life itself.

In a way, the first instance in which this excess would manifest itself was in Descartes' (mis)reading of Harvey's work. As perhaps the single most important vector in the spread of Harvey's discourse, Descartes embraced *De motu cordis*, but only by violently misinterpreting his key discovery of the powerful systole of the heart. On the one hand, Harvey's model of the circulation fitted well into Descartes' conception of the mechanical body. By 1632, Descartes had read *De motu cordis*, and its impact would be noted in the amendments made in his *Discourse on Method* of 1637. For Descartes, the movement of blood gave his new philosophy the most exemplar result on which the validity of his entire philosophy would depend – that of particulate motion (French, 2006: 181). Yet on the other hand, as a consequence of Descartes' anti-Aristotelian presumptions, he could not accept that the heart's systole was a self-generated motion. Because, for Descartes, all motion was transmitted, particle to particle, from an original (divine) source, 'it was important for him that the heart was the sole source of motion in the body and equally important that it was *not* self-generated motion' (ibid.: 185; my emphasis). Despite the two philosophies that developed around circulation, it was because Harvey's ideas tied in with those of Descartes that they were brought to new audiences and fuelled by the ensuing debates. Yet, in all of the arguments for and against Descartes' natural philosophy, Harvey's doctrine of circulation lay to a certain extent at their root (ibid.: 205).

Nevertheless, it was by confronting a Harvean notion of circulation with the Cartesian discourse on mechanical motion that a crucial element of circulation was able to emerge: *mechanical motion plus circularity*. *De motu cordis* stands as a kind of diagram of this new conception that would allow itself to depart from the natural sciences and to circulate among the various discourses and debates of the seventeenth century. References to Harvey and his circulation began appearing in poems, theological texts and philosophical works. 'Litterateurs like Hobbes, More, Harrington, Birkenhead, Cowley, Dryden, and Fuller would not have dropped Harvey references into their works if they had not had reasons to feel that the literate public had some vague understanding of his accomplishments' (Frank, 1979: 134). Harvey's 'discovery' marks a kind of turning point in which the metaphor of the circle, without losing any of its divine impact, had spawned a more profane derivative of itself in a model of circulation that would begin to affect the more earthly, secular operations of the world. And perhaps its greatest impact outside natural philosophy lay in the discourses of trade and in the early philosophies of the state – debates that both preceded and succeeded the publication of *De motu cordis*.

CIRCULATION AND STATE REASON

As early as the late sixteenth century, a clearly modern conception of circulation had begun to play a crucial role in the construction of an early theory of the state that went beyond metaphor, providing an outline for a new form of secular power that would underpin the construction of the modern European state from this point onward. Giovanni Botero, one of the earliest to identify this emergent configuration of power, authored two texts of note: *Della ragion di stato* in 1589 (*The Reason of State*, 1956), and *Delle causa della grandezza delle città* in 1588 (*On the Causes of the Greatness and Magnificence of Cities*, 2012), both of which were translated into English as early as 1606 and widely read across Europe. Botero's work, in direct opposition to that of his intellectual nemesis, Machiavelli, is a kind of proto-liberal recognition of the importance for a state of maintaining its subjects' happiness and health. In this respect, *On the Causes of the Greatness and Magnificence of Cities* provides a prescient bridge between a premodern cosmos and the nascent, geometrical space of modernity under the managerial disposition of the state, as we shall investigate further in the following chapter. Botero's text explores the various factors that affect and influence the glory and power of the city. Disclosing a kind of proto-Malthusian conception, Botero shows clearly in his *Reason of State* that the central factor through which all others proportionately relate or are determined is the city's population. Thus, one could associate the terms greatness or magnificence with establishing a positive population growth rate. Because a city's citizenry (the primary measure of its 'greatness') must be nourished by a constant intake of food and made wealthy by exchange, Botero looks to establish all the relationships between resources, wealth, physical geography, exchange, circulation, and so on, that would in some way play a determinate role in increasing or decreasing the number of inhabitants of a city, and thus its magnificence.[5] Thus, the importance of religion, for example, lies in the church's ability to lure and fix large numbers of people in one city. Of note is Botero's privileging of the city's domestic spaces and its infrastructures of circulation, highlighting an early relationship between production and reproduction and foregrounding an administrative concern the object of which, as Foucault has shown, would later be know as 'population'.

Book 1 considers the basic conditions that make a setting for a great city. It considers, as it were, the original forces that draw people together to form a city, a set of factors that spans from physical conditions that favour the sustenance of a large population to the social conditions in which civilization emerges. These factors are largely divisible into two categories: those affecting manufacturing and those affecting exchange, or the 'commodious' circulation of goods. Like Cerdá, Botero attempts to historicize the conditions under which the 'first' cities were formed, drawing together large numbers of people, 'little different from brute beasts, without laws, without conformity to customs and manner of civil conversation' (Botero, 1956: 227), under the authority of a certain few wise, eloquent leaders, who thus constitute the first governments. The origin of the city, for Botero, would consist of the discovery of the efficient and commodious manner in which humans could live by coexisting in a relationship of *civil commerce*. Their governors 'declared to the rude and barbarous multitude how much and how great profit they were likely to enjoy if, drawing themselves to one place, they would unite themselves in one body, by an interchangeable communication and commerce of all things that would proceed thereof' (ibid.). Thus, if Botero can be said to have discovered an early notion of population – the civilization within the 'multitude' – it would consist of the simultaneous establishment of a city and its government.

If the historical origin of the city for Botero is based on the founding of a kind of government of exchange (almost in the way Cerdá would historicize it three centuries later), it would do so only through the effective administration of its 'natural' infrastructures (e.g. rivers, passes, coastlines). And, like the physiocrats who would follow him, although wealth, for Botero, derived from the 'fruitfulness of the soil', he recognized that this wealth must also circulate. Thus, for him, the land outside a city was not only a site on which wealth would be cultivated for the city's inhabitants, but it had also to be transformed to suit the needs of the perpetual movement of wealth *between* cities. 'It sufficeth not enough therefore to the making of a city magnificent and great that the site thereof be necessary, but it must withal be commodious to other countries that are borderers, or near unto it' (ibid.: 235). Botero went further to underline the necessity for a kind of interconnected network of infrastructure that serves 'commodiously' the needs of international trade (by which he means trade between cities). He considers all means of transportation of goods: on foot, on horseback, by carriage and by water. A certain zeal for circulation comes across in the following passage, which would be echoed nearly two centuries later by Adam Smith: 'It seems in very truth that God created the water, not only for a necessary element to the perfection of nature, but more than so, for a most ready means to conduct and bring goods from one country to another' (ibid.: 237). He continues, outlining his hopes for a kind of universal society that such trade had the power to create:

> For His Divine Majesty, willing that men should mutually embrace each other as members of one body, divided in such sort His blessings as to no nation did he give all things, to the end that others having need of us, and contrariwise we having need of others, there might grow a community, and from a community love and from love a unity between us. (Ibid.)

Anticipating both William Petty and Richard Cantillon, Botero goes on to show how the basis of a city's power is articulated on its ability to quickly move its merchandise. In that way, not only is it important for a city to store quantities of its products and of those imported, but also to provide the infrastructure whereby such products can circulate easily and quickly in and out of the city. Ports thus require efficient design and security of loading and offloading merchandise. Highways that are paved and maintained further increase the 'greatness' of a city by way of improving the circulation of goods within and without (see ibid.: Book II, § 8).

Over half a century later (and following Harvey's discovery), in the pages of the *Leviathan*, we see Hobbes develop a similar principle regarding the administration of wealth, which he incorporated into his theory of the Commonwealth. However, unlike Botero's work, these ideas would now make direct reference to the model provided by Harvey:

> And in this also, the Artificiall Man maintains his resemblance with the Naturall; whose Veins receiving the Bloud from the severall Parts of the Body, carry it to the Heart; where being made Vitall, the Heart by the Arteries sends it out again, to enliven, and enable for motion all the Members of the same. (Hobbes, 1986: 301)

That Hobbes alludes to the circulation of blood as a system is not surprising. Many have noted the relationship that he had with Harvey (of particular note, see Keynes, 1966). Hobbes held Harvey in the same esteem in which he held Galileo and Copernicus (Frank, 1979). He was a close friend of Harvey's, and it is likely that Hobbes sat in on some of Harvey's famous lectures and vivisections in which his discovery was demonstrated (French, 2006: 61; Hobbes makes reference to this in the section 'On the Causes and Effects of Heat and Cold' in his *Decameron Physiologicum*, 1845). What is surprising then is that, despite his relationship with Harvey and the admiration he had for his work, Hobbes adopted a traditional, Galenic model of circulation that operated in a clearly Cartesian mechanical world. He likened the gold and silver flowing through the 'conduits' and 'ways' within the Commonwealth to blood circulating within his mechanical, artificial man, whose heart, the 'Publique Coffers', enriches this blood. Circulation, for Hobbes, had become a kind of de facto component in the mechanics of his *Leviathan* – a system among others. As with Botero, Hobbes's Commonwealth established the object of such circulation as the maintenance of vitality of its subjects: 'For naturall Bloud is in like manner made of the fruits of the Earth; and circulating, nourisheth by the way, every Member of the Body of Man' (Hobbes, 1986: 300). By circulation's endowment with both power and vitality, the modern European state that would emerge along Hobbesian lines had, like in Botero's writings, identified a central concern on which it would base its political calculations. For Hobbes, circulation had already been identified as a concept in its own right. Harvey's demonstration of the microcosm at work in the body seemed to be sufficient for the concept of circulation to stand as a self-evident truth that existed in excess of its scientific specificity, instead providing the Commonwealth with a universal measure of power.

Unlike Botero's emphasis on the practicalities of administering circulation, for Hobbes, circulation operated as a subcategory of an epistemological system of truth: *motion*. Inspired by Galileo, his mentor and friend, Hobbes had become obsessed with motion as the basis of all veracity. Indeed, the entire argument of *Leviathan* rested on the category of motion in the same terms Galileo had set out:

> That when a thing lies still, unlesse somewhat els stirre it, it will lye still for ever, is a truth no man doubts of. But that when a thing is in motion, it will eternally be in motion, unless somewhat els stay it, though the reason be the same, (namely, that nothing can change it selfe,) is not so easily assented to. (Ibid.: 87)

Leviathan represents an effort by Hobbes to construct a comprehensive *science* of politics grounded in a rational, Galilean understanding of motion together with Cartesian mechanics. The result would be both a 'mechanical' explanation of how man behaves and a means by which he could be made to behave to form a Body Politique. *Leviathan* would propose nothing short of a geometrical order between sovereignty and subjectivity based on obedience. To achieve this, he employed Galileo's 'resolutive-compositive' method of scientific deliberation (see C.B. Macpherson's introduction to Hobbes, 1986: 25–6), splitting his work conceptually down the middle.

The first stage, the 'resolutive' stage, would resolve all of political society as the net result of the motion of its elemental, individual parts – the simple, 'invisible' motions that, in sum, compel each individual subject to act. Hobbes believed he could resolve each of these simple forces in the same way that Galileo had, 'in imagining motions which could not be observed but which, once postulated, could be shown mathematically to be sufficient to account for the complex observed "motions" he wanted to explain, such as the trajectory of a cannon ball' (ibid.: 26). Embracing a Cartesian model of particulate motion, Hobbes set out the first part of his work, 'Of Man', in order to construct the basis of his mathematical science, which would in turn allow him to explain the more complex 'motion' of society. Hobbes proposed that the human being could be reduced to a mechanical apparatus composed of sense organs, limbs, muscles, speech organs, imagination and memory. Each individual mechanical body moved in response to various objects impacting it. He reasoned that such motion was not self-moving, but moved instead as a result of a greater, pre-existing chain of external motions impacting themselves on the body and on its constituent parts. 'Neither in us that are pressed, are they anything else, but divers motions; (for motion, produceth nothing but motion.)' (ibid.: 86). Nevertheless, internal to all these simple motions at work within each body is an in-built desire for each part to remain in motion – what Hobbes called endeavour or appetite. 'These small beginnings of Motion, within the body of Man, before they appear in walking, speaking, striking, and other visible actions, are commonly called Endeavour' (ibid.: 119). Taken together, these desires or endeavours, either emerging as innate, instinctual drives (for food, etc.), or as learned desires proceeding from experience, are the bases of human activities, or 'motions'. 'Life it selfe is but Motion, and can never be without Desire, nor without Fear, no more than without Sense' (ibid.: 130). Driven by such passions, 'man' enters an arena of competition for power, each man struggling to assert himself over the others, which, in the state of nature (the state of being without an artificial order), leads to Hobbes's well-known war of all against all.

With the second, or 'compositive' stage, Hobbes would put forward his proposition for the Commonwealth – a great 'Artificiall Man', a single 'body' capable of sublating the sum total of subjects' desires and motions into the single will of the sovereign.

Because Hobbes was influenced by Cartesian anatomical mechanics, the appearance of circulation would take on a different character to that of movement in Botero's writings. *Leviathan* fuses human, animal and machine into one figure, bringing in all models of contemporary natural philosophy – mechanical, anatomical and animal *motu* (Schmitt, 2008: 19). As Carl Schmitt notes, 'Hobbes transferred – and that seems to me to be the gist of his philosophy of state – the Cartesian conception of man as a *mechanism with a soul* onto the "huge man", the state, made by him into a machine animated by the sovereign-representative person' (ibid.: 93–4; original emphasis). Hobbes would incorporate Harvey's anatomical notion of circulation in this artificial, mechanical *Leviathan*, as it was through Harvey's discovery that circulation first appeared as a *comprehensive, closed and mechanical system*. Like the *Leviathan* itself, circulation would materialize as an essential component in the construction of an earthly, secular form of power – one that bears a self-evidently virtuous character in its systematic, rational and scientific truth.

The Hobbesian Commonwealth differed significantly from Botero's network of commodious city-states. Hobbes wrote the *Leviathan* in the shadow of the English Civil War and in the wake of bloody religious civil wars across Europe – a political context vastly more unstable than that in which Botero had written. Religion had grown hazardous to the maintenance of order, and in its place Hobbes saw that mathematics and natural science provided a more universal source of indisputable truth. Turning to geometry, Hobbes's *Leviathan* would not only sketch the mechanics of the new absolutist form of state, but it would describe a new logic of spatiality that would fill out this 'Body Politique'. It was a logic that would unfold across Europe over the course of the next three centuries – a period in which the relationship established between circulation and sovereign power would only grow integral, in turn appearing increasingly *necessary*.

CIRCULATION AND TRADE

If the concept of circulation reverberated in these early writings on the state, it had a far broader purchase on the various discourses of trade of the seventeenth century.

By the eighteenth century, it would find itself one of the central concepts for the physiocrats and would later play a fundamental role in the birth of political economy. Only five years before Harvey would publish *De motu cordis*, Edward Misselden had written his *Circle of Commerce* in which he expounded upon a nascent principle of circulation that he believed underpinned commercial trade: 'all rivers of Trade spring out of this source and empty themselves again into this Ocean. All that waight of Trade falles to this center, & comes within the circuit of this Circle' (Misselden, 1623). A mere 15 years later (10 years after the publication of *De motu cordis*), Lewes Roberts would dedicate his 1638 *Merchants Map of Commerce* to Harvey and his five brothers (who were all involved in trade; Webster, 1979: 27, n. 84). Historian of medicine Charles Webster observes, '[t]here are certain suggestive analogies between dynamic conceptions that emerged in the two fields of economics and physiology at the time of Harvey's work on circulation' (ibid.).

Central to the adaptations of Harvey's work in matters of both trade and the state would be Sir William Petty. Petty had been a Reader at Cambridge and an enthusiastic supporter of Harvey. In 1651, the same year Hobbes published *Leviathan*, Petty delivered a public lecture in which he directly praised Harvey's work (French, 2006: 344). His own ground-breaking work on 'Political Arithmetick' towards the end of the seventeenth century would see at its core a suggestively Harvean idea: the 'velocity of money'. What made this work important was that it changed the terms of the various discourses of trade, providing a new framework in which the blossoming realm of economic thought could unfold. What had preceded both Petty's contributions and the well-known discourses of the second half of the seventeenth century (mainly in England) was a text that both set the tone and laid out a general framework for these works to follow: Antonio Serra's *Breve trattato delle cause che possono fare abbondare li regni d'oro e d'argento dove non sono miniere* (*Brief treaty on the causes that make kingdoms that lack mines abound with gold and silver*) of 1613. Serra's work aimed to establish the principles by which the amount of gold, silver and other resources within the Neapolitan kingdom could be assessed (Schumpeter, 1972: 195). It was the first attempt to construct a scientific treatise to develop policies and analytical principles to evaluate and balance the outflow of gold and silver from the kingdom. Indeed, Serra went beyond simply explaining these fundamental principles to establish 'a general analysis of the conditions that determine the state of an economic organism' (ibid.). Much like Botero, Serra based the terms of all subsequent discourses of trade and their analytical frameworks on an *abundance of commodities*: 'natural resources, quality of the people, the development of industry and trade, the efficiency of government – the implication being that if the economic process as a whole functions properly, the monetary element will take care of itself and not require any specific therapy' (ibid.).[6]

In work from Serra's to Josiah Child's late contribution of 1693, there exists a recognition of, or an intention to construct, an analytic apparatus founded upon the abundance of goods. Yet Petty's work – in particular, his 'Political

Arithmetick' – would establish a different set of criteria from all other discourses of trade of his time, presenting a model that would have an impact far beyond its time, for it introduced an analysis of wealth based not on a fixed entity (gold or silver), but rather on money and the *velocity* at which it passes through a given state. In his work, Petty helped to identify a key factor that would answer the various problems which had been brought to light by the vast amount of precious metals pouring into Europe from its colonies. The characteristic of money as a material quantity and the mobility of prices were seen to be tied to one another. This led to the problematic conclusion that money was *also* a commodity that comes at a price which depends on how much of it there is in circulation, bound up in what Foucault called a 'circle of preciousness' (Foucault, 1994: 175). 'The standard of equivalences is itself involved in the system of exchanges, and the buying power of money signifies nothing but the marketable value of the metal' (ibid.: 171). Petty's solution to the lack of sufficient money was to increase the 'velocity' of its circulation, which, he reasoned, was equivalent to an increase in the amount of money in a country. For this, he proposed to install banks that would facilitate the circulation of money, thus increasing its effective amount. By identifying the velocity of money as the object of both analysis and intervention, Petty's work helped to untie this knot by reversing the relationship between money and wealth:

> Whereas the Renaissance based the two *functions* of coinage (measurement and substitution) on the double nature of its intrinsic *character* (the fact that it was precious), the seventeenth century turns the analysis upside down: it is the exchanging function that serves as the foundation for the other two characters (its ability to measure and its capacity to receive a price thus appearing as *qualities* deriving from that *function*). (Ibid.: 174; original emphasis)

In this framework, the analysis of wealth is no longer a matter of accounting for the various precious metals in circulation, but rather *the analysis of wealth is based on circulation itself*. Foucault explains: 'When goods can circulate (and this is thanks to money), they multiply, and wealth increases; when coinage becomes more plentiful, as a result of a good circulation and a favorable balance, one can attract fresh merchandise and increase both agriculture and manufacturing' (ibid.: 178). In other words, by the end of the seventeenth century, money had become a universal representation *and* analysis of wealth, and, for this reason, '[n]ow that money and wealth are both included within the area of exchange and circulation, mercantilism can adjust its analysis in terms of the model recently provided by Harvey' (ibid.: 179).

For Hobbes, the venous circuit of money's circulation concerns taxes and duties, which return to the 'heart' of the state coffers in order to be made vital, and then the other circuit of money's circulation, analogous to the arterial circuit of blood, is that of the 'exchange of wealth, manufacturers and agriculture' (ibid.), which is the circuit in which the money, made vital by the first circuit, is then made available as analysis of wealth through its circulation. The circulation of money provides the measure by which wealth, at any point in time, can be mapped against itself and objects can be put in relation to one another. Petty's velocity of money, therefore, would lend a new object of analysis in the history of economic thought. Although he was the first to identify this figure of analysis, the first to apply it to circulation (*la vitesse de la circulation*) would be the physiocrat Richard Cantillon (Schumpeter, 1972: 317), who demonstrated that increasing the speed of circulation was equivalent to increasing the quantity of money. These developments marked the transition point from a world of 'trade' to one of '*œconomia*'.

'It was but slowly that the fact began to dawn upon analysts that there is a pervading interdependence between all economic phenomena, that they all hang together somehow' (ibid.: 242) – thus, the fate of seventeenth- and eighteenth-century economics, according to Schumpeter. He points out how the best of the seventeenth-century discourses of trade would cultivate a growing awareness of this, while nevertheless remaining unable to compose a model in which each of such phenomena could form a contiguous, systematic whole – a fundamental lapse that only a scientific approach would render clear to the practical frame of economic thinking: 'the first discovery of a science', as he puts it, 'is the discovery of itself' (ibid.). Such a totalizing, systematic and *macro*economic analysis received major contributions first from Petty's rationalism in the seventeenth century and then from the physiocratic doctrines of the eighteenth century, in particular those of Richard Cantillon and François Quesnay. The most significant development in this came with the introduction of the *tableu économique*.

By 1730, the date around which Cantillon would publish his *Essai sur la nature de commerce en generale*, Harvey's concept of circulation had already developed significantly through the contributions of Marcello Malpighi and others. Yet it was still fresh (ibid.: 240, n. 9). Cantillon's work would base its primary assumptions and its entire analytical framework on circulation, owing its greatest debt to Petty. For Cantillon, the circulation of wealth through the social body provided the clearest measure of a state's actual wealth. Through an understanding of the process by which money circulates (specifically, within a closed economy), a picture of the whole economy could finally emerge.

In order to construct such a diagram, Cantillon needed to set out the basic assumptions by which such an economy functions. First, he developed what he called the 'normal price' (*valeur intrinsèque*), which he opposed to the market price as a means to fix value to both the land and labour, which together go into the production of commodities. Like his physiocrat successors, he saw all wealth as originating in agriculture. 'The Land is the Source or Matter from whence all Wealth is produced. The Labour of man is the Form which produces it: and Wealth in itself is nothing but the Maintenance, Conveniencies, and Superfluities of Life' (Cantillon, 1959: § I.I.1). For Cantillon, 'society' in France at the time could be simplified as a composition of three distinct, 'natural' classes that arise from the fact that ownership of the land is based on an original, violent sequence of appropriation, distribution and production. From this, society organizes itself as landlords, farmers and labourers. Central is the landowner class as, he claims, 'all classes and inhabitants of a state live at the expense of the Proprietors of Land' (ibid.: § I.V.3). This was because it was owing to the riches of the lands owned by the landlords that a state was able to maintain those dwelling within it. Following this, Cantillon attempts to develop a holistic market-theory model in which villages, towns, cities and capital cities had emerged over time both as a function of his economic sociology and having been fashioned in part by 'Nature' and in part by the common mechanism by which this model operates: the circulation of wealth within the state.

Cantillon's theory of the circulation of wealth begins by assuming that farmers earn three 'rents' from the sale of their produce grown on the land they cultivate, which serve as the 'mainspring' of circulation in the state. One of these rents pays the landowner class for the use of its land, and the second pays for the upkeep of the farmers' tools, clothing, and so on, going to the 'undertakers',[7] or entrepreneurs, in the city. The landowning class also contributes to the wealth of the city by paying 'in detail' for the commodities it regularly buys over the course of a given economic cycle. Finally, the class of undertakers, artisans and labourers of the city produces a net return to the farmers by buying the latter's produce. According to Cantillon, pure rent yields the net return, which in turn is explained by the productivity of scarce natural resources. It follows that this net return is singly the product of agriculture, which yields the entire net income of a given society. Cantillon emphasizes that this net income must be spent quickly to keep the cycle of economic production in process, which is where his theory of circulation comes in. As Petty had previously suggested, Cantillon prescribes the use of banks: 'It will then be understood that all the advantage of Banks, public or private in a city, is to accelerate the circulation of money and to prevent so much of it from being hoarded as it would naturally be for several intervals' (Cantillon, 1959: § III.VI.11). Furthermore, the landowning class would remain independent of the actual circulation and exchange of goods: these processes would be conducted by the other classes, as the landowners are a kind of paternalistic class of caretakers of the very source of wealth in their 'natural' ownership of the land (ibid.: § I.XIII.18).

This schema can be seen to follow a kind of post-Harvean model cycling between city and country. In eighteenth-century France, it would have been easy to adopt the common theme of the state as body – a single, closed entity – that is nourished by the circulation of money. From this point of view, the model of circulation follows (ibid.: § II.III.11): money, originating from the large (arterial) sums paid as rent by the farmers to the landowners is then paid 'in detail' (capillary) in the city to the entrepreneurs, labourers, artisans, and so on, in exchange for commodities. These small payments are distributed across the population of a city (which, Cantillon claims, accounts for half of a state's population). From there, these small payments are then brought together again to return in large (venous) sums to the farmers, where they are reinvested in the next cycle of cultivation and thus made vital (profitable) by the 'heart' of the economy, which is the land. For Cantillon, it was clear that that the landowning, sovereign class played precisely the same role that Hobbes had attributed to the capital city as a kind of 'heart' that, through its paternalistic care-taking of the source of wealth, makes vital the net return of the entire state. All this circulation takes place between city and country, replicating a kind of circular movement from centre to periphery – a movement that inevitably not only nourishes the population ('maintenance') and thus the riches of the state, but also serves conceptually to make whole and complete the state itself as a *closed entity*.

Cantillon, like Botero, sees a state's population as a crucial factor in its economic wealth. He advises a maximization of the population according to an early notion of territorial carrying capacity as a governmental strategy related to the complete economic cycle. 'The natural and constant way of increasing Population in a State is to find employment for the People there, and to make the Land serve for the production of their Means of Support' (ibid.: § I.XV.31). And, like Botero, Cantillon sees this task of government to be intimately related to the state's infrastructural network. Anticipating Johann Heinrich Von Thünen's ring theory, the transportation of goods in and out of cities becomes an obvious and central factor in an analysis of a state's wealth based on circulation and exchange. For Cantillon, the cost of transportation not only is calculated as a cost of labour, but it forms a central constraint in his economic sociology, determining the hierarchy between cities, villages and their surrounding countryside – a factor Botero would take for granted. 'Great Cities are usually built on the seacoast or on the banks of large Rivers for the convenience of transport; because water carriage of the produce and merchandise necessary for the subsistence and comfort of the inhabitants is much cheaper than Carriages and Land Transport' (ibid: § I.VI.2). Indeed, circulation is read by Cantillon as *traffic*, which is the key underlying factor of a state's measure of power. 'After all it seems to me that the comparative Power and Wealth of States consist, other things being equal, in the greater or less abundance of money circulating in them hic et nunc' (ibid.: § II.VIII.14).

In a way, what Cantillon's analysis of wealth manages to combine is a kind of economic sociology and population theory of Botero, wedded to the morphology of cities and structured around Petty's velocity of money, all conceived within a closed, territorial state. These conditions provided a historical moment in which to experiment with a model that, for the first time, would attempt to construct a synthetic whole of the economic processes within a state. Cantillon's predecessors and contemporaries made general statements and described principles that drive the economic process, but, as Schumpeter says:

> they leave it to us to visualize this process itself as it runs its course between social groups or classes. Cantillon was the first to make this circular flow concrete and explicit, to give us a bird's eye view of economic life. In other words, he was the first to assemble a *tableu économique*. (Schumpeter, 1972: 222)

Of course, it would be François Quesnay who would be most widely known for his particular *Tableau économique* of 1758 (1972 (1758)). This work took Cantillon's a step further by drafting a diagram that was only implied in Cantillon's *Essai*. In many ways, Quesnay's work remained a reproduction of Cantillon's.[8] Nevertheless, Quesnay's overall recommendations can be reduced to two: *laissez-faire* economics and free trade (a general condemnation of governmental regulation) and a single tax on the net income (*produit net*) from the land. His economic principle revolved around a belief that the greatest satisfaction (*jouissance*) is to be attained with the smallest expense of labour – what Schumpeter called the 'maximum doctrine of perfect competition': '[Quesnay] held that the maximum satisfaction of wants for all members of society, taken together, will result if, conditions of perfect competition prevailing, everyone be allowed to act freely upon his own individual self-interest' (Schumpeter, 1972: 233). Such perfection within a competitive society, for Quesnay, would achieve a universal harmony of class interests, and, as such, Quesnay's overall economic equilibrium turned upon the explicit condition that '*everybody should promptly spend his net receipts upon consumers' goods*' (ibid.: 235; original emphasis). He believed that, if some people took their money out of circulation for the purpose of saving it, then it would directly impact another person's income, thus destroying the perfect balance between classes. Furthermore, like Cantillon, Quesnay's model constructs a kind of farmers' paradise. He based his programme on a call to abolish the commons, letting them instead to farmer-entrepreneurs while taxing the landowning class, thus making several assumptions: For one, the farmer-entrepreneurs, he believed, would 'buzz with energy'; second, this 'farmer paradise' would not be undersold by similar systems abroad, as France in the eighteenth century was a fairly closed system; and third, there would be a large supply of cheap capital fuelling this system.[9] This could be said to contribute to the development of capitalist theory in that it is the capitalist class that provides such advances for the sake of production. It is of note that Adam Smith would critically absorb Quesnay's theory on this point (ibid.: 237).

As a tool, Quesnay's *tableau* was a simplified, pictorial representation of the economic cycle – very much like Harvey's model of circulation, which provided such a representation of an anatomical process – and was thus able to condense and translate ideas of economic circulation that had been developing since the early renaissance.[10] With his early utilitarianism and proto-harmonism, his *laissez-faire, laissez-passer* critique of intervention and his embrace of entrepreneurialism, Quesnay would lay the foundations for nineteenth-century economic liberalism, providing Smith, its greatest exponent, with a solid footing, as well as lending Marx a central reference for Volume II of *Capital* – a text dedicated solely to the analysis of capital's circulation (see, in particular, Smith, 2008: Book IV, chap. IX, and Marx, 1993).

Smith would accept the basic tenet that the land (to which he added the sea) is the ultimate source of a nation's wealth, but he would also take the circulation of money as a force by which wealth is increased. 'No fixed capital can yield any revenue but by means of a circulating capital' (Smith, 2008: 167). For Smith, as for Cantillon and Quesnay, money does not have intrinsic value in itself. It is an instrument for the generation of wealth. 'The great wheel of circulation is altogether different from the goods which are circulated by means of it. The revenue of the society consists altogether in those goods, and not in the wheel which circulates them' (ibid.: 175). Smith would go beyond the proposals of his predecessors by suggesting the abandonment of any intrinsic value in money and the substitution of paper money for gold and silver coins. With this, he would break the 'cycle of preciousness' once and for all, while also maximizing the portion of a nation's wealth to remain in circulation. For him, only circulating capital is able to put industry in motion. It is active, productive capital.

Just as for Hobbes, money is once again made vital when it is put in circulation. It is to the virtue of circulation that the state (or in this case, the 'nation') owes its measure of power. This pattern has continued to develop from the second half of the eighteenth century until the present day, bringing about another adaptation of the concept of circulation at least as significant as that of the early seventeenth century. Circulation, as the following chapters show, would lend itself to the development and growth of communication, 'publicity' and the political use of public opinion. In short, circulation would prove to be equally as fundamental to the development of capitalism as it was to the birth of the public realm.

From its long-standing role as metaphor, the emergence of *circulatio* offered the early modern European world a powerful principle that would occupy discourses of state and of trade – realms of human thought so essential to the establishment of modern European power. Yet what remains to be examined is how circulation as a concept entered into and animated the material transformation of the modern world. The remaining chapters of this book will look to address this question.

NOTES

1 There may be some conceptual obscurity to my use of the word 'metaphor' when talking about the circle. What I am dealing with here is the fact that the circle has a distinct history as a metaphor. It also has a history as a concept – a concept that is not only embedded in the argument this chapter elaborates, but may well penetrate in particular the social practices it examines.

2 The authorship of the Aristotelian *Mechanica* is disputed, although it is widely believed not to have been written by Aristotle. A recent argument has been convincingly made by Thomas Nelson Winter, who names the author of *Mechanica* as Archytas of Terentum (see Winter, 2007).

3 This conception remained roughly intact in the Galenic tradition of medicine, which would not be overturned until Harvey's 'discovery' of the circulation of blood in 1623.

4 Generally, this notion is attributed to the twelfth-century treatise by Hermes Trismegistus, *Liber XXIV philosophorum* (see Small, 1983: 90). However, the historical validity of this figure is disputed.

5 In a way, the greatness or magnificence could be said to indicate an early notion of the 'health' of the city, as all factors are valued strictly by their nominal, immanent or ontic nature.

6 Of the various discourses of trade that began to appear decades after Serra's *Breve trattato*, Sir Josiah Child's discourse of 1693 was, according to Schumpeter, the most significant in that it exemplified the general tendency of this body of works, which would, under different political circumstances, become the 'rational of the doctrines of laissez-faire liberalism'.

7 This term is what Higgs, in his translation of the original *Essai*, uses to speak of 'entrepreneurs'. It is now commonly understood that Cantillon was the first to use the term 'entrepreneur'.

8 For Quesnay, the *produit net* would substitute for Cantillon's *produit de la terre*. In both cases, as Schumpeter points out, these terms refer to 'the fact that the rent of the land contains [. . .] the only net return in existence' (1972: 238). The three social classes that make up Cantillon's tableau are replaced by nearly equivalent classes in Quesnay's: he now calls the farmers, *la classe productive*; the landowners, *la classe propriétaires* (or *classe souveraine* or *classe distributive*); and the entrepreneurs he calls *la classe stérile*. Labourers, which Quesnay, like Cantillon, treats as a passive class, either form a fourth class or are added into the second or third classes (ibid.: 223–43).

9 This was a point on which he went into substantial detail, proposing what he called '*avances foncières*', or initial expenditures on preparing the land for farming, and so on.

10 Before becoming a philosopher-economist, Quesnay was a physician whose earlier works, *Observations sur les effets de la saigné* (1730) and *Essai sur l'œconomie animale* (1736), provided a direct model of circulation to be applied to an 'economic government' (see Mattelart, 1996: 26–30).

4

A World in Circulation

How is it that, in its transpositions from metaphor to model, circulation would become a category useful to the perception and ordering of space? What effect would such a shift have on the thinking on the city, on architecture and on the emergence of modern territory? How can we understand all of this in terms of the development of Western politics? These questions tend to escape the scope of modern histories of the city and of architecture and are only peripherally the object of geographic enquiry. Indeed, why should we presume there is a connection between political form and the physical movement of objects and people when there are much more obvious relations of power at hand in seventeenth-century Europe?

But, just as questions of science, ontology and theology were of equal pertinence to sixteenth-century natural philosophy, so too in the seventeenth century were those of state form, trade, government and the city bound together in a single epistemological knot. It was only by the late eighteenth century, with the rise of such categories as civil society and political economy, that these various strands were first seen as strategically useful only if analysed in a degree of isolation from one another. The development and progressive compartmentalization of knowledge has only increased since then, and it is no surprise that modern historians of the city often project the outlines of modern disciplinary boundaries back on to the material they assess. In the process, it becomes possible to view knowledge of architecture and the city as though relatively isolated from that of trade, of the formation of the state and of governmental administration – forms of knowledge that, if anything, appear to pre-exist the material configuration of the world and thus of the city. As a historical object, the city appears as a domain in its own right – a site the history of which progresses according to the accumulation of knowledge born, as it were, within its walls. It persists in this light as an entity within a field of causality, adapting itself to the sway of only the most directly linked forces: the applied rationality of cultural experts, architects, artists, theoreticians, engineers and their patrons. Knowledge, in this dominant perspective, moves along straight lines, rarely laterally. And for this reason, the history of the city (and of space more broadly) tends to remain an ontologically *passive* figure capable only of registering the greater epistemological forces that traverse it.

According to such orthodoxy, the city of the Renaissance is typically the body that responds to the will of plutocratic patronage or later serves to glorify the power of the baroque court. Likewise, the modern city is understood as a technical problem that must accommodate the needs of communication, health, exchange and circulation – categories of human practice that all supposedly emerged only in the nineteenth century. The city, in other words, is a 'barometer' of history.

The task of this book, then, is to look at this history as a far more reflexive process constituted by the relations between political form and spatial order, between conceptual formations and concrete organizations, where knowledge is not merely the product of directed, enlightened thought but is also produced through the cognitive and heuristic experience of the material world. In this sense, architecture, the city and indeed the territory can be seen not only as products of a certain rationality, but as fields of latent ideas in themselves – objects that, in the commotion of history, become unintentionally useful tools in the formation of a broader epistemological horizon. From this perspective, certain patterns in history begin to emerge, confirming not a causal coherence, but a much looser, non-linear relationship between space and order, or between the concrete and the ideal. Thus, if we forego any art-historical tendency to categorize periods, or any impulse to reduce the history of the city to one framed around functional terms, then immediately new configurations and relationships begin to appear. Such an approach is predicated on understanding history through a fundamental *nomos* – the notion of a uniquely sensed relationship that exists at any given time and place between concrete spatial order and political form (for the term *nomos*, I rely on Carl Schmitt's understanding (2006)). Within a given *nomos*, the city, its architecture, the territory and space in general reverberate reciprocally with the development of human thought: concepts that manage to take hold of human rationality often do so because they find their confirmation in the material order of the world, entering into an oscillation between thought and observation, intellect and projection. And it is in this way that such categories also enter into the realm of the political. As Carlo Galli argues, space is (and perhaps always has been) an inescapable dimension of politics:

> [P]olitics cannot but measure itself with space, that the control of space is one of the stakes in the game of power. [...] It is, in other words, *politics* that arranges *itself* in space and that, moreover, arranges *space itself*, determining it, not only insofar as it represents space in thought, but also because it politicizes, produces, and structures space in reality. (Galli, 2010: 5; original emphasis)

The rise of circulation that this book is attempting to sketch here could not have been politically significant were it to have remained at the level of thought alone.

Likewise, the gradual recognition that space itself can be made to 'circulate' was fundamental in translating it from an intellectual category to a fully political one. From the break of the sixteenth century, a vastly new perception of space would indeed lurch forward across Europe in equal pace with the construction of a new human order governed by a temporally grounded politics:

> No sooner had the contours of the earth emerged as a real globe – not just sensed as a myth, but apprehensible as fact and measured as space – than there arose a wholly new and hitherto unimaginable problem: the spatial ordering of the earth in terms of international law. (Schmitt, 2006: 86)

As we shall see, it would be this new perception of space that would at once destabilize the ancient status of the European city while also fixing it within a new space ordered by the nascent logic of circulation.

This chapter examines the effects of the greater epistemological shift that both accompanied the rise of the modern state and provided a new model of circulation applicable to multiple realms of thought. More specifically, it will examine how such models (which also 'circulated' throughout Europe) would come to realize themselves in the planning and administration of the city, binding political order with the movement of objects seen increasingly as a register of the state's power and thus transforming the city into both a *site of circulation* and an *analytic device* of increasingly larger and more complex political spaces. It will look at this epistemological configuration within (and between) the cities of Europe in relation to the rise of the category of modern territory.

MODERN SPACE AND CIRCULATION

The prolific cognitive spaces that blossomed around the metaphor of the circle and flourished following the notion of *circulatio* that we saw in the previous chapter eventually found purchase in the construction of a real space the physical constitution of which in turn allowed for this concept to manifest itself: At the turn of the sixteenth century, circulation would slowly begin to find a place in the space of the world precisely by making the space of the world a domain of circulation. Yet the construction of such a world governed by circulation – a world with a centre of gravity that would be occupied by trade and traffic, by *movement* – was not a self-conscious process. Rather, the modern world as perceived from Europe stumbled into being in the desperate aftermath of two great crises that shook the very foundations of its premodern cosmos apart (Galli, 2010).[1] Its precarious new configuration was the response to, on the one hand, the decentring of the Mediterranean world brought about by the seafaring mastery of the Atlantic and the 'discovery' of the Americas – a decentring only compounded by the displacement of the world itself into its heliocentric planetary system. On the other hand, it was the reaction to a world torn apart by the crisis of the *res publica christiana* in the wake of the Reformation. These two simultaneous breakdowns of frontiers, one through rapid colonial expansion and the other through the rupture of the Church, resounded throughout both 'new' and 'old' worlds alike, destabilizing long-standing perceptions of space and time. In their place, an entirely new spatio-temporal configuration emerged predicated on an unstable balance of a new European political power.

For Galli, the premodern world bears a space that is eminently and naturally 'qualitative'. It is marked through natural manifestations of what already exists in it. Its order derives itself from the qualities and attributes of the natural world. Borders, divisions and passageways are intrinsic to space – mountains, rivers, valleys, seas – and it is thus that space itself gives a measure to politics: the space of the premodern world is *immediately political*. It is the natural world that divulges its divine order in the immediate presence of signs, omens, traces and marks. Its laws are given by divine projections that literally sculpt earthly space, providing it with a natural orientation and an inherent sense of law (Schmitt, 2006: 42). Fences, enclosures and walls result from an agricultural demarcation of the Earth, binding an inner measure of the Earth's 'justice' with the products of human labour (ibid.). Similarly, the city in the premodern world would become a privileged figure the enclosed space of which is positively qualified against the space outside through the performance of rituals and sacred acts, the endowment of citizenship and the activity of politics. In fact, as Galli argues, premodern space *is* the space of the city. The *polis*, for him, is the political space of antiquity par excellence in that it is 'not a space defined by the physical border of walls but as a group of citizens who meet and act in the "high" places of politics, the agora and the theater' (Galli, 2010: 12).

The birth of the modern world – of modern spatiality – is rather the *reconquest* of the spaces of antiquity in the wake of their ruin. At the turn of the sixteenth century, this traditional world entered a simultaneous, sustained crisis with, on the one hand, not so much the 'discovery' of the Americas, but the encounter with a vast new 'empty' space, presumed infinite in dimension and devoid of civilization – a discovery paired with the erosion of the Christian empire on the other. The traumatic experience of the Other inhabiting the Americas, compounded by the waning of the Church's eschatological authority over time and space, delivered a profound sense of insecurity to the European world. In response to this, what emerged was a desperate and violent effort to stabilize, neutralize and, above all, to *order* a world bound up in internal conflict and deprived of its traditional horizon of temporal expectation. Modern spatiality, one could argue, arises as a reaction, an attempt to construct a new cosmos in which human certainty is no longer fixed by the divine centrality of the universe. Such a cosmos would instead be founded along a new horizon of scientific reasoning, calculation and prognosis.

As the natural world was colonized by the expanses of human intellect, it would reveal itself to be equally mouldable to the latter's need for order and security. The perception made available to the new human subject, conceived as a single point in a great web of human intellect, could only coincide with the gradual evacuation of space of its natural consistency.[2] Space, for such a subject, would instead be given over to rational calculation and scientific assessment, being emptied of its natural features and existing sense of orientation. As early as 1586, this had become obvious to Bernardino Telesio:

> Space can become the receptacle of any being, and in the case of the beings occupying it withdrawing or being driven away, it does not withdraw and is not driven away, but remains perpetually identical, ready to receive all the beings which replace the others, and promptly assumes the dimensions of all the beings that are placed in it, and is always similar to the things that are placed in it, but is never identical with any of them, nor identified with them, but completely different from all of them. (Telesio, 1586, quoted in Benevolo, 1978b: 586)

It would become increasingly a dimension *available* to the requirements of mankind's earthly existence. For this reason, in the wake of the Reformation, there is a reciprocal effect produced by these crises:

> By setting the inessential space of exteriority against the infinite abyssality of an inner life that is, by definition, devoid of space, the Reformation produces a subjectivity that is, in effect, liberated from space. More precisely, it produces a Protestant subject who, when projected outside himself, is able to place himself anywhere, to take control of any land, precisely because he is not at home in any place. (Galli, 2010: 17)

Over the course of this period, this increasing 'senselessness' of space corresponded to the subject's escape into the limitless virtual 'space' of human reason – an inner 'utopia' (*non*-place) of rational cognition – which constructs a subjectivity that responds to the emptiness of the natural world outside with an increasing degree of scepticism. If the erosion of the Christian empire, coinciding with the gradual collapse of macrocosm into microcosm, gave rise to a kind of relativism of individual centrality, space too would become relativized, its natural variations drained of their eminently political quality. Spatial variations from this point on would simply appear instead as *variation*, as indifferent differences. The space of the modern world 'is no longer the bearer of politics, nor is it organically full of complexity. It is instead de-qualified and undifferentiated – empty of any measure' (ibid.: 16). In turn, it 'assumes a sort of "perspectival" value: the initially relativized and senseless space of absolute alterity becomes a space "for us", a space newly legible, but only from the point of view of Europe's new artificial and mathematical rationality' (ibid.: 19).

Modern spatiality and modern politics are thus the twin offspring of a twin crisis, each an artificial armature seeking at once to 'geometrize' a nature full of senseless difference in the same measure as it strives to neutralize a world steeped in human conflict. It was for this reason that Schmitt would qualify the whole of modernity as the 'age of neutralizations and depoliticizations'.[3] The rise of modern spatiality saw the construction of a figure both universal in its capacity to guarantee such neutrality and also serving as the instrument that would determine the geometrical (and thus political) disposition of its space: the centralized state. As Koselleck writes, '[n]ot until the state had suppressed and neutralized religious conflict could progressive reason unfold in the newly vacated space' (Koselleck, 1988: 34). In fact, one can interpret Schmitt's understanding of 'the political' with reference to the originary dual crisis at the heart of the modern era (Schmitt, 2007). The political can be seen as the perpetual violent effort to reinstate the order and peace of a world whose immediate relationship between order and orientation had been destroyed by this 'original' catastrophe – a crisis the effects of which will continue to haunt the state, while nevertheless remaining hidden from it. Because such a task will remain unresolvable, modern political thought will perpetually undermine itself by each subsequent order it sets in place. This ceaseless re-establishment of political order, in turn, propagates a new chasm that courses through all the modern world, pitting on one side *artifice* and on the other *nature*. Such a new, volatile division would penetrate the depths of the modern world, separating the state from the state of nature, the subject from his or her set of beliefs and, most importantly, the natural world from the political.

To the logic of the modern state, space presents itself as an infinitely empty terrain available to the needs of political calculus. Space is a *quantity* open to the perspective of state reason, and its projection of borders, meridians, divisions and passageways gives new measure to an increasingly *quantifiable, governmental* form that power takes in the modern world. Yet, although all of this appears as a pure reaction to the perils of a world deprived of its previous sense of certainty, its entire composition is nonetheless founded on its incorporation of the very crises that gave rise to it in the first place.

In this sense, in direct response to the religious civil wars unleashed, modern spatiality would rest on the categorical distinction it makes between 'interior' and 'exterior' as the primary characterization of a space of guaranteed peace. Interior space is that which has been neutralized, *depoliticized*, that from which civil, creedal war is banished once and for all. Once it is possible to define an 'interior', modern spatial logic will then unwittingly rediscover the very same 'emptiness' that had been discovered in the spaces of the Americas – an emptiness it will then reproduce as a condition of possibility for modern politics in the spaces of Europe.

> At its inception, then, modern political space is defined by an internal space in which *nothing is possible* (the internal sphere of the State, which has been depoliticized and made 'smooth' and safe) and an external space, Europe, in which *everything is not possible* (which involves, that is, a relatively ordered external space. (Galli, 2010: 40; original emphasis)

Likewise, condemning war within its interior only reproduces it as a permanent condition at its periphery in the form of political conflict of adversaries – of 'war in form'. Together, the modern state arises as a figure endowed with the capacity to safeguard its new human: the centred and rational subject.[4] 'And he that carryeth this Person, is called Soveraigne, and said to have *Soveraigne Power*; and every one besides, his Subject' (Hobbes, 1986: 228; original emphasis). No longer an entity predicated on universal salvation, as the *Res publica christiana* had been, it would be the art of government, the territorial space of the state and *raison d'état* – the tautological essence of the state itself as well as the knowledge of its affairs – that would always already define the modern world. Founded only on its guarantee of universal peace, the state, as Foucault observed, had neither origin nor objective – the only end of the state was itself: 'We now find ourselves in a perspective in which historical time is indefinite, in a perspective of indefinite governmentality with no foreseeable term or final aim. We are in open historicity due to the indefinite character of the political art' (Foucault, 2009: 260). However, the theme of universal peace as defined by the unity and spirituality enjoyed in the Christian empire no longer applies: instead, in the realm of *raison d'état*, universal peace will be a condition of precarious stability achieved between a plurality of states according to a balance that prevents the domination of one state over others.[5] Because the fate of the state is no longer a matter of providential intervention, its future becomes determined by a class of administrators guided by a new type of sovereign knowledge: rather than a knowledge of the law, the sovereign must possess a knowledge of things (ibid.: 274). Out of this new formation of political space, power would be measured increasingly by the state's ability to manage and order the totality of objects and resources moving throughout its interior. The space of the modern state, empty and homogeneous, driven by necessity, will find itself evermore penetrated by the nascent logic of *planning*.

Precisely for this reason, circulation appears as a self-justifying phenomenon – a manifestation of political vitality *in itself*. Beyond metaphors, what is now at stake are the relationships forged when traffic becomes a concern of government, when infrastructure becomes central to the spatial configuration of the state, and when territorial planning begins to correlate directly to state power. From the end of the sixteenth century until well into the eighteenth century, this new *nomos* of movement would unfold not just over Europe, but across the surface of the Earth.

GIOVANNI BOTERO

In many ways a forerunner to Hobbes, Botero used spatial imaginary that spans the threshold between a premodern political space and an eminently modern one. Botero's world is one whose spatial hierarchy is dominated by the city, and whose politics are qualitatively intrinsic to the existing configurations of space

itself. Yet, at the same time, in his administrative treatises, we see a clearly modern perception of space unfolding as well. Space for Botero at times appears
homogeneous and empty – open to a new administrative calculus and therefore
determined *by* its politics. As for Machiavelli, it is space that begins to receive its
intelligibility from politics (Galli, 2010: 21–4), not the other way around.
Furthermore, Botero is one of the first to identify and rationalize a new spatial
technology in which an emerging and increasingly 'economic' state power will
operate: *territory*.[6]

In his treatises *On the Causes of the Greatness and Magnificence of Cities*
and *Reason of State*, he would anticipate this new space that would fully emerge
across Europe half a century later. In his praise for agriculture as a direct factor
in the propagation of the city's population, he suggests that a kind of large-scale
agricultural planning should be taken on by the prince in which nature is made
available to the administrative needs of his kingdom:

> It is his business to initiate and direct all works that are for the public ben-
> efit, such as draining marshes, clearing and preparing for cultivation any
> forests that are useless or superfluous, and helping and assisting any others
> who are engaged in similar operations. [. . .] Since warmth and dampness
> are the necessary conditions for growth and plenty, the prince must also
> contrive to assist nature by leading rivers or lakes through his country.
> (Botero, 1956: 148–9)

Botero illuminated a new domain in which state politics could constitute itself
in the investment in management of a domestic population (*popolo*), transforming it into a political concern and thereby also a political force. Crucial to such
a logic would be the deployment of new arrays of infrastructure. Indeed, Botero's
treatises would open an administrative horizon within the logic of sovereignty
that depended increasingly on the organization of a controlled space in which the
circulation of material wealth, its vehicles, storehouses and the people needed to
sustain the city could constitute the basis of his *raison d'état*. Although the attention to an early notion of population remained a political force, it would do so
in a world where space had yet to be politically enclosed – parcelled off behind
militarized boundaries. Thus, although Botero's work may have anticipated the
modern concept of territory to an extent, it would only be in the next century
that this new space could be seen to correlate to the increasingly 'internal' disposition of territory – a secured, closed space both abstract and cleared for the
infrastructural penetrations of state-administered trade.

This space was, in Botero's world, still dominated by the figure of the *city*
(the city-state), whose control over the predominantly agricultural *territorium*
surrounding it was bound to a premodern conception of space[7] in which the
proposal for interstate trade would not have been terribly controversial. Because
wealth had yet to detach itself from the products and materials it represented,
the wealth of a city was tied to the production made available to it by its land

and the natural orientation of channels of its 'conduct' (rivers, passages, etc.). Nature, too, in Botero's spatiality, still dominates the human ability to move, and thus nature still holds rank over the ultimate magnificence of a city: 'For where there is not commodity of conduct the multitude of people cannot be great, which the hills and mountains teacheth us, on which we may well see many castles and little towns, but no store of people that we might thereby call them great' (Botero, 1956: 242). Indeed, for Botero, a city's grandeur is a direct factor of the fecundity and suitability of the land on which it was originally built (ibid.: Book I). From this basic quality, all other elements of a city's power (in particular, the city's population and its reproduction) follow. With Hobbes, however, this hierarchy of city and its surrounding lands would change altogether.

THOMAS HOBBES

For Botero, the vitality of the sixteenth-century Italian city-state was predicated on its physical relation to others, circulating goods both within and between them; with Hobbes, we have an inversion of this. For him, the state was secured and made vital precisely by constructing an interior, closed system of circulation within it. Circulation, for Hobbes, was always already a measure of state power, not simply a means to it.

Just as Giordano Bruno had observed that the blood only maintained its spiritual life force if it remained *within* the body, so too would the vitality and power of Hobbes's *Leviathan* become relevant only in its ability to safeguard its 'artificial' interior from the 'state of nature' surrounding it. From this notion springs the clearest materialization of a distinctly modern spatial logic articulating itself on a distinction between 'exterior' and 'interior'. The modern state, inspired by Hobbes, arises as a great machine – no longer a city, but a network of cities and contiguous lands enclosed and protected by a centralized governmental apparatus. The modern state – a single mechanical body composed of parts – is governed by the political technology of *territory*.[8] For Hobbes, it is imagined as a giant, artificial man equipped with the capacity to protect its subjects *from themselves* by enclosing them within its artificial boundaries, its space of social contract. Its exterior is a realm of peril, the state of nature in which the subject, given over to its own nature, regresses to the state of *bellum omnia contra omnes*.

Sovereignty for Hobbes would only be valid insofar as its universality was reflected and made visible in the equally universal smoothness and geometrical rationality with which the state's interior space was treated. The neutrality of this space comes, of course, at the cost of at once permitting war to continue indefinitely at its borders, where its universality collides with that of other states, and banishing the subject's 'passions' and beliefs to the dark, secret, interior realm of inner consciousness (Koselleck, 1988, chaps 2 and 3). The space in which the subject dwells, bound to its new destiny in rational calculation and the universal application of *raison d'état*, would, therefore, become drained of its naturally qualified complexity and hardened within a new, artificially controlled and geometrically grounded order. In other words, '[i]f politics is to make itself "absolute", it must make itself an exact and rational science, like geometry, and it does so by clarifying its own definitions and defining its own actors, and ends with a rigorous nominalism that excludes every claim to transcendence' (Galli, 2010: 30). As Hobbes would put it, '[t]he skill of making, and maintaining Common-wealths, consisteth in certain Rules, as doth Arithmetique and Geometry; not (as Tennis-play) on Practice onely' (Hobbes, 1986: 261). In turn, space, as Galli claims, would now be made available to politics and its precarious, geometric order – one that no longer operates in the metaphorical register, but 'consists in the application of a constructive rigor to the artificial space of politics' (Galli, 2010: 29). And, with this, territory would emerge as the primary instrument through which modern space could be given measure.

Yet, despite (or perhaps because of) the instrumental reason of this new configuration of power, it bears a sharp contradiction: 'Modern political space is that space in which State and Subject coincide, each with its own universality and its own particularity. It is a space *of* movement; but it is also [. . .] a space that is itself *in* movement' (ibid.: 37; original emphasis). In other words, modern spatial logic is coloured by the contradiction that, on the one hand, the subject's 'free' action and mobility within the interior of the state are constantly checked and frustrated by the closed borders and internal disciplinary divisions that articulate modern space, and, on the other hand, the borders and divisions that the state erects are never permanent, fixed entities, but rather characterized by their provisionality. The subject, a centred self, thus brings to bear a particular paradox on the heart of the state: within the disciplinary space of the state, the infinitely expansive space of human knowledge unwittingly produces its opposite: the infinite pursuit of liberty (ibid.: 29).

POLITICAL SPACES OF THE MODERN STATE

Whereas the interior/exterior ontology on which the state's rationality rested would be historically tested by this internal contradiction at the end of the eighteenth century, its closed, restrictive logic would be paradoxically underscored by the models of circulation that brought it its measure of vitality and power. Not only did circulation provide a means by which to literally order the space of the state, but its very vitality was predicated on the fact that it operated *within* a closed body. There was a great expansion of awareness of systems and objects under the sway of circulation, from Copernicus's finite universe to Harvey's demonstration of the circulation of blood, and all presented themselves as *closed systems*. Indeed, the inherent virtue seen in systems that demonstrate circular motion was that they all tended to be circumscribed in a given, finite spatial enclosure. Put another way, a circular system bears truth in that it also illuminates the completeness of a body in space. It was thus taken as a given that this new realm of power could, therefore, only be realized insofar as the 'body' circumscribing it could secure absolute control over this boundary, guaranteeing its vitality in the wholeness of itself with regard to the world outside. 'Security exists only in the state. *Extra civitatem nulla securitas*. The state absorbs all rationality and all legality. Everything outside of the state is therefore a "state of nature"' (Schmitt, 2007: 48). The very existence of ordered, secured channels of circulation, systems of infrastructure and the movement of traffic would in turn confirm the existence of a corporeal unity of the state itself.

Yet this spatiality alone – its interiority, its rationally geometric and homogeneously 'empty' quality – is not enough to justify the blossoming use of a circulatory logic operating within it. Even if it were simply a matter of absorbing an adopted concept, born of the scientific metamorphosis of centuries of contemplation, that alone cannot explain the sudden and widespread use of the notion throughout the modern European world. Furthermore, although this new sense of space was opening up across Europe during the seventeenth century, it was certainly not a uniform development. What I have outlined above is clearly a phenomenon restricted to specific histories of continental politics; the image of the *Leviathan* paradoxically became attached to monarchical absolutism typical of certain continental states (Spain and France, in particular; ibid.: 79), rather than in Hobbes's own England, which developed its state form along commercial imperialist lines.

We can postulate, therefore, that the distinction between interior and exterior is perhaps somewhat less essential to territorial state space than we have assumed. Indeed, the emergence of territory as it applies to the modern European (continental) state does not fully describe the spatial order that the European powers began to unfurl across the globe. For this reason, we cannot assume that the political ontology of interior/exterior is sufficient in itself to explain the general character of the spaces unfolding throughout the modern European world. A perhaps more significant distinction, for Galli (as for Schmitt), comes in that between *land and sea*, or the distinction made between powers deriving order from territorial, politico-military logic and those deriving it from naval power, respectively. For Schmitt, the foundation of the first truly global order – the modern '*nomos* of the earth' – would rest on this very tension created between these two spatial orders, a distinction that became visible immediately following Columbus's crossing of the Atlantic:

> The originally terrestrial world was altered in the Age of Discovery, when the earth first was encompassed and measured by the global consciousness of European peoples. This resulted in the first *nomos* of the Earth. It was based on a particular relation between the spatial order of firm land and the spatial order of free sea, and for 400 years it supported a Eurocentric international law: the *jus publicum Europaeum*. (Schmitt, 2006: 49)

More concretely, parallel to the distinction between interior and exterior that characterizes the spatial ontology of territory is the broader gulf between territorial sovereignty and British monarchical 'corporations'. Anglo-Saxon political form is distinguished by its 'non-closed spatiality' (e.g. constitutionalism, the open sea, etc.). 'These open political forms are compatible with a mobility that is not strictly public, or "imperial", but also "private". In this sphere, space is truly nature that is available to conflict, adventure, and the domination of pioneers and pirates' (Galli, 2010: 43). The opposition between these two spatial orders gave tensions and consistency to the newly formed *nomos* of the Earth – a global, Eurocentric order consisting of a territorial space of geometric landscapes and fortifications on the one hand, and a maritime space of the free sea outside any state's jurisdiction and open for the free seafaring individual – a space open for those courageous enough to engage in trade, fishing, piracy and the free pursuit of maritime wars (Schmitt, 2006: Part III, chap. 3, 172–84).[9] 'The English isle became the agency of the spatial turn to a new *nomos* of the Earth and, potentially, even the operational base for the later leap into the total rootlessness of modern technology' (ibid.: 178). As Schmitt goes on to say, this agency was proclaimed by the term Utopia itself, which, he argues, could have only emerged from England in the sixteenth century. 'Utopia did not mean any simple and general nowhere (or erewhon), but a U-*topos*, which, by comparison even with its negation, A-*topos*, has a stronger negation in relation to *topos*' (ibid.). Together, these two logics articulate a general distinction that would colour the entire history of the modern world, transcribing a distinction derived from the experience of two spaces into two vastly different conceptions of warfare: one that is concealed in moral intents (*justa causa bellum*) and the other of explicitly pursued power (*jus bellum*) – between the smooth, Atlantic-based power on the one hand and the striated, continental power on the other. More than a territory of firm ground, the island of Britain was itself like a giant free ship on the open ocean.

Over the course of the seventeenth century, the distinction enjoyed between the continental, territorial state and the open imperial space controlled by England would begin to circle itself, constituting a dialectic that would resound throughout Europe and its colonial spaces. This dialectic would reproduce itself both within the state and without, applying logics born of one space to that of the other. Over this century, a consistent ontological resonance can be traced between representations of ocean space and constructions of territory on land (Steinberg, 2009). On the one hand, the dialectic between land and sea would leave its mark on the distinction between public and private law, the establishment of the market and free trade, and in the construction of modern universals pertinent to the subject in its perpetual struggle against the state (Galli, 2010: chap. 4, 54–68). On the other hand, it would be this relationship, born of a spatial distinction, that would in turn constitute the spatiality of the modern world, setting in motion the rapid explorations and colonization in which nearly all European powers would engage.

It was upon England that, for Schmitt, the entire *nomos* of the Earth would balance, as England was the only European country whose power and orientation allowed it to determine this global order from the perspective of the sea. Yet, for precisely this reason, the spatiality opened up by English seafarers – an *empty* space owned at once by no one and everyone – would become a space dominated not by England's sovereignty itself, but rather by its non-state fleets of merchant traders. Empire, as it re-emerged in the sixteenth century, would be the first regime predicated on travel, transportation and traffic. If land appropriation lay at the base of the territorial power of the state, sea appropriation would take the form of commercial trade routes and colonial shipping lanes. Its space was a space of movement, a realm of free, reciprocating traffic. For this reason, although trade remained a measure of the territorial state's power, for England, it was a source and the object of its new global, imperial power. Space understood from an English perspective could be said to be state space turned inside out that, for that reason, encompassed the entire globe. Yet, from a certain perspective, the two spaces may be seen as joined in a process of co-production, for what remained common to both conceptions of space and would span the entirety of the modern world was the dependency of each on modes of mobility – on the category of circulation (Steinberg, 2009).

Within such oppositional concepts of law, of freedom and of state power, the two spatial orders born in Europe, which would largely shape a singular, global spatiality, were traversed by a certain necessity common to both: the perpetual movement of goods, precious metals and bodies throughout each one's spatial domain. Thus, although they differed greatly in terms of spatial disposition, the modalities and geometries of traffic that were developed both on land and at sea proved increasingly essential to bolster state power *in general*. It comes as no surprise then that this relationship became more explicit, not only in the early theories of the modern state, in its evermore administrative countenance, but in the discourses and policies for which circulation was more directly relevant: transatlantic trade. In part, this was because early theories of state and the plethora of 'discourses of trade' in the seventeenth century were, in a certain sense, indistinguishable from one another: for England, a discourse of trade was also a treatise on state form. If the roads and highways that criss-crossed the territory of a state were a testament to the virtue and wholeness of the 'Body Politique', on the open sea, the movement itself of trade vessels was the direct experience of a universal freedom made possible by England's 'open' oceanic dominion. In both cases, it was circulation – the perpetual and cyclical movements within a defined grid of roads, routes, passages, cut by global lines, meridians and *rayas* – that would increasingly give geometric permanence to the emerging spatial order of the modern world. 'Authentic traffic can only come about with a network that makes a given zone accessible, whether as *terra cognita* or *mare cognitum*, for routine crossings' (Sloterdijk, 2013: 34).

Within each spatial order, one can witness elements of the other replicated at different scales. For example, protectionism brought about by England's global colonial empire would effectively reproduce the same closed-circuit diagram of administered circulation that upheld the aspirations of both monarchical, territorial states and commercial empires founded on sea-power (Schmitt, 1997, 2006). Although England may have remained an 'open' imperial state in its rejection of a kind of territorial, Hobbesian state form, it would nonetheless seek to shore up its power by closing off its expansive maritime network of trade from any foreign intervention, in just the same way that France, for example, under the rule of Jean-Baptiste Colbert, would seek drastic protectionist measures at its borders to maintain its control over the traffic moving through the closed, interior network of circulation. It is no small coincidence that *Leviathan* was published in the same year that Cromwell's Navigation Acts were also passed. The grip that England would begin to exert over its trade routes was a result of the fact that the early British Empire lacked the kind of spatial, territorial coherence that the newly formed states on the continent had. As Schmitt notes,

> [s]uch a way of thinking directs itself not towards a certain coherent space and its inner order, but rather, above all else, towards the security of the connections of the scattered parts of the empire. It is more common for the jurist [...] of international law of such a world empire, to think in terms of roads and traffic routes than in terms of space. (Schmitt, 2011a: 91)

Whereas the idea of circulation had a firm conceptual grounding as an increasingly important source of state power in the mechanics of territory, in England, an analogous Hobbesian notion of security would circumscribe not its territory, but the various circulatory routes of trade that composed England's world empire outside it. 'The English world began to think in terms of bases and lines of communication' (Schmitt, 1997: 51). In either form, from the sixteenth century onward, colonial trade would, of course, become an increasingly decisive factor on which state power was to be based. And, for this reason, circulation would only grow more fundamental to this new, precarious configuration of an increasingly *global* power.

Nicolas Barbon, who very clearly recognized the contrasting spatialities emerging in Europe, argued in his 1690 *Discourse of Trade* that trade had become 'as necessary to Preserve Governments, as it is useful to make them Rich' (Barbon, 1690). Before him, William Petty's writings had addressed the direct relationship between trade and the art of government. From 1682 until 1687 (the year of his death), Petty developed several foundational essays under the concept of 'Political Arithmetick', which could perhaps best be defined by one of his 'ablest' followers: 'By Political Arithmetick we mean the art of reasoning by figures upon things relating to government . . . The art itself is undoubtedly very ancient . . . [but Petty] first gave it that name and brought it into rules and methods' (Davenant, 1771: 128, quoted in Schumpeter, 1972: 210). Still earlier, Josiah Child had begun work that would forge a link between trade and the government of an expansive empire, encouraging a large population through the act of naturalization. This basic connection between trade and government was not restricted to the construction of the Atlantic empire of England. As we have seen, the work of the physiocrats would address this same relationship in their treatises and *tableaux*, and its form was conditioned instead by the closed geometric territory of the state. Indeed, the entire body of pre-classical economic thought that blossomed in the early modern world is predicated on its fundamental presupposition that the circulation of wealth (whether as goods, resources, precious metals or people) is an essential and self-evident fact of political power. As Foucault would write, '[w]ealth is a system of signs that are created, multiplied, and modified by men; the theory of wealth is linked throughout to politics' (Foucault, 1994: 205).

Thus, with the construction of modern Europe and its global pretences, we see a political spatiality constructing itself that is increasingly governed by forms of *movement* – a world in which *traffic* would become a category of power, materializing the relationship between commerce and statecraft. Whereas, on land, the invention of modern territory would create a space that could respond to the demands of a world in circulation, such a shift of power would interminably transform the city, reconfiguring the monopoly it held over political, cultural and economic life for centuries. In turn, the city and all collective forms of human settlement would increasingly appear as hierarchical components within a coordinated system tuned to measure, modulate and valorize the circulation of wealth.

NOTES

1   In this claim, Galli is building to a large extent on those made in Carl Schmitt's later work, in particular his 1950 *The Nomos of the Earth* (2006) and his 1954 *Land and Sea* (1997).

2   Reinhart Koselleck writes: 'Progress opened up to a future that transcended the hitherto predictable, natural space of time and experience, and thence – propelled by its own dynamic – provoked new, transnatural, long-term prognoses.' See 'Modernity and the Planes of Historicity' (Koselleck, 2004: 22).

3   This is the title of the essay that appears in Schmitt (2007: 80–96).

4   Galli calls the Subject the 'universal particular' in that it is the particular that strives towards universality, towards crossing borders. The State Galli refers to as the 'particular universal', as it is an entity defined by its unconditional universality, but remains a particular among the many homogeneously defined states of Europe.

5   'Peace will no longer come from unity, but from non-unity, from plurality maintained as plurality' (Foucault, 2009: 300).

6   The notion of *territory* that I will make use of throughout this text derives largely from Stuart Elden's work on this concept. In particular, to reiterate his argument, territory is understood here as a 'political technology', that is, the network of different techniques, knowledge and technologies required to produce, measure

and uphold both the land, as an economic, proprietary category, and terrain, as a military-strategic control of the spatial extents of state sovereignty. See Elden (2013; in particular, see pp. 268–75 for his discussion on Botero).

7   For more on the notion of *territorium* and its relation to the city, see Elden (2013: 11, 13–14, 116, 218–28).

8   Although Hobbes does not develop the notion of 'territory' explicitly, his work for the present research is essential in the way it sets out a clear political ontology of the territorial state as a spatial order. Much more explicit in the modern articulation of this concept itself and its relation to emerging forms of sovereignty, however, is the work of Leibniz (see Elden, 2013: chap. 9).

9   This distinction is underpinned by the contrasting thought of More and Hobbes, or, more specifically, the conceptual difference between the absolute war implied by a 'Utopia of Ought', on the one hand, and limited, 'bracketed' war predicated by Hobbes's *Leviathan*, on the other, based on restricting war to a permanent conflict at the border of the state.

5

Circulation, Territory and the City

It is hard to place the role of the city in the spatial hierarchy of the continental, territorial state or in the fluid world of England's maritime empire. With the irruption of the modern European world, the construction of a space the political consistency of which privileges either the 'empty' spaces of the territory on the one hand or the open navigable ocean on the other, what possible status can the figure of the city hold? We can begin to chart its transition into modern history by looking at how certain authors of state and economic theory treat this category. Of note is that, in almost all texts, from Botero to Smith, there emerges a tendency to categorize cities within a given kingdom, territory or state. Botero classifies cities according to their renown, to which administrative, educational or ecclesiastical institutions reside in a given town. Almost a century and a half later, Cantillon, on the other hand, classifies cities in a ranking of importance to the territorial state and their role in the generation of wealth.

If the city had dominated the political spaces of the premodern world in its spatio-historical plurality, by the sixteenth century it began to play a far more utilitarian role within a hierarchically defined spatial entity that extended far beyond the reach of any particular city. Cities began, in other words, to adopt mechanical characteristics such as Hobbes had bestowed upon those in his *Leviathan*, incorporating them as elements in the greater machinery of the state. The classificatory nature that we find the city taking on reveals a remarkably generic, replaceable quality – one that no longer bears a kind of historical significance, but hints rather to the influence of a larger process in which it plays a part. In that sense, it is not simply that the city is now one figure among many that compose the state, but rather that it takes on increasingly 'scientific' attributes, fulfilling a *calculable*, machine-like function within a much larger, more complex spatial body composed of an interconnected array of other cities together with the lands in between them.

In the early Renaissance, the city's pre-eminence as a political figure meant that it enjoyed the status of a defined 'body'. For centuries, throughout the Western world, the human body had served as a reference in the construction and idealization of the figure of the city. The last vestiges of this tradition in the likes of Francesco di Giorgio Martini's late fifteenth-century *Trattati di architettura* (1967) depict the deep relationship sustained between the human body and the ideal disposition it lends to the form of the city extending from Vitruvius, reiterating an early modern interpretation of the ancient relationship between microcosm and macrocosm that would persist until the late sixteenth century. Its ideal proportions, established by the divine model, provided the city and architecture with a measure from which the processes of human activity, of trade, of dwelling, of craft, of festival and of ritual would align in perfect synchronization with the cycles of the Earth and the heavens, in what Jacques Le Goff has called a 'political physiology' (1989). Likewise, it would be with reference to the human body and its ailments that problems in the city could be illuminated, not least of which the circulation of bodily fluids:

> The state or kingdom, then, is like a human body. . . . As, therefore, the body is disordered when the humours flow too freely into one member of it, so that that member is often thus inflamed and overgrown while the others are withered and shrunken and the body's due proportions are destroyed . . . so also is a commonwealth or a kingdom when riches are unduly attracted by one part of it . . . neither can a kingdom survive whose prince draws to himself riches in excess as is done by altering the coinage. (Oresme, 1956, quoted in Lowry, 1974: 435)

Over the course of the seventeenth century, the modern figure of territory that took over the rank of the 'body' occupied a much larger, more abstract, fluid and mobile agglomeration of space. As such, this 'Body Politique' – new to the modern world – was imperceptible in an immediate sense – it lost its spatio-formal qualities as a physically recognizable entity – and, through the simultaneous development of technologies of cartography, the perception of the state became an increasingly scientific task to represent it in its planimetric abstraction. On the frontispiece of Hobbes's *Leviathan*, the figure of the state as a body appears as an endless mass of obedient subjects whose consistency seems to extend beyond the horizon. In both the representation and experience of space, within either the territorial states of Europe or the maritime empire of England, space increasingly adopted a certain perceivable quality of infinity – a quality, as such, completely alien to the presence and experience of the ancient city and the closed universe that illuminated it.

Yet, despite the apparent 'demotion' of the city to a mere constituent element within the territorial body of the state, the latter did not displace the city's centrality within the actual mechanics of state power. Far from it. Indeed, it was perhaps the repositioning of the city from a central, political-strategic figure of the state to a more abstract, systematic entity of the territory that gave it a new, albeit somewhat oblique, identity. With the growing importance of wealth's circulation for the strength of the state as well as the emergence of an increasingly administrative 'state reason' that it took on in managing this power, a new importance of the city appeared: no longer a 'body', the city re-emerged as a kind of 'organ' of circulation. This role was already evident in Hobbes's *Leviathan* when he described the movement of wealth channelling through the 'veins' and 'arteries' of the artificial body of the Commonwealth (1986: 301): this is no metaphor. For him, this movement was something that materialized in the physical spaces of a new, self-enclosed configuration in which the city was the essential organ (the heart, in this case) for the movement and valorization of wealth throughout the entire state. Circulation of wealth became a crucial means of, on the one hand, connecting and 'enlivening' all of the corporeal 'parts' of the state and, on the other, making visible the structure and order of this new spatial entity: the only way to actually perceive the state in its new vastness was to move throughout it. The role of circulation involved a new mathematical, physiological calculus of state reason, not only through the various 'arteries' and 'veins' that traversed the body of the state, but in the role that cities would play in the accumulation and valorization of that wealth – in other words, in providing a marketplace for the commodities produced in the landscape. Far from retreating, the city in this shift established a new centrality precisely because of the importance of circulation. Foucault writes:

> But the transference of this physiological metaphor was made possible only by the more profound opening up of a space common to both money and signs, to both wealth and representations. The metaphor of the city and the body, so assiduously put to work in our Western culture, derived its imaginary powers only from the much deeper foundations of archaeological necessities. (Foucault, 1994: 179)

From the seventeenth century, the city's role in the circulation of wealth would thus become functional in the sense of providing the space in which wealth could 'return'. It was precisely in the *capital city* that, by 'returning' in the form of taxes and duties, wealth could then be made 'vital' by sovereign authority before its 'arterial' redistribution. In this way, the (capital) city now also begins to function as an *analytic device* in the circulation of wealth.

ALEXANDRE LE MAÎTRE

One of the first to begin theorizing the role of the city within a clearly territorial epistemology was the general engineer for Brandenburg, Alexandre Le Maître. In 1682, he published *La Métropolitée ou De l'établissement des villes Capitales*, *de leur utilité passive & active, de l'Union de leurs parties & de leur anatomie, de leur commerce, etc.*, in which he established the importance of the capital city for the functions and unity of the state. This treatise is an attempt to establish the economic and political role in the founding of a capital city, as well as the overall structural order of cities within the state as a spatio-political whole. Mapping out a territorial logic of cities, it marked the beginning of a tradition that was carried into the next century. As the title suggests, Le Maître clearly endorses the corporeal metaphor of the state, and it becomes quite apparent that he is operating within a Hobbesian 'anatomy' from the beginning:

> The Prince sacrifices his time and care to protect the honour, the life and the resources of his Subjects, who are in turn obliged to sacrifice, if need be, their own property and their many small veins, which will in turn flow into His treasuries with great riches over all parties of his Estates. (Le Maître, 1682: 5; my translation)

What is also clear from the title is the emphasis Le Maître places on maintaining the unity between parts that now had become important for the state – a notion raised repeatedly by Hobbes. In the framework Le Maître sets out, the territorial unity of the state is founded precisely on a hierarchical relationship between the capital city, smaller cities and the villages and hamlets that extend into the surrounding countryside. The form this takes is a great circle, the centre of which is occupied by the capital city. The state then can be divided into three social ranks consisting of the sovereign and his officers, the artisans and the peasants. Le Maître assigns an appropriate type of residence to each of these orders, which he then distributes across the circular hierarchy of space.

> As well, the first order (the Peasants) will live in the villages and the hamlets, the second (the Artisans), in the towns, cities and small cities [*villotes*], and the third (the Regency and Officers of Justice etc.), for the purposes of the State and of eminence, will reside particularly in the Capital, which is the President and Chief of affaires, as even Tacitus says. *Caput rerum, unde in omnia regimen*. (Ibid.: 24; my translation)

Peasants, Le Maître asserts, should not live in any city as they are designated to work the land, cultivating the riches of the state. They dwell in villages and hamlets distributed throughout the state, far from the capital. Likewise, the artisans, as required by their trade, should restrict themselves to living primarily within the smaller, secondary cities (*villotes, bourgs*) distributed in a circle around the capital city. Only the most 'absolutely necessary' artisans will be allowed to reside in the capital (ibid.: 24).[1] Lastly, the capital city is, of course, the residence of the 'superior order', the sovereign and his officers, the seat of justice, and so on. Le Maître makes concessions for intellectuals to reside in the capital city as well, as it should be there where the great institutions and academies will also be situated. Taken together, this structure achieves a unity and order Le Maître likens to the human body:

> What the head is to the Body, the Prince to the subjects, Heavens to the Earth, a Metropolitan city is to the towns and townships, villages and hamlets. The Head operates to connect all the other members and all the parts of the body to work together, acting in concert to maintain the Chief. (Ibid.: 5; my translation)

The relationship between the three socio-spatial divisions revolves around the pre-eminence of the capital city and the 'sympathetic' glory it radiates across all of the state (ibid.: chap. 12). The presence and status of the capital symbolize the entire state (ibid.: chap. 34), the whole of which works as a unity, which Le Maître likens to the water cycle, as many before him had done. In this, the capital city gives in order to receive, just as it receives in order to give (ibid.: 26):

> As brooks form rivers, and these in turn form great rivers; that rivers spill into the Sea, which again overflows with the same waters, and that the lakes and ponds are the sources from which they themselves are derived, Nature having given to the water a continual ebb and flow, Capital Cities receive their life and their glory from all parts of the State, which in turn gives back the same to all Provinces. (Ibid.: 5; my translation)

What makes this text substantial is the way Le Maître treats the circulation of wealth (*commerce*) as the primary means to achieve this unity. Trade underpins nearly all the claims he makes. From the beginning, it is already clear that the purpose of the capital is not only to house the political seat of the state, but to serve as a great hub of trade: 'One must not be fooled by these hopes, this city then became the store of all the merchandise of Asia, Africa and Europe, and having the use of the Sea the Rivers and the Canals, and, as such, the ease to receive and to give' (ibid.: 3; my translation). Because it is the capital that consumes the most, it is the capital that must, therefore, be the seat of commerce (ibid.: chap. 25). Yet, more than historicizing this role for the capital, Le Maître goes on to argue that harmony and unity of the state as a whole are achieved only through the coordination of commerce directed by the sovereign. The sovereign, according to this logic, resides in the capital city precisely because there he can oversee trade, illuminating this process by his presence and providing it with security (ibid.: chap. 24); because he instils both fear and equity in his subjects, through his presence alone, the economy will function properly.

Le Maître makes clear that the purpose of this union achieved by a centrally located, well-connected capital is nothing less than the ease of movement (ibid.: 20).

> The purpose of the union, or its object, is the movement of all the members and all the parts of the Body, in order to work as a whole, which the parts could not have done separately. [. . .] In the same way, it is necessary to have an overall or general movement which is regular and precise, an internal moving force which is able to sustain and coordinate the union of the parts. As in the World, we see but one Sun, and in the Human Body, but one Heart, and one Sovereign or Regency, supreme in one State. (Ibid.: 56–7; my translation)

Unlike Botero's enthusiasm for movement, in which the circulation of wealth in and out of a city contributed to its magnificence, for Le Maître, such movement was essential for the grandeur of a body far larger, more abstract than the Italian city-state. Thus, the movement he refers to here is also more abstract than that which Botero had described. Furthermore, Le Maître develops his idea of movement not as a basic logic in itself, but within a clearly Cartesian mechanics. In fact, he goes on to flesh out this movement with several much more pragmatic prescriptions for the administration of the circulation of wealth, the planning of cities and the ordering of the state's infrastructure. As a first measure, not only should the capital city lie at the centre of the state, but it must also be served by the greatest roadways.

> The Capital City would be foolishly placed if it were situated away from the principal route, in woodlands or a dangerous desert, a wet marshland or on mountain or any remote setting [. . .] It would deprive it of the advantages which will make the Capital flourish and prosperous, of commerce, of the ease of correspondence, of the approach of foreigners, and finally the ease of communication itself with the whole State right here on its own principal street, where the mail passes, and where travellers find their route, to have the necessary correspondence, and that it may profit from the approach of Foreigners, to be less sombre and more populated by affluence of people and Commerce. (Ibid.: 132; my translation)

More than the benefits afforded to a well-connected city, Le Maître, like Botero, recognized that the continuous circulation of goods, money and people would depend on certain institutional measures within the (capital) city. He knew that a state that abounded in foodstuffs and manufactured goods would suffocate without the necessary means to unload it or sell it off. For this reason, trade was to be regulated by the administration, allowing for neither corruption and dishonesty nor the formation of monopolies (ibid.: chaps 47, 56 and 58). To support this, Le Maître recommended the establishment of banks within the capital (ibid.: chaps 49–51). As Petty had recognized, and as Cantillon later advised, banks were indispensable for the maintenance (and, subsequently, the analysis) of wealth precisely because they can sustain and regulate its circulation. Furthermore, the regulation of this circulation for Le Maître could only be guaranteed if there was another institution – the stock market – that could centralize the business of trade and provide a further measure of state-monitored security (ibid.: chap. 52). He even went so far as to consider the configuration of the town square as a means to optimize the movement of trade (ibid.: chap. 62).

Yet behind what amounts to a proto-liberal theory of the early modern city, Le Maître also places an emphasis on luxury and opulence – a secondary concern next to commerce. In light of his stress on utility that appears throughout the text, as well as the importance he places on liberty (ibid.: chap. 46), it comes as something of a surprise that he claimed that the capital must also be the most opulent of all cities. He even relates these qualities directly: *because* the essential quality (the cause) of the capital city is public utility, it follows, for Le Maître, that it should, therefore, be the greatest terminus of luxury (ibid.: chaps 5 and 58). This is all the more peculiar because Le Maître operated within a protestant milieu: A protestant himself, he left France to take his post in Brandenburg, where he wrote *La Métropolitée*, publishing it in Amsterdam and dedicating it to the king of Sweden.

It is tempting to suppose that opulence for him was simply the requisite mark of rank and glory typical throughout Europe at the time. But this presumption does not explain Le Maître's correlation between opulence and utility, between luxury and the fluid operation of trade. The answer to this, in part, may be in the need for unity that Le Maître constantly returns to. In this sense, the role of the capital city becomes one of administering a kind of reciprocal relationship between the state's centre and its periphery. This is wholly new in that the state is now coextensive with a large territorial entity that it must measure, coordinate, discipline and structure as a single 'anatomical' technology. The grandeur and glory of the capital must be, Le Maître asserts, proportional to the grandeur of the entire state. It must represent this glory and project it outward to all reaches of the state's territory. The capital, Le Maître writes, 'will be the political heart giving life and movement to the entire body of the Province, through the fundamental principle of the ruling science, which forms a whole of several parts, without destroying them' (ibid.: 52). It will achieve this by managing the traffic routes and marketplaces where trade occurs (principally, in the capital) and by giving the state a new, modern visibility, one achieved by rendering perceptible the uniformity that can and must be seen throughout the state. The capital city, therefore, becomes the representation of the entire state, and, through its reciprocal exchange with the other parts, the entire state in turn reflects this glory. More than this, the capital represents a new form of power altogether, one that illuminates itself by controlling the movement of materials in the object world.

> It is [...] necessary that the Prince's Eye casts its rays over the movements of his people, that he observes their conduct, can note them closely, and that his presence alone keeps vice, disorder, and injustice in check. This can best be achieved only through the union of the parts in the *Métropolitée*. (Ibid.: 69; my translation)

In this way, the circulation of traffic serves two simultaneous functions: one of trade and the movement of goods and money; the other, a circulation of the symbols of power and control. Opulence thus becomes the necessary mark and vehicle of this power, which must circulate within a parallel network of representation. Both serve to unify the state and both mutually reinforce each other. As *Métropolitée* attests, the visibility of traffic as a form of conduct, both in direct and indirect means, will become an essential component of state power from the seventeenth century onward.

Only 30 years after the publication of *Leviathan*, *La Métropolitée* shows us only the status that trade had acquired as a principal tool and metric of state power. Once again, circulation in the space of the state stands as a self-evident and virtuous process that assists in making functional and whole its territorial interior. The lack of any formal framework for its analysis in Le Maître's work is not a mark of an undeveloped form of knowledge; rather, it is a tribute to the fact that circulation *in itself* sufficed as a kind of modern political truth within a territorial epistemology. Instead, it is perhaps that circulation as such could provide a framework around which a more scientific approach to trade would later develop, rather than the other way around. Le Maître's treatise offers a kind of idealistic socio-spatial template that would be filled in using more rigorous analytical thinking by the physiocrats in the following century.

Like Le Maître, Cantillon and Quesnay both saw society as consisting of three classes or 'estates'. In the case of Cantillon, as we have seen, he devised a similarly spatialized economic sociology, organizing the three estates into a general distribution where class, dwelling and function all coincide in a new disciplinary component of a territorial order. Cantillon took his cue in part from Petty, a contemporary of Le Maître's, who found in the city the perfect conditions to develop his Political Arithmetick. In the same year Le Maître published *La Métropolitée*, Petty wrote his first essay that dealt with the city: *Another Essay in Political Arithmetick, Concerning the Growth of the City of London*. Like the physiocrats, he came to see the city as a socio-spatial entity essential to the calculations of trade. His statistical analyses of London, Dublin, Paris and Rome introduced a kind of proto-Malthusian account of population, its rates of growth and concerns for its overall health (see Petty, 1899: Vol. II). Yet it was not until Cantillon's *Essai* that Le Maître's spatially distributed state found its place in an overall economic theory. Cantillon's entire *Essai* turns on a kind of territorial system in which wealth, extracted solely from the riches of its lands, directly determines a 'natural' order in which the state's subjects dwell.[2] Their relation to the world is based largely on an equally 'natural' circulation of this wealth.

RICHARD CANTILLON

For Cantillon, villages historically emerged around the cultivation of land as the necessary means of cohabitation and the sharing of responsibilities. The size of each village is directly determined by the productivity of the land on which it sits – a factor that determines the number of farmers and labourers each village can sustain. Likewise, villages are distributed in proximity to towns according to their productivity and subsequent population size. In this calculation, as in many others, Cantillon includes transportation distances and costs in this distribution. The village is to be occupied primarily by farmers and labourers associated with cultivation. Only 'necessary' artisans are also to live in a village. Second in rank is the market town, which occupies a central location within a given region. The market town originated as a village that, owing to its centrality, established at one point in time a regular market at which other villagers from surrounding villages would sell their produce. The centrality of the market town helps to reduce the costs of transportation of produce from the neighbouring villages, and also to maintain Cantillon's notion of the 'just price' through this overall spatial organization. The size of the market town, like the village, is a result of the number of farmers living in its surrounding villages, as well as the number of artisans, merchants and landowner staff that the town attracts to live in it (Cantillon, 1959: Part I, chaps III and IV).

Next are the provincial cities, which, for Cantillon, are founded not on the productivity of the land, as with villages and towns, but rather on conquest. They are residences of nobility who have acquired land through 'discovery' or through battle – approximating what Marx called 'primitive accumulation'. Because of their status, they 'naturally' attract all other classes to live within their presence, setting up industry and business. 'For the service of these Noblemen, Bakers, Butchers, Brewers, Wine Merchants, Manufacturers of all kinds, will be needed. [. . .] There is no great Nobleman whose expense upon his house, his retinue and Servants, does not maintain Merchants and Artisans of all kinds' (ibid.: § I.V.2). Cities, for Cantillon, can also be founded by the establishment of governmental judiciary institutions or industrial ports within existing market towns, their status elevated by the influx of various classes they would attract. Yet all of these cities differ from that in which the nobility, heads of government and the Supreme Courts of Justice come together with the 'largest' landowners of the state. This city, bringing together political representation and economic structure, is, in Cantillon's terms, the capital city.

In this way, Cantillon relates economic production via the cultivation of a state's lands to political power, centralizing both in the capital, just as Le Maître had advised. 'Thus all the Lands in the state contribute more or less to maintain those who dwell in the Capital' (ibid.: § I.V.1). And just as for Le Maître, such grand cities can only be established where there are naturally ample means for transportation. 'Great Cities are usually built on the seacoast or on the banks of large Rivers for the convenience of transport; because water carriage of the produce and merchandise necessary for the subsistence and comfort of the inhabitants is much cheaper than Carriages and Land Transport' (ibid.: § I.IV.2).

Although his sociology of villages, towns and cities derives from the need to cultivate the land, it is organized by a political structure founded on the violence of land appropriation. Cantillon's entire theory of wealth fits well within the triad of appropriation, distribution and production that, as Schmitt argues, underpins every *nomos*. As we have seen, the articulation between the political and economic sides of his sociology – the cities and the web of villages and market towns – creates a system for the circulation of wealth, relating centre to periphery, city to countryside in a closed circuit (ibid.: Part II, chap. III). Because the wealth in circulation within a state is, for Cantillon, equivalent to its political power (ibid.: § II.VIII.11), these two faces of his theory remain tightly bound together in one indistinguishable whole. The circular relationship that Cantillon establishes between city, town, village and land, all organized within a territory, is *in itself* an apparatus for the vitalization and valorization of the state's wealth. That it is contained within the closed body of the state immediately transcribes this wealth into a measure of its political power.

Because Cantillon was the first to bring a kind of mathematical analysis to bear on a theory as totalizing as his, he introduced for the first time the possibility of relating an overall spatial composition of the state (as a distribution of villages, towns, cities and lands) to an analysis of wealth via its circulation. More rigorous than Le Maître's *Métropolitée* ever dared be, Cantillon introduced factors such as distance between villages, towns and cities, the type of produce cultivated on a given plot of land, its yield, the cost of labour for both cultivation and transportation, the annual investment in agricultural tools, the expenses and earnings made by artisans, and much more, brought them all into a single economic calculation. Traffic, in all of its forms, is not only the material confirmation of a state's glory and vitality, but it is now part of a mathematical analysis of its power. Furthermore, it became one of the key components available to the state's disciplinary apparatus of *planning* that unfolded over the course of the eighteenth century. Cantillon opened a world in which traffic, flow and circulation of all things material would present itself as the harmonious confluence of the greatness of a state and the rational calculus of its brute strength.

JEAN-BAPTISTE COLBERT

Although it was not until 1730 that such a comprehensive theory of territorial state trade emerged (1730 is the approximate date of publication of Cantillon's *Essai*), the appearance of such thinking had been firmly put into practice by one of France's most infamous administrators some 60 years before Cantillon's *Essai*: Jean-Baptiste Colbert. Indeed, not only did Colbert introduce a new, economically grounded system of planning into the French capital, but his government laid the foundations for a much greater institutional and professional transformation to take place in the next century – one fully prepared to embrace the physiocratic ideals of Cantillon, Quesnay and, later, Turgot to connect the entire realm of France in a single machine of circulation and exchange. In fact, it was perhaps Colbert's administrative control over Paris as minister of finance under Louis XIV that initially provided Le Maître with a model for his *Métropolitée*.

Colbert's agenda, more than anything else, was to promote the economic standing of France within the new political formation of Europe. 'He saw clearly, with his Cartesian temperament, that the power of the government was a consequence of national prosperity; at the same time he considered wealth as a fixed datum, and prosperity as a phenomenon of concentration, not of development' (Benevolo, 1978b: 724). It is, of course, the centralization of state affairs for which Colbert is perhaps best known. For this reason, as *La Métropolitée* later advised, Colbert's treatment of the capital was indistinguishable from his management of the state of France: Paris was, for him, the command centre for the entire realm of France. In a letter to his son, he wrote, 'Paris, being the capital of the realm and the dwelling place of kings, sets the whole of the rest of the kingdom in motion, and it is here that all businesses have their beginnings' (quoted in ibid.: 737).[3] His authority as minister of finance gave him titles ranging from superintendent of buildings and protector of the academy of architecture, to minister of royal palaces, to minister of the navy and colonies. On taking up his post in 1664, he began a radical reformation of the instruments of public control such that the most distant reaches of France were pulled under the authority of a single administrative apparatus. During his time in office, he conducted everything from the planning of Paris to the overseeing of France's foreign policy.

As one of the first chief civil servants of a modern state, Colbert saw his administration as one that should operate according to an economic rule of profitability (Picon, 1992: 100–1). As such, one of the most important facets for him was to greatly improve France's existing network of transportation. His administration immediately began a vast project of standardizing, constructing and managing the roadways that extended throughout the state, unifying them into a centralized, disciplined, mechanical whole. As a first step, he abolished the former *corvée* system, which delegated the management of roadways and canals to local authorities, and replaced it with a single set of standards that could be applied to all parts of the realm. Roadways connecting towns were to be straightened and widened and classed into two categories measuring 60 and 68 feet, respectively, and classified on the basis of their economic importance (ibid.: 101). Colbert also began massive works to improve the network of canals throughout France. In his first year in office, Colbert authorized the construction of the Canal du Midi, connecting the Mediterranean with the Atlantic (ibid.: 733).[4] Furthermore, he launched a programme to found new cities and upgrade existing ones according to the needs of his violently protectionist trade policy.

In his second year in office, he began organizing a team of engineers (*génie*)[5] and specialists (ibid.: 727–37) under his command to build a series of ports for use as naval bases and trading centres, located on all coasts of France (Rochefort, Brest, Lorient, Sète). Second, he expanded and fortified cities along the borders of France. He did this not only to defend the state from the encroachment of its neighbours, but because he wanted to concentrate trade along the borders, adjusting it to accommodate the most prosperous industries of each neighbouring state. These militarized borders thus served a second purpose of promoting the exportation of France's own trade in luxury goods (ibid.: 727). For this, Colbert commissioned Sébastien Le Prestre de Vauban, the former *ingénieur du roi*, to carry out this vast project. Gifted in the art of war and the construction of bulwarks, by 1678, Vauban had already completed the fortification of more than 30 towns – both new and existing – along France's northern frontier alone. In addition, existing border towns had to be not only fortified, but also expanded in order to cope with the new demands of militarized state trade. For this, Vauban, a pragmatist, developed new planning techniques that eliminated the geometrical idealism of the humanist tradition embodied in the notion of the ideal city, preferring instead a more rational, practical approach to polygonal fortifications and internal grid layouts, often combining several systems in each (ibid.: 735–8).

Colbert's approach to the capital was consistent with his overall management of the realm, but, for that reason, different from his approach to the fortified cities and ports at its periphery. The capital would be the domain of order, cleanliness and propriety. It would epitomize the ambitions and glory of the entire kingdom while also concentrating and coordinating its commercial activities. In contrast, the role of Versailles became crucial as the emblem of the seventeenth-century state in its greatness, and many accounts of this history set Colbert's pragmatic programme for Paris at odds with the grandeur of André Le Nôtre's project at Versailles. Although the separation between the capital and the residence of the king represented a clear chasm between the demands of sovereignty and those of governmental administration, this apparent opposition between the two entities belies a degree of continuity between them that unfolded in Colbert's planning of Paris.

His planning of Paris was far-reaching and can be read as two parallel programmes: the management and improvement of the old town and the opening of the city to its outskirts. Between these two strategies, he managed to establish a kind of template that developed into an administrative apparatus for urban planning that was, in turn, adopted by many in the nineteenth century. In 1666, Colbert established a new institution that was granted authority over the control of public order as well as the planning of the city's infrastructure: the council of the police. A year later, he appointed Nicolas de la Reynie as *lieutenant général de la police*; he was, as Benevolo contends, the person truly responsible for the planning of Paris (ibid.: 755). A short history of the activities of de la Reynie's council of police should suffice to characterize the role of what we might call a proto-*urban* institution:

[I]n 1666 it organized the cleansing and public lighting of the streets, in 1667 it fixed a height limit for buildings and forbade projections on to public spaces, in 1668 it required owners to install latrines in every house and laid down rules for the cleansing of drains. From 1666 onwards it studied the means to increase the water supply, granted permits for building other pumps along the Seine, and other aqueducts; in 1671 it ordered the building of fifteen more public fountains. [...] The banks of the river were laid out with quais and the hitherto non-existent embankments. Some new roads were traced, some old ones widened and straightened. (Ibid.: 756)

Its remit included the beautification of streets, gardens and public squares, the regularization of architectural facades, the planting of trees, and so on. As Foucault has shown, the activities of the police also involved the regulation and management of the market. It would oversee the buying and selling of merchandise and establishment and regulation of prices. It would provide order within the marketplace so that exchange could continue without disruption, and it would control the circulation of goods by directing the flows of traffic, both those within the city and those exiting and entering it, while also repressing thieves, vagrants and others who may obstruct the movement of traffic. As Foucault put it, the seventeenth-century police dealt with the problem of disciplining and ordering the 'coexistence of men and circulation of goods' (Foucault, 2009: 335). Colbert's council of the police was the first of its kind in the modern world operating under the aegis of *raison d'état*. It served as the conditional complement to the permanence and universality of sovereign law. It stood as a governmental paradigm for the creation and maintenance of neutrality that Hobbes had seen as the essential characteristic of his commonwealth. Following Colbert's council, other states began developing similar institutions. Prominent administrators wrote lengthy theories and treatises on the function and duties of the police throughout the eighteenth century (see, for example, De La Mare, 1729, and von Justi, 1782 (1756)).[6]

The other facet of Colbert's programme for Paris was its expansion. The founding of the council of the police revealed Colbert's awareness of the primacy of circulation within the political space of the capital. This remained at the level of policy – of the actual socio-political mechanisms for maintaining authority over the circulation of all kinds of traffic within the capital. His work on the planning of Paris proved to be equally as ground-breaking as his work on France's territory and again reflected the demands of its modern political status. Unlike the expansion techniques that Vauban had developed for cities such as Strasbourg or Brest, which had to accommodate themselves within systems of advanced fortification, Colbert treated Paris as a city at the geographical centre of a politically secured territory. Before Le Maître had theorized the role of a capital city, Colbert already understood that its organization and composition would have to exhibit a fundamentally new status no longer as a 'body' itself, but instead as the principal organ within a much larger, interconnected and functional spatio-political anatomy. Paris, for Colbert, would function as the centre of a vast new system of circulation and, for this reason, it would need to be a city *open* to the landscape outside it.

Between 1670 and 1676, Colbert authorized the demolition of defensive walls on the right bank. In their place, he commissioned Pierre Bullet to design broad, tree-lined roadways, which would come to be known as the *grands boulevards*. Beyond this ring of boulevards, Colbert had a network of roadways laid out with an eye to strategically connect Paris to all parts of the realm and beyond. Into this scheme, he began to incorporate the techniques of gardening pioneered by Le Nôtre at Versailles in order to unite his more pragmatic strategy of roadways with the splendour of Louis XIV's power. Indeed, Le Nôtre played a pivotal role in Colbert's scheme, laying out the most important elements of this peripheral network, the Champs-Élysées to the west of the city, along with the series of radiating roads (currently, the Rond Point) as well as the Cours-La-Reine along the banks of the Seine. Other radiating roads and avenues were also planned and constructed, giving monumental access to the city from all sides, including the avenue Saint Denis, the avenue de Meaux, avenue de Vincennes and the *grandes routes* of Fontainebleau and Orléans radiating to the south of the city (Benevolo, 1978b: 756). This system of roadways constituted a strategic and aesthetic foundation for Colbert's programme for Paris, and he accompanied it with a plan for an array of architectural objects to occupy and order this new landscape. He commissioned Jacques-François Blondel and Claude Perrault to carry out the construction of monumental entrances, gates and triumphal arches leading into the city (ibid.: 757). Together, this system of corridors, gardens and monumental follies was coordinated and consolidated into a single, regulated plan by an edict of 1676, which was eventually carried out by Blondel and Bullet (ibid.: 757–8).

CONSTRUCTING LANDSCAPE

It is noteworthy that the majority of Colbert's projects for Paris took place on its outskirts, in the reorganization of its immediate environs, focusing on the connections between the city and the surrounding countryside, between the state's capital and its territory. It was an experiment in combining the strategic logic of opening the capital up, functionally connecting it to the realm, with the demand for greatness that accompanied Louis XIV's reign. The unity Colbert achieved between these two aspects in the improvement of Paris proved resilient and gave grounds for future administrators to succeed him (including Haussmann)[7] because it brought together a rational policy of planning (although this term would not be used until the eighteenth century) with a monumental scheme for its execution, all housed under a strong administrative framework. In his management of the old city through the council of the police and his expansion of the city's outskirts, Colbert managed to unite the rational with the magnificent, the economic with the political. Colbert's programme for Paris remains a paradigm for modern planning because it went far beyond the concerns and scale of the city itself, answering both the economic and political demands of state reason.

Figure 5.1   Pierre Bullet and François Blondel, Plan de Paris, 1676

Source: Bibliothèque nationale de France. Reproduced with permission from la Bibliothèque nationale de France

Through this model of administration, Colbert transformed the city into the capital of a modern, territorial state and wove this entity into the rational planning of the entire realm, binding the territory, the space and form of the city and the activities of its population into one regulated, disciplined and calculated system of administered movement. Such a configuration would be indispensable for the formation and performance of modern Western governments from the seventeenth century onward:

> If the governmentality of the state is interested, for the first time [in Western history], in the fine materiality of human existence and coexistence, of exchange and circulation, if this being and well-being is taken into

account for the first time by the governmentality of the state, through the town and through the problems like health, roads, markets, grains, and highways, it is because at that time commerce is thought of as the main instrument of the state's power and thus as the privileged object of a police whose objective is the growth of the state's forces. (Foucault, 2009: 339)

Colbert's time in office saw the strategic restructuring and expansion of many cities in France, together with a massive deployment of infrastructure connecting them, all according to a hierarchy derived from the imperatives of *raison d'état*. The innovation his model achieved was in its ability to coordinate the needs of the state with those of the capital. In a way, Colbert treated the entire territory of France as though it were a large city: part of this was in order to militarily fortify the borders, sealing off the interior from the exterior while characterizing the new diplomatic relationship between the two as one of precarious, interstate trade. He would unify the interior of the state through the rational improvement and coordination of its cities and towns in a single infrastructural network of economic circulation. The entire whole would fall under the control of the capital, the *regulatory* power of which, underwritten by the sovereign, would radiate itself to distant parts of the realm through the presence and activity of the police. As Foucault asserts, '[p]olice consists therefore in the sovereign exercise of royal power over individuals who are subjects. In other words, police is the direct governmentality of the sovereign qua sovereign' (ibid.: 339). Such a regulatory apparatus would be required by reason of the sheer scale of territory over which the sovereign was to rule, in addition to the actual functional management of the vast system of circulation and exchange that would in turn underwrite the sovereign's power. Thus, although the domain of the police remained largely attached to the city and market town, its effect was integral to the administration and political power of the state as a territorial whole:

When *raison d'État* takes European equilibrium as its objective, with a military-diplomatic armature for its instrument, and when this same *raison d'État* takes the singular growth of each state power as its other objective with, at the same time, commerce as the instrument of this growth, you can see how and why police is inseparable from a politics of commercial competition within Europe. (Ibid.: 337–8)

Colbert's administrative apparatus left a legacy that can be traced in its scale of both town planning and the planning of the entire territory. Not only did Haussmann benefit from it two centuries later, but the establishment of the École des ponts et chaussées in 1747 – the body of state civil engineers – was a direct outcome of the Corps de Génie inaugurated by Vauban in 1672 under Colbert's direction. Furthermore, it was Colbert who integrated the category of 'landscape' (via Le Nôtre's work) into the planning of Paris, recognizing at once a scale and a class of space not only useful for the glorification of the king, but that proved to be useful in the formulation of a single, coherent framework for policy that had been the hallmark of his administration. In this new class of space, Colbert saw perhaps the first instance of a quantifiable instrument for planning, comprehensible in its ability to be measured and integrated into a larger economic calculation. It was, for him, the medium of circulation and exchange and the commensurate instrumental space within the larger political technology of territory. 'In a world that was still under the sway of custom, the idea arose of space described by the circulation of men, ideas and commodities, and covered by services which respond at a distance' (Picon, 1992: 101).

This category of space, fundamental to the formation of state reason and the principal site of its administrative activity, became the central domain of activity for the Corps des ponts et chausées at the beginning of the next century. With the birth of territory as a primary spatial and epistemological instrument of state reason, a new distinction between architects and engineers arose. The engineers associated with the ponts et chausées emerged as a distinct group of architects charged with the task of developing and managing the territory. Increasingly, with the growing prominence of the Corps throughout the kingdom, the division between architects and engineers grew more apparent in terms of both the time and scale of the projects each took on. Although the projects taken on by engineers operated at a scale much larger than those of architects, they also had to accommodate a timescale that architects in the classical sense never had to encounter. It soon became clear that engineers operated with respect to processes embodied in the logic of planning that not only directly reflected the policies of the state, but forced the creation of a form of knowledge that could cope with such spans of time. More than the imitation of nature or the glorification of the king, engineers were responsible for a domain more extensive in both scale and use than architects, one 'formulated in terms of a perspective involving the conquest of nature and of social progress' (ibid.).

The origin of this new arm of the state reveals the unity it maintained between its practices and the governmental administration of the state from its beginning. The special group of elite military engineers organized by Vauban, crucial to the fortification of France's borders, provided the model on which, in 1716, the Corps des ponts et chausées established itself (Benevolo, 1978b: 735). The ponts et chausées began as a group of 21 engineers – one to oversee each region of France – working under the supervision of three inspectors and one chief architect (Picon, 1992: 102). Although this structure condensed the efforts of planning under one organization, it still lacked a certain coherence in enforcing a single, unified system of territorial planning. Thus, it further centralized its efforts in 1744 with the establishment of the Drawing Office, a managerial body set up to consolidate and standardize the processes of mapping the territory and planning its bridges, roadways and canals.

> It appeared to be the first technical state structure whose competence
> extended throughout the whole country. The maps established by the
> employees of the Office featured the roads which they proposed to build.
> The pinpointing of geographical features was linked to concrete projects,
> thereby helping to fashion a new approach to planning. (Ibid.: 104)

As an institution of the state, it was given the further responsibility of training
pupils in addition to maintaining a professional status. In 1756, the Drawing
Office, seeing its role as increasingly pedagogical, adopted the title of École des
ponts et chaussées. Its teaching remained grounded in the completion of actual
projects, blurring the boundary between student and professional. The École created a unique form of knowledge, grounded in 'reality', that could respond to the
fluid contingency of site, geography and economy, rather than adhering strictly
to universal principles of geometry, proportion and harmony. It was a corpus of
management of the entire physical 'reality' of the kingdom, making a powerful
technological apparatus available to state reason for the first time (ibid.: 105).

Over time, because of its claim of mastery over space, the École began to
concentrate on the development of a consistent science of engineering that came
to be more substantial than the actual practices of engineering themselves. The
progression from a rational approach of the practice to the formulation of a true
science of engineering, both of which were intended to be deployed across the
entirety of the state's territory, led to a system of rationalization. This system – a
kind of doctrine – provided a discursive vocabulary by which any project could
be described in its totality and fitted within a single calculable framework. 'While
the architects sought to base their vocabulary upon the imitation of nature, the
engineers located their work within a continuous process, from the initial moment
of invention to the effective realization on the building site' (ibid.: 107). This kind
of descriptive totality contained in the cataloguing of the building site provided
a model for engineers to then analyse and qualify the territory as well. The territory appeared as an 'inventory' of resources available to the state through its
new technical arm of engineers, while also legible as a space-in-process. Nature
and human artifice coincided in this category to form an instrument of state-
administered extraction and production.

Of course, the engineers of the ponts et chaussées existed in a time in which
such references to nature were commonplace. Most importantly, the influence of
physiocracy on the development of the École became clearly marked in their use
not only of the category of nature, but of reason as well. Whereas architects had
long seen their work as reflecting or even imitating nature, in light of physiocratic
thought, the engineers engaged with a nature now seen to be 'productive' as a
source of wealth and the medium from which reason was to be derived. In this way,
Cantillon's *Essai* and, more particularly, Quesnay's *Tableau Économique* had their
most significant effect, despite their more limited reception in the political realm.

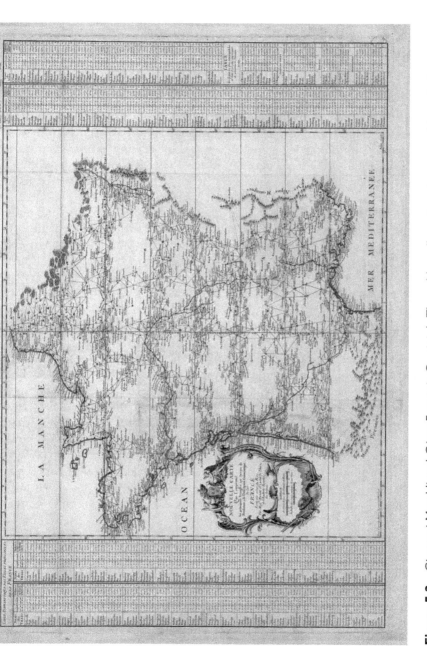

Figure 5.2 Giovanni Maraldi and César-François Cassini de Thury, Nouvelle carte qui comprend les principaux triangles qui servent de fondement à la Description géométrique de la France (New Map that understands the principal triangles that serve as a foundation for the geometric description of France), 1744

Source: Bibliothèque nationale de France. Reproduced with permission from la Bibliothèque nationale de France

Embracing physiocratic ideals, the engineers drew on the tautology that society was formed as a result of its natural ability to organize exchange. Free-market ideals appeared as a means to reform the state, which, to the eyes of a burgeoning civil society, had begun to appear corrupt, *artificial*. '[W]ithin the smooth, determined space of the State, we see the emergence of a [. . .] smooth indeterminate space of the market. The former spaces are artificial, the latter supposedly "natural"' (Galli, 2010: 63). The engineers' work was rooted in its capacity to 'fulfil' nature's mandate through artifice in the improvement of the state's circulation. The contradictory status of this logic was not lost on historian Antoine Picon: 'Nature was to be perfected by means of bridges and causeways; society had to be transformed also, so as to facilitate exchanges between men' (1992: 109). Such a 'perfecting of nature' was at the basis of the engineers' work, whose presence served as a kind of concrete correlate to the laissez-faire policies pursued by the physiocrats (Picon, 2009: 28). The construction of bridges, the dredging and straightening of canals and the vast regularization of roadways according to the demands of trade opened a space in which the imperative to lift tolls and customs barriers could become equally natural. These references to reason, nature and the universal communication set the engineer as a figure in eighteenth-century France who could attain a status of virtue. This claim to truth was forged with the assistance of the *esprit de corps* that provided a bond between engineers and their work in the name of goodness and the unification of society and, most importantly, in the category of utility.

Utility serves as an indicator of the growing differences between architects and engineers at the time. On the one hand, whereas architects remained within a certain restricted relationship of patronage, drawing on the long-held precepts of taste, proportion or *bienséance* to persuade individual patrons, engineers saw themselves as a kind of collective whose task was to fulfil a responsibility that 'society' itself (via the state) had bestowed on them. The engineer 'addressed himself to a human group whose needs and laws he had himself defined' (Picon, 1992: 109) according to a universal notion of humanity akin to that conceived by the *philosophes*. At the same time, a gradual shift in attitude had been taking place towards the basic values of the architect. Under the pressure of the economic spirit of the time, a fundamental wedge was driven between architects and engineers around the notion of utility. The category of utility prescribed how a project was made useful in itself, and it 'determined the form which the engineers' design would assume in the social domain' (ibid.: 112). As a principle, it remained bound to the economy, as its pretensions were based on the ability to constantly be assessed in an economic framework of cost, productivity and profitability. For engineers, it became apparent that their work would rely first and foremost on its utility to the greater needs of a society in perpetual circulation and exchange. 'Character had therefore come to seem supplementary, as far as the engineers were concerned, whereas taste continued to be upheld, albeit in a fairly vague way' (ibid.: 113).

The achievements of the engineers of the ponts et chuassées assisted in the subordination of the core principles of the architect to that of utility for the first time. What became clear over the course of the eighteenth century was a distinction that has continued, in a broad sense, to the present day: the architect's relation to power derived from the ability to reflect the glory of the ruling political class, whereas the engineer would manifest a relationship to power in the planning and construction of the networks and landscapes that would give material and economic order to state and society alike. Furthermore, the knowledge of the territory embedded in the techniques of cartography had forged a bond between a political space and the space of representation. Architectural representation had begun, for the first time, to lose ground to a truly modern form of spatio-political knowledge.

Such a shift is noticeable in the techniques employed by the students of the ponts et chaussées. It was no longer a matter, as it was for architects, of imitating nature, but a matter of mapping it. The drawings made by the engineers aimed to represent nature in its exactitude and totality. Like Quesnay's *Tableau*, these maps became catalogues of nature itself. 'Learning to draw a map involved, first and foremost, learning to read nature, and to decipher the signs which she [*sic*] lavished upon an attentive observer' (ibid.: 217). 'Reading nature' meant creating a cartographic register of all productive lands, minerals and resources distributed throughout the land. The map of the territory was a map of wealth and energy; wealth had to be set into motion, and this is precisely how the work of the engineers came to correspond so tightly to the thought of the physiocrats. Creating a scaled facsimile of nature was only useful if it could become a template on which to project an abstract geometric order composed of roadways and canals across its surface. The grammar of geometric forms and symmetry of which the engineers made use drew inspiration from existing models (in particular, Le Nôtre's). The gratuitousness with which such designs were treated reveals a strange desire to control and discipline the very same nature that was so thoroughly venerated for its riches and order of reason. It was as if the discovery of the state's interior in the late seventeenth century, in the same spirit as the 'discovery' of the new world, was accompanied by an equally powerful anxiety to dominate and neutralize the very nature discovered therein.

It is telling that the star-like networks of roadways radiating from *carrefours* and the symmetrical march of grids of *parterres* rarely could be constrained within the boundaries of a single drawing. Lacking any clear centrality, the drawings of the ponts et chaussées students depict roadways projecting off the edges of the paper into the imaginary spaces beyond. Garden layouts creep into the frame of the drawing only to hint at their invisible magnificence. Great walled cities, foregrounded by systems of infrastructure, disappear off into the infinite plane beyond the drawing. The drawings they often produced contain no centre, no boundary condition and no limits. Hierarchy – and thus order – exists in the spaces between the natural and the artificial, in the space of infrastructural domination over the natural world. They lacked a certain figurative, formal composition, a lack that was compensated for by the relationship between the natural and the artificial: nature, in these maps, is subjected to the logic of circulation.

In addition, the character of the projects engineers undertook embraced a startling scalar breadth. In the service of connecting the territory, engineers were predisposed to work at hugely varied scales. 'Intervening locally or in the territory amounted to the same thing; the actions governing the lay-out of a portion of a road or the constitution of the general network of traffic paths were fundamentally identical' (ibid.: 220). Engineers were able to produce work that traversed all intelligible scales of construction. When circulation and exchange are elevated to the natural precondition of society, the distance between artifice and nature conceptually collapses in on itself, and the two begin to coexist as a limitless quality visible in the constant slippage into the infinite depicted in the drawings of the ponts et chaussées. As Benevolo has shown, infinity had already been integrated into planning with the arrival of the category of landscape (1978b: 719; 1994). However, the character of 'infinity' explored by the ponts et chaussées reveals a far more strategic, utilitarian and indeed political quality than Le Nôtre's work had opened up.

THE CITY IN *RAISON D'ÉTAT*

Within this new professional and institutional setting, the figure of the city and its relationship to the territory received a renewed, although increasingly negative, attention. The notion of territory had been made legible in part through the work of the ponts et chaussées, its visibility an undeniable measure of political power. As the attention of economists, philosophers, political advisors and engineers pored over the fecundity and riches of the countryside, while becoming acquainted with the power legible in its cartographic representation, the city seemed to have receded from view. After all, when Cantillon had written about the circulation of goods, produce, money, he was not speaking about the circulation of the 'detailed' flows of exchange within a city, but, crucially, about the circuit of wealth's flow in the territory outside the city (1959: § II.V.13). The city for the physiocrats only existed as a site of exchange that can, therefore, only be comprehensible in the larger territorial system in which it resides. By the middle of the eighteenth century, the city was often seen as a kind of necessary evil – a site of corruption, disorder, disease, justifiable only in terms of its use in the process of exchange. The abbé Marc-Antoine Laugier, in his famous *Essai sur l'Architecture*, characterized the state of disrepair of Paris in terms of its status as capital of France: 'Strangers who pass [Paris's] tollhouses are thunderstruck when they are told: "Now you are in the Capital of France"' (Laugier, 1977: 124). Indeed, although both the planning and theorizing of the state as a unitary, administrative entity had advanced well into the spatial realm, the city as a theoretical project in itself had yet to adapt to this new political and *œconomic* horizon. Nevertheless, the lapse in attention paid to the town in a period intensely preoccupied with questions of spatial and material order paradoxically opened the door to such thinking. Over the course of the second half of the eighteenth century, the city, from an architectural perspective, once again became the object of theoretical speculation, notably in the writings of Laugier, Blondel and, of course, Pierre Patte. And, as before, it was around the notion of circulation that this discussion unfolded.

Although Laugier contributed relatively little to the thinking on the city, his overall criticism of the inadequacy found in the cities of his day, as well as his conviction that a new approach to 'improving' the city had to conceive of it as a whole, was shared by many. For him, the city had been neglected and lacked the same holistic, systematic planning that had been devoted to the territory, resulting in a situation he saw as unfit for the times. 'Our towns are still what they were, a mass of houses crowded together haphazardly without system, planning or design' (ibid.: 121). Despite his preoccupations with architectural composition, decoration and *bienséance*, Laugier placed great emphasis on the town's layout ('*distribution*') of streets. Of particular concern for him was the free flow of traffic entering and exiting the city, as well as the 'narrow and tortuous streets' of the city centre, 'where the encounter of carriages causes constant obstruction' (ibid.). In fact he makes clear his priorities in the following order: 'The beauty and splendor of a town depends mainly on three things: its entries, its streets and its buildings' (ibid.: 122). For him, the first priority was to provide a number of ornate entries to the town, evenly spaced around its walls. Interestingly, Laugier, like Colbert, began to rethink the city by focusing on the avenues leading to it, rather than the streets *within* it. The 'entries of towns' not only refers to the placement and design of the gates, but also – more importantly, Laugier stressed – the layout of the avenues leading up to them, considering above all how to avoid crowding of traffic and improving access *to* the city. Given such a favourable layout can be achieved, one can then consider the streets inside the city: 'It is not enough that the avenue be wide and as far as possible without bend and deviation; the gate and the street inside, which corresponds to the avenue, must also have these advantages' (ibid.: 123).

Inside the city, the layout of the streets should follow a similar logic: 'The streets of a great town cannot make communication easy and convenient unless they are sufficiently numerous to prevent lengthy detours, sufficiently wide to forestall any obstructions and perfectly straight to shorten the way' (ibid.: 127). To solve this problem, he turned to the only paradigm of design that approximated the scale of the city, incorporating both rational geometry and attention to beauty: landscape design. 'One must look to the town as a forest. The streets of the one are the roads of the other; both must be cut through in the same way' (ibid.: 128). For Laugier, the problem had a simple answer. One needed merely to transpose the same reasoning and logic of landscape design employed by the engineers of the ponts et chaussées (and, by extension, Le Nôtre) to the planning of the city. 'Let us carry out this idea and use the design of our parks as plan for our towns. It is only a question of measuring the area and making the same style roads into streets and *carrefours* into squares' (ibid.). In this, Laugier could solve two pressing problems of his contemporary city – efficient circulation and architectural beauty – through the device of landscape. 'The essential beauty of a park consists in the great number of roads, their width and their alignment' (ibid.).

Le Nôtre had become a point of reference for both the engineers of the ponts et chaussées and architects, and so it is no surprise that Benevolo observed that '[t]own-planning as it is understood today [. . .] first appears, at the time of the Sun King, in the form of landscape design' (1978b: 741). For Laugier, it was clear: the knowledge needed to 'improve' the city would be imported from outside it, a knowledge that would penetrate architectural theories and treatises for the first time, introducing the predominant logic of circulation into the repertoire of architectural principles. Most importantly, it would enter into the arena of architectural thought on the back of a form of knowledge foreign to the city, but destined to become integral to its reconception: territorial planning. Like the territory, the city, too, would have to be taken as a theoretical object to be regulated, made whole and subjected to the kind of cataloguing typical of the engineers' work if it were to become visible as an object of modern theoretical enquiry. From the perspective of the engineers, '[t]he town ceased to be a world turned in on itself, and came to seem a particularly dense zone for the network of services' (Picon, 1992: 223). Indeed, it was the town in which the interests and expertise of both engineers and architects could again find common ground. Over the course of the eighteenth century, the architectural perception of the city was, for the first time, altered by the logic of planning, beginning a long process of opening the city up to its integration within a space given over to state reason – a process the results of which remained unclear until well into the nineteenth century.

If the city finally featured in the work of architectural theory with Laugier's *Essai*, it was in the work of Pierre Patte that it achieved a clearer status as a discursive object in itself. Patte argued for holistic improvement of Paris, taking his cue from Laugier's *Essai*, but going well beyond it and advocating the complete '*rectification*' of the city. In 1765, he published his first major work, *Monumens érigés en France à la gloire de Louis XV*, which contained his famous engraving of Paris, complete with a constellation of 19 previously unrealized projects by various architects. Opening with a survey of the arts and sciences, it consists of a damning critique of the current state of Paris, made in the same vein as that of Laugier, before finishing with the plan for its embellishment. Addressing the problems of the city, he advanced a new perspective by viewing it through the lens of a single plan. Patte drew from the techniques his former mentor, Blondel, had developed in his plans for Metz and Strasbourg, thus treating the wholeness of his plan for Paris as an agglomeration of individual architectural projects. By relying solely on this classical architectural knowledge of embellishment, Patte was unable to resolve the problems he had nonetheless raised. Just four years later, Patte published his *Mémoires sur les objets les plus importants de l'architecture*, in which he attempted to carry forward his efforts from *Monumens*, towards a '*plan total*' (Patte, 1769: 5). Architectural historian Françoise Choay noted that this work is 'irreparably shattered' into chapters with seemingly little congruity between them. Spanning from his thoughts on the city, repeating his concern for a holistic planning method, to a discussion on the architectural orders, to a discussion on the construction of bridges, foundations and quays, among others, this work struggles to maintain its own coherence. Interestingly, departing from previous thinkers and architects, the relative status of beauty (*bienséance*, etc.) in Patte's '*nouvelle ville*' is never reconciled with that of practical necessity (*commodité*), setting it adrift as a category somewhat emptied of its classical import while signalling the urgency that circulation had acquired. This discrepancy traverses the entirety of Patte's text, from the fragmented arrangement of chapter topics to the very approach to the city he took, juxtaposing architectural prescriptions with techniques of assessment employed by engineers – specific architectural details with generalized principles of distribution.

If there is one conceptual foundation that stands out in Patte's work, it is his use of the notion of circulation. Already, the concept of circulation had not only been embraced by the work of the physiocrats, but had also reached near-messianic status in the circles of elites who championed the growing public sphere in which circulation had become associated with the Republic of Letters and the formation of public opinion (Habermas, 2010: chap. 2). If, for Laugier, circulation had been a predominant concern in his scheme of town improvement, for Patte, it was clearly the principle around which his entire theory turned. Indeed, Laugier's critique of the city remained generally occupied with an aesthetic assessment that had only a limited interface with the movement of traffic. His critique of Paris was formed more around the concerns that a lack of circulation would contribute both to the city's poor hygiene and to the inconveniences for traffic associated with trade. For Patte, his *nouvelle ville* would respond to the world of laissez-faire economics – a character that was central to his work and already clearly visible in his *Monumens*. As Picon notes:

> Whereas the classical squares represented a form of sumptuary expenditure, serving to interpret the tissue of the town in such a way as to glorify the monarchy, the spaces opened up by Patte were designed to increase wealth by facilitating traffic and exchanges. The architect also dreamed of installing public granaries around the city. (Picon, 1992: 194)

For Patte, the city must intercommunicate – its network of streets must not only be made intelligible, rational and laid out according to reason in themselves; the unmistakable implication is that they must also be unified as a system (see Choay, 1997: 219).[8]

Foreshadowing Cerdá's work, Patte prescribed an exhaustive set of regulations and technological requirements with which to transform the city. As with Cerdá's approach, Patte's regulations were driven by the two pillars of the modern rational city yet to come: hygiene and ease of movement. Despite his inability to achieve a 'total plan' for Paris, let alone a generalized theory of city improvement (akin to Cerdá's), Patte was able to synthesize these two concerns into a single model that responded to both. Perhaps his most emblematic contribution to the history of architecture, Patte's design and layout of generic city streets proposed a system that would integrate the two concerns in a single structure.

The system he put forward – remarkably close to the system of *vias* and *nudos* Cerdá would design a century later (1999: 111–13) – was represented by a kind of idealized street system with corners that had been chamfered to assist the free movement of traffic and with breadth that had been rationally partitioned into specific lanes for either horse-drawn or pedestrian traffic. Down the centre of this ideal street would run an underground system of sewers and aqueducts, integrating both waste from the neighbouring houses and drainage from the street,

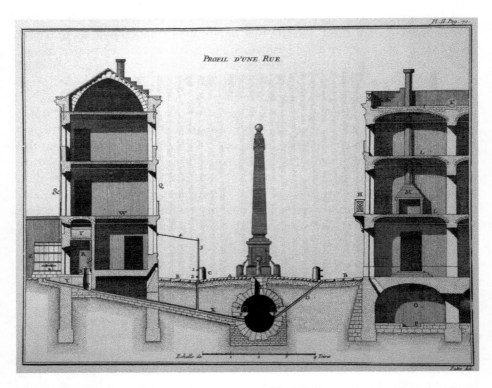

Figure 5.3 Pierre Patte, Section of a street, 1769 (*Mémoires sur les objets les plus importans de l'architecture*, Plate II)

Source: Canadian Centre for Architecture. Courtesy of the Canadian Centre for Architecture

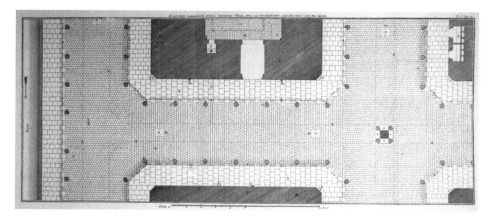

Figure 5.4   Pierre Patte, Plan of a crossroads of a new city with the distribution of either streets or embankments, 1769 (*Mémoires sur les objets les plus importans de l'architecture*, Plate I)

Source: Canadian Centre for Architecture. Courtesy of the Canadian Centre for Architecture

together with a system for the supply of fresh water for the city. The intersection of the street could be 'improved' by a fountain being placed at its centre, which would also draw fresh water from the underground aqueduct.

All of this was designed, from the overall composition of technologies to the specification and placement of bollards, the differentiation of paving, roof construction to assist in the drainage of water and the distribution of lamps along its length. He even included spaces for public toilets. Almost a century before Cerdá published his work, Patte had already proposed a model based on two parallel systems of circulation working as a unified infrastructure, integrating street, sewerage system and the design of the houses flanking it in a single, mechanical gesture – all of which is famously depicted in the first cross-section of a street. 'Just like a productive work, the street became a machine regulating a set of flows: the flowing of water and the traffic of vehicles' (ibid.).

Mémoires appears not just as a declaration of the desire to transform the 'physical composition' (Patte, 1769: 61) of the city, but as a kind of tableau of the ideal characteristics a town should aspire to contain, based on reason. 'His conception of the town resembles nothing so much as a catalogue of urban technology' (Picon, 1992: 197). Despite his attempts to set out a totalizing method to grasp the problem of the city, Patte was only ever able to operate by working either with general principles (street system, regulations) or detailed, isolated prescriptions (technical apparatuses, machine design). His principles remained stunted in the form of a series of solitary strategies or operational devices 'universally applicable to old cities as well as to "new cities"' (Choay, 1997: 219). Pre-empting the urbanists of the next century, Patte nevertheless was the first to approach the city as a single, technical object viewed through a scientific lens.

'In his *Mémoires*, the city is already partially transformed into an instrument' (ibid.: 220). Perhaps for this reason, he saw that the city would need to be permanently policed: Patte's rational city consisted of an extensive list of prescriptions, regulations and technologies, the functional unity of which could only be held together by the same police structure Colbert had first set in place a century before. As Picon points out, '[t]he relations between the building and the town then came to involve the subjection of both to rules for the control and management of space' (Picon, 1992: 204).

As we would see in the century to come, the ambitions Patte upheld were carried forward by the germination of engineers, reformers and administrators who succeeded in realizing total systems, categorically transforming cities into urban bodies. The overarching sense of 'truth' implied in the work of Cerdá and Haussmann alike can also be found in Patte's. Truth in his text is based on an appeal to reason of science and technical application, just as it would later be for nineteenth- and twentieth-century urbanists. Although Patte constantly makes mention of society's needs, he nonetheless takes them to be a single, homogeneous set that can be understood in its totality and met through the technical rectification of the city. He speaks on behalf of all of society in the name of this truth and with the sense of self-assuredness common to eighteenth- and nineteenth-century reformists. His concerns for hygiene, order and the establishment of unimpeded circulation all arise as a symmetrical response to his exaggerated critique (ibid.: 188) of Paris – a form that is unmistakably part of the utopian tradition of critique (see Chapter 1 of this volume), which, as we have seen, provided both structure and vindication for the nineteenth-century theories of urbanization.

For all its strengths, Patte's *Mémoires* did not overcome a weakness that had begun to render architecture torpid over the course of the eighteenth century. With the continued success of the engineers of the ponts et chaussées, a certain privilege had been given to the planning of the territory. By translating the principles of the physiocrats into spatial terms, they managed to transform the territory into a geometrized landscape of utility, justifying their actions in the name of 'perfecting' nature. Drawing on Le Nôtre's legacy, the gap between the natural and the artificial was closed in the realization of a system of communication extending its abstract geometry throughout the countryside. The result was a dazzling confluence of natural topography and human networks of exchange. Yet this left the figure of the city with an uncertain status. To the engineers, its spaces lacked the facility in which rational geometric and infrastructural schemes could be laid out. Furthermore, the city neither served as the source of wealth, nor did it show the self-evident qualities of goodness that the countryside bestowed in the riches of its lush vitality. As two separate technologies of the state, a stark contrast between the city and the territory grew, and, increasingly, the city could be rationalized according to dominant eighteenth-century thought only as a space of exchange – the site where the 'capillary' flows of wealth distributed payments to society 'in detail'. It was these terms that Patte emphasized in his *Mémoires*, opening spaces for trade, rationalizing traffic and improving the capacity for circulation within the city. If nature in the space of the territory needed to be perfected by the engineers, the city could at least by 'rectified' by Patte's street system and machines in order to allow 'nature's' passage into the city in the form of economic circulation. Trade, traffic and the movement of merchandise in and out of a city would be the manifestation of a 'natural' and thus virtuous process otherwise relegated to the spaces outside its walls and *portes*.

From the sixteenth century until the end of the eighteenth, there was a great transition in the status of the city as but one of the outcomes of the greater emergence of what Schmitt has called the '*nomos* of the earth'. It is a shift that can be traced in the representational devices used to depict and project the dominant spatio-political entities over this period. From ancient portrayals through its appearance in the early Renaissance, the privileged figure of the circle had played a dominant role in representing the city, both in its idealized form and in the architecture that composes it. The ancient city stood for centuries as an immediately political entity – a *body*, the unity and integrity of which confirmed its political capacity. Yet it was not only in its representation or description that its stature could be comprehended. The ancient city declared its political status in the very materiality of its defensive walls, not simply protecting it from foreign threats, but carving out a space separated from the natural world in which the coordinates of a political life could be made legible. Its relationship to the world outside its walls was not one of such sharp categorical distinctions as it would come to be, but rather it was predicated on its intrinsic correspondence with its site and its surrounding qualities. Because political order was an inherent condition of the natural world, the existence of the city could never be considered as separate from it, but would instead derive its ontological conditions of possibility in conjunction with the natural configuration of its site.

Expansions, fortifications, improvements and early forms of planning blossomed from the sixteenth century to the eighteenth, and during this time a completely new set of demands was placed on the city. By the seventeenth century, the city began to fulfil an entirely new capacity, and the figure that had taken its place and political significance in the world was, of course, territory. Its early representational appearances, both as 'body politique' in Hobbes *Leviathan* and as a concentric network of circles in Le Maître, are a register of this shift. In contrast to its ancient counterpart, the city would now mark its political status precisely by *demolishing* its walls and projecting a new instrumental network of roadways across a landscape deprived of its natural, autonomous consistency. The political shift towards territory had begun, and architects and administrators across Europe would struggle to grasp the city's new identity in this configuration.

Colbert was the first administrator to have recognized the new spatial requirements of the modern world. His opening up of Paris by demolishing its defensive walls was not only a practical consideration: it was the recognition of the new political space unfurling across Europe's new territorial order. This space was to be explored and conquered by boulevards, networks of roadways, avenues and canals penetrating the 'emptiness' of the landscape outside the city. It developed from the perimeter of the city outwards, tying the city as an entity into the rationalized system of circulation that Colbert would develop and control at the same time. In contrast, the city itself, impervious to such planning, remained the domain of 'police science', the awkward realm in which architectural beautification would complement the disciplinary control of space. This division between the city and territory persisted for almost two centuries.

In the face of this, architectural experiments (within Europe) remained tied to a scale that prevented them from advancing a new paradigm that could answer to such demands. Instead, architecture, together with small-scale improvements and policy-making, coped with this changing world by modifying the space and form of the city in a limited, piecemeal manner that drew from a classical repertoire of tools. In this way, the city for architects began a slow retreat from view. It became *relativized*, just as the perception of both space and subjectivity had (see Chapter 3): the city now defined itself *with respect to* the territory outside its walls. Only by its doing so did the first inkling of a modern conceptual framework of the city surface. Although such a view eventually began to emerge in the latter half of the eighteenth century, as we have seen, these efforts remained insufficient and fragmented. The status of the city had been reconfigured from the outside, as it were, and no one as yet had been able to answer the new demands placed on it from within.

By the eighteenth century, the somewhat weakened status of architecture that we have seen reflected the larger crisis into which the city itself had fallen ever since the emergence of the modern state. Although economists, advisors and administrators wrote about the city more than ever before during this period, its status as a political body had clearly changed. The town remained irrational, whereas the territory, because of its 'emptiness', was infinitely accessible to the rational, geometric planning devised by the engineers. The naturally heterogeneous composition of the landscape discovered through cartographic technologies could at once be neutralized by the techniques of planning that its discovery also made available. Its 'indifferent differences' could be instrumentalized by the superimposition of a continuous web of roadways, canals, bridges and tunnels on top of them. The city, by contrast, remained closed to such techniques. It had become a displaced object, inserted into a greater mechanical structure whose space was no longer perceivable without cartographic knowledge and whose order was only manageable through vast new governmental apparatuses. 'Perfecting nature' meant filling out the space of the state with a spatial order fit for the logic of its management, and infrastructural planning was the only tool with the capacity to do so.

The knowledge of the city generally associated with its 'modernization' that matured from the end of the seventeenth century until the turn of the nineteenth – the rationalization of the city, the perception of systemic wholeness, the introduction of a technologically instrumental order – so often attributed to 'enlightened' thought, appears rather more haphazard, feeble. Indeed, up until the latter half of the eighteenth century, the city was all but forgotten by such thinkers. Over the centuries-long construction of the modern world, the city as an object of theoretical enquiry only plunged deeper into obscurity. Architectural theorists found it nearly impossible to grasp as a figure in its own right with the existing knowledge offered by classical architecture. Nor was the city treated as the object of pure reason alone. The utopian critique drawn upon by the likes of Laugier, Patte or Mercier not only signalled an attempt to historically restore the city to an elevated status of times past, but also revealed the reactionary and incomplete means by which to do so: if a holistic approach to the city could not yet provide it with order, order could be forced into it through the perpetual policing of its space. In this way, the utopian critique imported another ambition into the theorizing of the city, opening it to both medical knowledge and the permanence of the police.

In part, large-scale town planning – what Cerdá will call *urbanización* – would be impossible without the mechanism of free capital and without broader coordination between administrative and legal devices – issues that, as we have seen, were resolved in the nineteenth century. Yet more pressing was the deep perceptual and epistemological rift that hardened over the seventeenth and eighteenth centuries between the status of the city and that of the territory. Although it was clear that these two spatial entities played distinct roles in the formation of the state, it became equally clear that, unlike territory, the city lacked a positive theoretical foundation. For the engineers of the territory, the city had grown increasingly opaque, appearing almost as a geological feature among others, but also as one impenetrable to their strategies of circulation, communication and connectivity – resistant, in other words, to 'improvement', or what later became 'planning'. Thus, while the demands of traffic grew within the space of the state, this gap prevented the development of a single form of knowledge adapted to the administration of *both* city *and* territory. In part, this was because the police had largely taken the role of managing the processes associated with good circulation throughout the city, establishing and enforcing a series of principles, regulations and (by)laws to do so (for an overview of this, see Foucault, 2009). Nevertheless, it was precisely this divide that fostered the conditions in which a synthesis of the two would amalgamate: in order to establish a knowledge of the city that answered to the requirements of modern political space and the expanding pressures of circulation, architects and engineers found themselves turning to the techniques and technologies of territory in order to conceive the city anew. In other words, it was only when the city was encountered as a strange entity *from without* – from the gaze of the territorial engineer – that a modern perception of the city as an entity *within a territory* presented itself.

In the spatial shift that unfolded over this period, we see a growing functional importance given to circulation not only as a principle to fulfil administrative requirements, but also as a means to maintain the conceptual unity of the state.

From metaphor to administrative policy to the development of a spatial practice, the principle of circulation lent credence to a plethora of state agencies that,
together, constructed a spatio-political order that advanced over the course of
three centuries. In both land- and sea-based powers, spatial and political unity
had been achieved through the ability to control the coveted networks of circulation, whether transatlantic trade routes or a system of roadways and canals
that fill out the territory. In turn, these spaces could stand as direct expressions
of the power of the state. In either case, the broader relativization of space had
exposed the material world no longer as a realm in which order is discovered
within the differences inherent in its natural variation, but as one in which
they are mere conditions to be quantified and put to use. Although theories
and treatises registered this change, the work of the engineers of the ponts et
chaussées was the first to make this 'senseless', fractured space legible to power,
cataloguing the boundless diversity of its features in their *tableaux*. Their
depiction of imagined landscapes,[9] composed with an exaggerated emphasis
on natural variation, only draws attention to the new status of nature as a
'senseless' category, empty of its own measure and made available to the calculations of economic utility. If this space was overlaid with an endless network
of infrastructure, the qualitative diversity of the landscape could be rendered
in quantitative, interchangeable and increasingly mobile terms within a single
economic space. In this way, the state developed an apparatus that could make
use of the productive density of the natural world by projecting a new, mechanical order on to it.

Turning away from the perils of a feudal world ruled by divine order, the new
governmental knowledge of the state formed around the fastidious administration of earthly objects in a space of movement. For this reason, over this period,
political order began to coincide with the planning and management of a state's
infrastructural network. Circulation now increasingly made the state's power
legible, visible. Circulation, traffic and the movement of the material world filled
out the empty space of the state, giving its geometrical disposition a physical confirmation. As opposed to the inherent density of the natural world, the circulation
of traffic by the seventeenth century came to both stand in as the manifestation
of this natural order and also serve as the object of a clearly more artificially
ordered world. Indeed, with Cantillon's *Essai*, we have arrived at a perception
of space fully inverted from that of ancient and premodern cultures: nature, for
him, does not exist in the qualities and consistency of the natural world as it presents itself to mankind. Rather, nature exists in the social relations of exchange,
in the networks of traffic and the circulation of wealth that result from them,
all of which he historicizes as the essential composition of human society. For
Cantillon, nature does not obtain as a perfect condition in itself that can be read
in its existing qualities, but remains a *latent order* yet to be perfected by human
rationality and intellect: human civilization began founding villages, towns and
cities as a result of an innate, natural sensibility towards the cultivation of the

wealth locked up in the Earth and its subsequent need for harmonious circulation. In short, nature, for Cantillon, is the artificial ordering of the world in the rational interest of trade and commerce. It is an odd condition, both pre-existent and yet to be achieved.

Whereas the movement of traffic manifests a certain power of the state's increasingly governmental temperament, the naturalization of circulation in physiocratic terms would have profound consequences for the future of the modern state. The physiocrats based their economic models on intrastate cycles of trade, but they also advocated for the circulation of produce *across* state borders as a means to regulate the 'just price' and to stave off scarcity (Foucault, 2009: Lecture 2 (18 January 1978)). Their intervention, brief as it was, thus presented *as a necessity* the opening of state trade to a 'world market' based on laissez faire, laissez passer policies. The predominant view of nature they adopted saw freedom in economic terms, as the freedom of circulation, which they justified on the grounds of the natural, self-regulating mechanisms inherent in commerce. In fact, Quesnay surpassed Cantillon in his development of the '*Droit naturel*', an immutable law that purported that all human actions within the course of physical events regulate themselves according to 'moral law' (Schumpeter, 1972: 229). Kant later adopted such thinking in his own moral philosophy (see, for example, Kant, 1991: 'Perpetual Peace', Appendix 1) in which he would expand on the physiocratic notion of freedom in his pursuit of a civil ('cosmopolitan') union of humanity. For him, freedom was the result of the enactment of individual will in accordance with natural law, and, for this reason, international trade appeared as the ideal mechanism around which the nascent liberal state could take shape and perpetual peace could be achieved. Of course, by this time, circulation had also been taken up by the fledgling civil society, which transcribed the same universal conception of it into the shaping of the public sphere,[10] all of which amounted to an indirect critique of the *ancien régime*. The utopian critique, born in this milieu, became the chief weapon in the struggle to rationalize the absolution of politics in the name of enlightened morality. Indeed, the contradictions born in the precarious unity between state and subject had become insurmountable, and the centred, critical subject, in its drive towards a *world space*, now posed a threat to the stability of the former.

> This world space is specifically smooth in its form, constricting little by little precisely to the degree that the domain of traffic, commerce, production, and universal consumption expands. [. . .] Unlike the Hobbesian model, international space is here not dangerous and amorphous; it instead is qualified by the 'good' of the universal circulation of wealth that is proposed by the anti-protectionist and anti-colonialist model of classical political economics. In the balanced increase of profit lies the potential for the progress of civilization, which, in substance, measures itself by legal guarantees, the spread of commerce, and private international law. (Galli, 2010: 63)

As we know, circulation underpinned the most essential assumptions of freedom and liberty that formed the basis of civil society as it emerged from the ensuing political crisis. The state it erected after the fall of the *ancien régime* nonetheless inherited its predecessor's basic spatiality, the political coordinates of which, as we have seen, were mapped on to systems of movement. Yet, by retooling itself according to the most coveted ideals bequeathed to it by enlightened thought, the liberal state of the nineteenth century could now present circulation as a social good, expressive of the power of an emergent subject: the so-called *homo œconomicus*. In its re-emergence in the nineteenth century, washed over by ideas provided by economists and philosophers of the enlightenment, circulation was portrayed as a moral duty essential no longer for maintaining the political unity of state and territory, but for constituting the *social* unity of the very fabric of civil society itself. In its transposition, the material experience of networks of circulation would now be complemented by the analogous expansion of a virtual, spaceless network of the public realm that manifested itself precisely by transgressing the physical boundaries of state territory. With this, a new idealism emerged around circulation, elevating it to a status unlike ever before: circulation now verified the essential condition of a morally virtuous, metapolitical existence of society. Reappearing in such terms and fortified by a burgeoning capitalism, it suddenly revealed itself to be a category *without* history and stripped of any political force. The virtual realm of the public sphere now provided an essential point of reference in the construction of the material world. And, in this way, circulation became ever more hardened in the mechanics of the modern world, the effects of which continue to shape life today.

NOTES

1 'Que comme dans la vie Champêtre ou dans les villages il n'y a que les païsans, on devoit distribuer les Artisans dans les petites Villes , & n'avoir dans les grandes Villes, ou les Capitales que les gens de tête, & les Artisans absolument necessaires.'

2 In this, we see an early example of how land is incorporated in territorial rationale as a category of territory related to wealth, property ownership and cultural heritage. For a distinction between 'territory' and 'land', see Elden (2010).

3 It is worthy of note that, of course, Colbert's king did not reside in Paris, but in Versailles – a disagreement that served as a thorn in the side of Colbert's entire career in office.

4 The canal du Midi was not completed until 1681 – two years before Colbert died.

5 It should be noted that, at this point, there was no significant professional distinction between an 'architect' and an 'engineer'. The two categories were generally seen to both be within the remit of a single individual, and engineering was regarded as a branch of architecture.

6 De La Mare was de la Reynie's *commissaire* at Châtelet between 1673 and 1710.

7 On the legacy of the council of the police, Benevolo notes: 'Thus the administrative solution from which Haussmann profited two centuries later was already in existence' (1978b: 755).

8 Of course, such a 'systematic' approach to the city would not appear until the middle of the nineteenth century, principally with the work of Haussmann, followed closely and more radically by Cerdá.

9 These 'imagined' landscapes were the products of competitions that were often held within the École des ponts et chaussées in the late eighteenth century. They allowed its students to display the entire breadth of tools available to planning and explore speculative representational techniques (see Picon, 1992: chap. 9).

10 Central to this was the role played by the *Encyclopédistes*, the Republic of Letters and the Masonic lodges. These groups all identified themselves as non-state entities who, rather than mounting a direct political critique of the state, articulated an indirectly critical judgement of the state based on moral grounds. See Koselleck (1988) and Habermas (2010).

6

The Becoming-Territorial
of the City

At the end of the eighteenth century, the European city had entered its first general crisis. Initially a crisis of epistemic proportions, by the early nineteenth century it became impossible to deny the socio-political dimensions this crisis entailed. Provoked by the internal demands that the space of the state exerted and made visible for the first time as a conceptual problem within it, the city seemed to be a space lacking a positive form of knowledge to allow its rationalization within the state – a governmental problem that was made manifest by the increasing incapacity of its physical spaces, organization and administration in the face of a now dominant *œconomic* state reason. Architects and elites such as Laugier, Patte and Blondel struggled to come to terms with the totality of the city; despite their attempts (see Laugier, 1977: chap. 5), their work remained fixed in pre-established forms of architectural knowledge, relying on the political institutions that had underpinned its practices and that their practices, in turn, endorsed. In this way, the rationalization of space that had helped give birth to territory as a political technology of the state was, in the space of the city, reduced to a commitment to rationalized architecture of geometric purity (Blondel, Patte). Still others at this time, such as Claude Nicolas Ledoux, approached this same epistemological problem by attempting to reconstitute the city as a bucolic organization embedded in the pastoral qualities of the landscape, registering a moralized condemnation of the existing city. Architectural knowledge, in short, had failed to achieve either theory or practice capable of grasping the city as not only a whole, but as a component of the broader temporal, processual space of planning that had been developed in the territory. And, as a fledgling capitalism began to flourish, complicating the physiocratic relationship between city and territory and transforming the city into both a factory and a marketplace of consumption, what began as a crisis of theoretical dimensions would irrupt into a socio-political crisis that surfaced in the visceral conditions of class conflict, pollution and disease within the city, along with the increasingly violent police apparatus used to maintain social divisions in the name of state order.

A long, complex history of the relationship between the territory and the city has perhaps yet to be written. Although the relationship between the two is, today, still unclear, trapped in the proliferation of cliché and historiographic dogma, part of the task of this book has been to ground both territory and the urban as interrelated spatio-political orders, historically and politically bound up with the emergence of circulation. Their relationship to one another will be the topic of this and the following chapter. As I argue, the two are not only intimately related, but indeed the urban could only come to light as a kind of modification of the mechanical abstraction of space that had occurred in the territory: If territory is the instrument by which modern state space was first given universal measure, the urban arrives in the nineteenth century as an augmentation of territory that would give new resolution and extension to this political technology

Contrasting the work of Georges-Eugène Haussmann (Chapter 6) with that of Cerdá (Chapter 7), I would like to depart from the typical depictions of innovation surrounding each figure by emphasizing that the transformative nature of both figures' work came as a result of integrating territorial techniques into its space of the city for the first time and modulating their effects at the scale of private property. This chapter will re-examine Haussmann's work in Paris to show how a model of territorial strategies (including their economic and political ambitions), developed from the legacy of Le Nôtre (Vauban, École des ponts et chaussées), could for the first time find its site of application in the city. In contrast to this, Chapter 7 will reflect on how, for Cerdá – a contemporary of Haussmann – such techniques were inspiring but remained incomplete. For this reason, Cerdá looked to another model founded in a parallel logic of territorial appropriation, distribution and production in the 'New World': the colonial (gridiron) settlement. By combining the two models (emblematically encapsulated in the title of his project, the *Reform and Extension* of Barcelona), a truly new paradigm was made visible in which the distinction between territory and city that had persisted for centuries could now be discarded ('Ruralize the urban: urbanize the rural: . . . fill the earth').

Most histories of the 'modern city' or of 'modern urbanism' begin with Paris. Historically speaking, its reconstruction by Haussmann in the middle of the nineteenth century inaugurated a new generation of planning projects throughout Europe and beyond. It was also the project that best embodied a concerted and violent governmental reaction to the socio-economic and environmental crisis into which the city had fallen, culminating in the first major, citywide reorganization strategy. Indeed, it was perhaps this project that, more than any other, allowed administrators, architects and engineers to imagine for the first time that the city could be reduced to a single, systematic entity through its strategic reconstruction.

However, in focusing on the *effects* of the crisis that were so painfully brought to the fore in this project, historians of the modern city all too often overlook the significance of this imaginary, or, at the very least, fail to understand its implications. What Haussmann accomplished in his reconstruction of Paris, and what underpinned the transformation of the city into a kind of kaleidoscopic machine of capitalist modernity, was to approach the city *as a territory* for the first time. In perceiving the city as a single, homogeneous mass – a kind of grey landscape of irrationally accumulated *faubourgs* and *quartiers* – Haussmann was able to institute a distinctly *territorial* array of infrastructure, from boulevards, *rond-points* and strategic axes, to sewerage and rail networks, to landscape and geological techniques, all of which would in turn coordinate the city as a 'whole', accomplishing what the engineers' work had over the space of the territory.

But precisely how did such territorial techniques come to rescale themselves to organize a city? Most histories of Haussmann's reconstruction of Paris take for granted a fundamental concept that shaped this entire project: that of the *réseau* (network). Only a few decades prior to Haussmann's appointment, this concept would have only been mentioned to describe systems of flow in hydrological or medical sciences. Yet, within Saint-Simonian discourse, *réseau* was generalized into a spatial imaginary that made questions of boundary and scale appear irrelevant. Thus, to better understand the territorialization of the city that Haussmann's work achieved, this chapter will trace the emergence and foundational role that network (*réseau*) played in the many spatio-political transformations that played out in the nineteenth century. As we will see, this concept not only allowed for territorial techniques to enter into and reimagine the city, but it also allowed for a crucial reimagining of territory itself, one that will play out in the following chapter as well.

SAINT-SIMONIANISM AND THE SECULARIZATION OF CIRCULATION

We find ourselves on the cusp of the period from which this book first departed. It is a moment in European and American history celebrated for its great novelty. Not only materialized in a flood of new technological commodities and scientific discoveries, but also rendered through new political formations such as the nation-state, the promise of a future that could achieve perpetual peace, personal freedom and social mobility had opened out into a radically new set of experiences, not restricted to the material world, but including those that would also condition the comprehension of time itself (Koselleck, 2004). The vast production of histories that has taken place from the nineteenth century until today underscores this sensibility by inscribing a kind of historical autonomy around constructs such as 'modernity' or 'progress' that serve to define and thus cleave the 'premodern' world from our own. From the philosophies of history of the eighteenth century, such a perspective becomes a kind of self-evident teleology that ideologues of the modern continue to adopt even today. However, rather than reject this historical autonomy as ideological, I will examine its genesis in some detail. For it is not merely an effect of a historical discourse, but also a real sensibility that, underwritten by the liberating qualities attributed to technology, capitalism and liberalism, charged many debates of the early and mid nineteenth century.

As we have seen, Cerdá's privileging of technology as a force of social liberation was itself an outcome of this perception common to nineteenth-century liberal positivism. It was possible for him and others to attribute a messianic quality to technology because of the spirit of historical autonomy enjoyed at the turn of the nineteenth century amid the post-revolutionary temper of Europe and the United States. Such an investment in science and technology inscribed a pragmatic perspective in the historical comprehension of the world that emerged at the same time. By the early twentieth century, it had become commonplace to imagine that all problems had their solutions in modern science and technology, domains that opened out to the modern world, promising to organize a society free of political domination. By the twentieth century, ideologues of liberalism, such as Giedion or Le Corbusier, could speak of entirely new material orders without making reference to political form whatsoever. Instead, it would be the economy that would condition an ethics for society through constructing its space of free exchange. It would yield a consensus around the notion of 'progress' as a complex of technological and industrial (and thus social) development. For this reason, the same ideologues could detach circulation from its long history in the realm of state control and domination and view it instead as a principle born in the context of biology and rooted as the basis of modern social liberation, a common goal guaranteed by a benevolent capitalism.

We might refer to this transposition of the concept of circulation as its *second secularization*. Despite originating in the metaphor of the circle as a principle of divine order – a direct expression of divine *œconomia* – it underwent its 'first secularization' when it was 'invented' as a scientific concept in the late sixteenth century, transposing a principle previously restricted to the works of God to one fully available to the earthly organization of human affairs. This model remained intact up to the late eighteenth century, in particular in the work of the physiocrats. By the early nineteenth century, however, we can see another shift taking place in which the concept of circulation undergoes a second displacement. With the advent of biology and the human sciences – fields of knowledge that emerged in the wake of what Foucault called the 'general redistribution of the *episteme*' (1994: 345) – circulation in its former, early modern sense was allowed to fade out of focus, its historical ties to political power fading out of view and its deeper roots in divine order becoming almost imperceptible. Now, it appeared anew, reframed as a natural, neutral principle of biological processes and transcribed as the basis of the newly discovered social relations.

Circulation, secularized[1] once again, would now stand as a signature within an expanded field, the truth of which could only appear if it was empirically mapped on to the human sciences and that now spoke of politics in the name of individual economic freedom and technological progress. By viewing circulation as a biological and sociological principle that, like all other scientific principles, could only be known in its empirical consistency, it became impossible to speak about it as a political construct developed within the interstices of the modern state, let alone as the mark of a divine order. Rather, by naturalizing it as a principle born alongside modern biology or seen as the 'natural' state of capitalism, it was in fact *only* possible to see circulation as a concept both ahistorical and apolitical, devoid of any relationship to sovereign will or state power. As such, it could be passively embraced as the foundation for a new scientific and economic order of life. Although administrators, politicians and early theorists of the state had seen it as a self-evident virtue, by the nineteenth century, circulation had achieved an expanded status as a common and most natural principle of society as a whole – a key feature of the concept of 'progress'. Once forgotten as the tool of political oppression, circulation could now operate as a principle with which to vindicate the expansive forces of society advancing into the empty void of the post-revolutionary state.

SAINT-SIMON

To have imagined a world ordered according to the administrative needs of economic exchange, technology and a general socio-moral code by the twentieth century would hardly have been seen as idealistic. In fact, it was a world-view already firmly established by the early nineteenth century, well before Cerdá would prophesy the coming of an urban world given over to peaceful relationships mediated by infrastructure. A central proponent of this world-view was Claude Henri de Saint-Simon. Between 1802 and 1825, he constructed what would become the foundations for a doctrine – a 'terrestrial' religion intended to replace Catholicism and a social order that would make the state itself redundant (see the introduction to Saint-Simon, 1975). Both spiritual and temporal, his doctrine called for a positive 'science of man' (a kind of predecessor of what would become sociology), structured around the power of industry. Society would be governed by the 'union of commercial and manufacturing industry with literary and scientific industry' (ibid.: 161; from 'Déclaration de principes', *L'Industrie*, vol. II, 1817). Saint-Simon saw this as the only option capable of organizing the young society emerging in the post-revolutionary milieu of Europe – a fragile configuration that constantly threatened to disintegrate into civil war.

A child of the Revolution, Saint-Simon drew heavily on the Kantian conception of achieving a universal and perpetual peace, which he, like Kant, saw as the natural achievement of a unified Europe bound together in free trade and guided by politics structured by and accountable to higher morals. For him, society had emerged victorious from the ashes of the Revolution, yet it had failed to create a new order of its own and thus faced two perils simultaneously: anarchy on the one hand and the return of political domination (despotism) on the other (ibid.: 158).

Saint-Simon would go further than Kant's cosmopolitanism, however, calling for the abolition of the state altogether. Following Bacon, he argued that the only way for society to institute order, while preventing the return to a state of political domination, would be to move from the political dominion over 'man' to an 'empire of man over things';[2] to abolish government altogether, replacing it with *administration* – a task that he identified as an immanent condition already in existence in the parliamentary governments being set up throughout Europe. 'The establishment of this principle [that the rulers are only administrators] is undoubtedly a thoroughly capital step towards the organization of a new political system; but nevertheless this principle cannot, in its present state, have any really important consequence' (Saint-Simon, 1975: 207; from 'On the replacement of government by administration' in *Deuxième extrait de mon ouvrage sur l'organisation sociale, L'Organisateur*, pt. II, 1820). In place of government, he called for an empire whose power would come from scientific knowledge and products of industry and the arts. Like many of the enlightened elites of his time, he held the development of scientific reason to be the means by which society could be spiritually guided and the guarantee that such a society would be aligned with the movement of progress (ibid.: 208).

For Saint-Simon, the rule of administration would only be the rule of society, as the task of such an apparatus would be to perpetually fulfil the needs of society. Because such a configuration would naturally derive its decisions from the needs of society as they are generated, the overall order of society would preclude, by definition, the arbitrary nature of the political excess Saint-Simon despised.

> Furthermore, the aim and object of such an organisation is so clear, so settled, that there is no longer any room for the arbitrariness of men, or even of laws, because both can be exercised only in the realm of uncertainty which is, so to speak, their natural element. (Ibid.: 208)

By removing the notion of sovereignty as it had been historically practised – by precluding the exception on which it is based (Schmitt, 2005: 5) – order within such a society would arise directly from society itself, mediated through a pan-European system of international institutions. In such a society, a 'natural' order would emerge in which each individual would 'naturally tend to confine himself to the role for which he is most suited' (Saint-Simon, 1975: 209).

In this new industrial-social order, a society of individuals bound to the universal law of pursuing self-interest could only be threatened by the return of despotism or by anarchy (ibid.: from 'Déclaration de principes', *L'Industrie*, vol. II, 1817). For this reason, Saint-Simon, like Locke, placed an emphasis on the role of private property, which, he recognized, would, like industry, have the effect of keeping both threats at bay. Thus, '[t]he nature of the right to property must be fully understood, and this right must be founded in the way most favorable to the increase in the wealth and liberties of industry' (ibid.: 172; from 'Views on property and legislation' in *L'Industrie*, vol. IV, pt. 2, 1818). Indeed, Saint-Simon realized that the very existence of society depended upon the preservation of the right to property – a right that transcended even the law in which it was to be enacted (ibid.).

If the right to property was to protect the society of industrial individuals from lapsing into anarchy, the achievement of its progress would take root through a vast programme of circulation and communication across and beyond Europe. In fact, the fulfilment of perpetual peace that Kant had outlined had, in the eyes of Saint-Simon, already started to reveal its material possibilities in post-revolutionary Europe. Expanding networks of transportation and communication, which, for Saint-Simon, had already begun to undermine divisions between states in Europe, would only make them more dependent upon one another. Moreover, the rise of parliamentary governments in Europe was a further testament to the overall transition to a new government founded on industrial interests – a sure sign of a cosmopolitan future whose peaceful existence would be based on the technical means of its permanent intercommunication and interconnection. For Saint Simon, this technological order was already unfolding in the form of railway lines and canals, roadways and viaducts penetrating Europe's old political spaces and would confer a new spiritual, world-historical duty upon the emergent European society – one whose task was to 'extend the boundaries of civilisation to the farthest corners of the earth' (ibid.: 45). Although Saint-Simon's main contributions came through his writings, he did draw up plans to form a link between the Pacific and the Atlantic by carving a passage through Central America – a plan that foreshadowed the Panama Canal – as well as making a proposal to construct a canal connecting Madrid to the Mediterranean. However, the grand order he imagined for the world remained, as all his own proposals would, a latent project.

Saint-Simon's influence was only truly felt after his death in 1825. Challenged by financial setbacks, disputes and fallings-out, disregard and scepticism, he only succeeded in cultivating a small group of followers during his lifetime. Nevertheless, this group, which subsequently grew, was both powerful and international, and, through its politically diverse make-up, over the course of the decades following Saint-Simon's death, it would fulfil and surpass many of Saint-Simon's ideas, spreading them throughout European society, from bankers to engineers and from social reformers to emperors and administrators.

Part of the reason that Saint-Simon's ideas took hold with such force was because they were applicable to both sides of the budding political spectrum in Europe. By advancing an industrial society, Saint-Simonian thought, on the one hand, foreshadowed a hierarchical, bourgeois social structure in which capitalist interests were to be buoyed up by a strong administrative state. On the other hand, at the same time, because this society would be homogeneously dedicated to an 'industrial society', sharing a common interest in production, it would 'naturally' eliminate class conflict, thus attracting support from the reformist left. As the left and right began to define the shape of political modernity, both social reformers and conservative industrialists could draw upon his ideas.

By the revolution of 1830 in France, and particularly after the fall of the Bourbons in July of that year, Saint-Simonianism had both established itself as the country's most serious reformist movement (ibid.: 49) and given birth to a second group who entered directly into industry and finance and who would begin to reshape the economic and political space of Europe. The latter group 'regarded the construction of railways and the organization of credit facilities to be especially important, and devoted themselves to these tasks with an almost maniacal enthusiasm' (ibid.: 54). In 1832, Michel Chevalier, one of the more prominent followers of Saint-Simon, published in *Le Globe* a landmark text for the movement, *Système de la Méditerranée*, a plan that 'proposed nothing less than the creation of a "universal association" of the peoples of Europe and the Orient through a comprehensive network of railways, rivers, and canals, the finance of which would be provided by new industrial banks' (ibid.). Such ideas greatly influenced colleagues, including Émile and Isaac Périere, who became prominent bankers and entrepreneurs in Europe (and who subsequently funded a major part of Haussmann's reconstruction of Paris). Together with other associates (Henri Fournel, Léon and Edmond Talabot, and Barthélemy Prosper Enfantin), this group pioneered the railway industry, financing the construction of networks in France, Switzerland, Austria, Hungary, Spain, Italy and Russia (ibid.).

By the second half of the nineteenth century, this cadre of Saint-Simonians, with the support of Napoleon III (himself, an advocate of Saint-Simonian thought), established the Crédit Mobilier bank. Capitalized with 60 million francs, the Crédit Mobilier 'did much to foster economic expansion and industrialization in France, and which in subsequent years served as a model for new commercial banks in the majority of continental countries' (ibid.). The legacy of Saint-Simonianism can be seen in the realization of projects spanning from the Suez Canal – realized in part by Enfantin – to the Anglo-French free trade treaty of 1860 (the 'Cobden–Chevalier Treaty') – a treaty directly negotiated by Chevalier himself. Their influence spread throughout Europe and beyond, inspiring political reformist programmes, policies, the establishment of institutions and the construction of infrastructural projects alike.

What made their ideas so palpable in the early and mid nineteenth-century world was the way they were able to reinterpret the same notion of circulation that had been mobilized to structure two centuries of state reason, redirecting it both against absolutist politics and towards the construction of the individual bourgeois subject. Under the banner of a 'terrestrial religion', Saint-Simonianism provided the perfect vehicle in which to reproduce the same spirituality that had for centuries claimed a monopoly over the future while relegating the potentials of the material, temporal, earthly practices of humankind, bound up in the sciences, arts and industry, to the authoritarian management of state politics.

Saint-Simonianism would, by contrast, propose to invert this relationship, founding its spiritual claims on technology, science, the arts and industry, and thereby rejecting politics outright. This shift would create the odd combination of a religion founded on highly rational, materialist terms, yet whose spiritual practice inaugurated a movement of zealous disciples fixated on the technocratic *planning* of the future. Rhetorically, their work assumed a radically pragmatic lexicon, aligning itself closely with the sciences and engineering and lending a sense of reason to even the most outlandish of proposals. Their model was founded on a core principle: a universal system of circulation and communication that would promote a techno-industrial world of peace and exchange.

For Saint-Simon and his followers, industry remained synonymous with ways of communication, with infrastructure viewed as the means by which production and exchange could be directly stimulated. As Chevalier noted, 'Industry [. . .] is composed of multiple centres of production united by a relatively *material* connection, which is to say, by ways of transport' (Chevalier, 1832: 35; original emphasis, my translation). For this reason, the railway, 'the most perfect symbol of universal association', promised to articulate material interests and social conflicts, resolving any contradiction between the two realms through the unfolding of a new mobile, industrial order (Picon, 2002: 226–7). In addition, a programme of universal circulation enabling a world in constant motion and privileging the industrial individual would, in their vision, lead naturally to conditions of perpetual peace, eliminating class conflict altogether. In its most zealous moments, it conceived itself as a force capable of ending a phase of history in which a struggle had raged between the civilizations of the Occident and the Orient for 6,000 years. Chevalier, in his *Système de la Méditerrannée*, had no doubt that infrastructure alone, by allowing the free movement of peoples and finance across vast spaces and territories, would pacify the two 'civilizations' and neutralize the war that, they claimed, had continued since the beginning of history. Circulation was, by the nineteenth century, the irresistible and infallible capacity for human salvation, as it would be for Cerdá.

RÉSEAU

By embracing this principle, the Saint-Simonians were able to condense nearly all their ambitions into a single conceptual and representational model: the *network*.[3] Broadly developing from the knowledge formulated over the course of the eighteenth century by the engineers of the École des ponts et chaussées,[4] the notion of the *réseau* was a new way to conceive of circulation – one that was at once more abstract than the exhaustive and ostentatious geometries of the ponts et chaussées, but also provided a more practicable framework for the execution of large-scale planning. This dual quality of the notion of the network arose in part because it was a term borrowed directly from the medical sciences to describe the circulatory and nervous systems in abstraction, while it was simultaneously used by the military engineers of fortifications and systems of hydrology in a very concrete sense to help design dynamic systems of canals and defensive infrastructures (ibid.: 234).

Michel Chevalier was the first to adopt the term *réseau* as a generic spatial concept to describe railway systems in his *La système de la Méditerranée*, but it was the initial set of texts published in *Le Globe* that truly marked the moment in which the notion of the *réseau* was taken up to describe systems of communication (ibid.: 235). By the time Chevalier reinterpreted the term, the construction of a number of large-scale railway lines had already begun, giving a convincing example of how this notion could slip easily between abstract concept and material practice – something that the Saint-Simonians fully embraced:

> More than anyone else, the Saint-Simonians had perceived a character of the territory, at once strategic and tactical, that the railways had helped to shape. More than a simple formulaic ideology [*idéologie d'accompagnement*], their movement seemed to have conceived of a matrix within which to elaborate both representations and new practices of development. The notion of network made its appearance as the articulation of these representations and practices, as if to facilitate any adjustments of one to the other. In the history of this notion and of its dissemination, the Saint-Simonian contribution once more proved decisive. (Ibid.: 234; my translation)

Demonstrating the dual quality of the network, Chevalier was able both to propose a concrete system of railways, canals and roadways connecting Europe with the Middle East, North Africa and Asia, while at the same time indulging in metaphorical descriptions to refer to this network spanning the ancient world as a 'système de veines et d'artères' (Chevalier, 1832: 41). But the concept of the network was even more flexible than this. For, in Chevalier's use of it, it also becomes apparent that he conceived the railways themselves to be the material extension of the banking network that the Saint-Simonians had so vehemently called for (Picon, 2002: 237). Through the notion of *réseau*, Chevalier was able to demonstrate how circulation, communication and exchange, each collapsing into the concept of the network, all had a common reference point, yet again found in the universality of the circulation of blood.

> Founded on the notion of the network this ideology placed mobility at the heart of its concerns. The 'administration of things' that Saint-Simon and his disciples had called for to replace politics [*la politique*] would put in constant circulation goods, people and news. The philosophy of the Enlightenment had already stressed the importance of such a circulation based on the model of a nature in perpetual gestation. (Ibid.: 243–4; my translation)

This quality of the network played itself out in two principal ways: on the one hand, the principle of circulation would be elevated once again to a quasi-divine category, as the Saint-Simonian Pierre Jean George Cabanis would evoke in the following passage:

> Everything is in constant motion in nature, all bodies are in continual fluctuation. Their elements combine and decompose; they successively assume a thousand fleeting forms, and these metamorphoses, according to the necessity of an action that is never suspended, in turn renew and preserve the eternal youth of the universe. (Cabanis, 1843: 158; my translation)

At the same time, by understanding the network first and foremost as a medium of circulation, their spatial thought would assume a radically elastic quality. Many early projects undertaken by Saint-Simonians remained within the political and scalar frame of the territorial state, such as François Becquey's plan to extend a network of canals throughout France, making the country completely navigable.

Already present in Chevalier's *Système de la Méditerrannée*, through the concept of the network, a new scale of geopolitical thought had been produced beyond that of the state. In opposition to territory, which had until now expressed itself as a closed body bounded by a fortified border, the interior of which was made smooth by a landscape of quantified resources and a tightly regulated system of circulation, the configuration that Chevalier proposed would reconceive space as an *open medium* defined by the figure of the network. Although networks of circulation had certainly existed within the geometries of territorial infrastructures, their qualities as such would be understood instead through their formal splendour. For Chevalier, the virtues of the network were self-evident and transcended the absolution of a territorially bound space, allowing him to imagine instead a space defined completely by connectivity. Such an inversion would naturally disrupt the smooth pretences of territorial unity, closure and homogeneity precisely because a space defined first and foremost by a *réseau* would remain completely indifferent to the abstraction of territorial frontiers and state borders. With the *réseau*, he was able to imagine a new order of space for the Mediterranean seen not as a set of territories fronting a sea, but as 'a series of great gulfs, each of which is the entrance to a vast country on the sea' (Chevalier, 1832: 39; my translation). The character and order of this space would no longer be defined by abutting territorial powers – 'particular universals' (Galli, 2010: chap. 4) – but rather according to a hierarchy of networks, 'a primary network on which to stitch secondary networks, so as in particular to make converge the communications to the ports that serve as a centre of each basin' (Chevalier, 1832: 50; my translation).

The spatiality given by a network ontology would not only affect its organization at a regional or continental scale of the Mediterranean, it would aim to do so at *all scales simultaneously*. Chevalier's preoccupation with circulation led him to develop a theory of elasticity, dynamism and flexibility in which even architecture could become responsive to perpetual movement. Enfantin, in conversation with Chevalier, expanded this theory:

> Architecture, as a theory of construction, is an incomplete art. The notion of mobility, of movement is lacking. Time, solidity and movement or mobility are the three conditions of a building. This is what I would like to say in regards to mobility: there is a continual movement that stirs all construction, not least the shock of the air, the shock of the waves of light. All buildings must be made in the manner to both receive movement and to return it; one should not construct buildings with a view to resist movement. (Quoted in Picon, 2002: 272; my translation)

Such jumps in scale, attributable to the abstract quality of the network (and the incessant circulation it enabled), would reveal a kind of *scalar indifference* inherent in the concept of the network, liberating circulation from its previous privileging of landscape and unleashing a new spatial imaginary in which a single system of circulation could coordinate across multiple scalar registers simultaneously, from architecture to the networks that would wrap around the entire planet. For Chevalier, such a network elaborated in the *Système de la Méditerranée* consciously represented a crucial step in a broader process that would make of the whole world the 'abode [*demeure*] of man' (Picon, 2002: 239; my translation). As Picon describes, 'at the dawn of the industrial era, the Saint-Simonians presented the conquest of the globe not as a brutally violent process, but rather as the marriage of man and earth' (Picon, 2002: 244; my translation).

The concept of the *réseau* that the Saint-Simonians developed inherited another aspect from the knowledge of territorial circulation: that of unification. As we have seen, from Hobbes to Colbert to La Maître, the use of circulation, as either metaphor or concrete principle, fulfilled an essential requirement of the territorial state: in order for territory to maintain and represent the extents of sovereignty, not only did it need a fortified border, but the interior space that resulted had to be made smooth by its system of standardized roads and canals that could materialize its instrumental reason in geometric precision. Circulation in this space was a regulated activity, at once a practice and a measure of state power. Its capacity to unify the state was upheld insofar as it could homogenize its experience as a space relieved of its natural, physical qualities and differences, and traversed instead by apparatuses of rational calculation. Although derived from the natural philosophies, circulation became a principle by which to construct an artificial, mechanical space.

In contrast to this, the Saint-Simonian character of the network – abstract and scaleless – proposed a wholly different geopolitical conception of circulation. By the early nineteenth century, the term network (*réseau*) was used to describe natural systems of circulation and communication in the body's circulatory and nervous systems. The network was seen as a multi-scalar system the function of which was to extend itself across and coordinate the various activities of independent organs, tissues and substances of the body. When abstracted in this context, the 'purpose' of the network was not to unify self-enclosed elements in contrast to others, but precisely the opposite: to traverse the *different* functions and morphologies that constituted the physiology of the body, unifying them at the overall scale of the organism. Such a conception proved valuable as a spatial concept perfectly compatible with the geopolitical ambitions of the Saint-Simonians. The *réseau* transcribed territorial borders as the very object that their lines of communication would traverse, not only to undermine the absolution and abstraction of the state, but in order to achieve universal unification at the scale of the planet. In other words, unification for the Saint-Simonians could be achieved as far as the political autonomy of the state, marked in space by its territorial homogeneity, could be undermined, thus depoliticizing the status of territory altogether and integrating it into a new, smooth space of a socio-technological and economic mode of circulation. What the Saint-Simonians had discovered was that the most profound potential of the *réseau* lay in its capacity to radically overcome differences, a trait that, as we have seen, underpinned Cerdá's ambitions in his *Teoría*.

Although the concept of the *réseau* began to open up a new geopolitical imaginary for the world in the nineteenth century, its realm of action was not to be exclusively the super-territorial, regional or even planetary. Because this concept invited a new spatial imaginary through its deliberate indifference to scale and through seeking to unite humanity by overcoming 'obsolete' political differences, such qualities also exposed a more direct form of application within the space of the city. Indeed, a pressing question that had haunted the modern European world since the advent of the state was the epistemological gap that had formed between the territory and the city. This divide had direct ramifications for the reality of these two competing forms of polity. As Picon notes, '[t]he town had therefore split, appearing to be both a general design and a territory, in the sense that this territory demanded a specific approach, different from that of architecture' (Picon, 1992: 207). This was a question that remained unanswered by either architects and engineers such as Patte or Blondel or the entire École des ponts et chaussées, or even by the generation of so-called 'utopian' thinkers, from Ledoux to Charles Fourier to Robert Owen. In the first case, the architects and engineers remained bound to disciplinary dogma, unable to conceptualize a response equivalent to the demands of the problems that presented themselves. In the second, 'utopian' thought pursued a space completely removed from the reality of the problems at hand, investing instead in an architecture and spatiality in which the figures of both territory and city were no longer legible at all. Their claims about the city appeared reactionary, their positions on territory, vague.

Yet, as Picon argues, both spatial paradigms were nonetheless linked. 'To have grasped this contradiction, and the complementarity which it masked, would have meant acknowledging that architecture was not equipped to tackle the new object which it was now seeking to make its own' (ibid.). It was here that the

Saint-Simonians' development of the *réseau* played a crucial role in making this link for the first time and articulating it in a radically new spatial model in which the city's organization and the territorial space in which it sat could potentially be addressed by means of a singular knowledge and set of technologies. For them, the concept of the network could apply equally to city and territory, deploying a single logic at different scales, just as viable at the scale of the city as it was at the scale of the planet. The *réseau* was a model that promised to overcome the epistemological chasm between the two spaces, unifying all of space in a coordinated fractal geography of circulation and communication.

Equipped with this model, the Saint-Simonians would no longer see the city as a disorganized, choked space impenetrable by the technologies of circulation and communication, but instead as fluid, continuous space, bubbling with activity, movement and elastic architectural forms and dotted with a surreal monumentality, all of which intoxicated with the most advanced technologies. For them, the city was to function indistinguishably from the greater network in which it sat – a network nested within networks. It was to be a 'nodal point within a system of routes, canals, railways and navigable waterways conceived at the scale of the planet, the great city is itself envisaged as an ensemble of networks' (Picon, 2002: 245; my translation). Embracing new forms of transportation, they proposed replacing the old *portes* of Paris with a system of railway stations, with railway lines that extended out into and beyond the territorial limits of France – an idea that Haussmann would later execute. New canals would penetrate and organize the space of the city (see, for example, Girard, 1843),[5] unifying it with its surrounding territory as a single space of ceaseless fluidity. They envisioned a society that would emerge in such cities distributed regularly across the surface of the globe – 'nodes' within a network the material constitution of which would form the backbone of a new spatiality that would at once extend the knowledge and practices of territory into the city, while also undermining the territory as the privileged space of the state, co-terminous with sovereignty.

Yet this integration did not mean that the city was to be conceptually or phenomenologically indistinguishable from the territory surrounding it. Despite its scaleless contiguity, the Saint-Simonians' *réseau* was in fact ruthlessly hierarchical. Indeed, it was only in light of such a hierarchical distinction that they could arrive at a conception of the city as a whole – as a complex 'organism' (Picon, 2002: 225) – for the first time. Beyond simply integrating a territorial notion of circulation into the city, the Saint-Simonians went further. Their obsession with technologies of circulation brought a whole new 'scientific' approach to the city, treating it as a single entity that, very much like a territory, could be cut through, organized and *planned* around abstract networks of movement.

But such a conceptual reinterpretation had to find its application in precise, scientific rigour. Moving from metaphor to method, it would be by applying hydrological mathematics to the planning of a city's networks of circulation that such a shift could occur, borrowing knowledge developed by the engineers of the ponts et chaussées to construct vast networks of waterways and canals. In his entry on 'Ville' in the *Encycolpédie nouvelle* of 1841, Jean Reynaud would elaborate this hydrological model of planning around the greatest possible flow of circulation. To drive such thinking on the city, 'one is mathematically led to the conception of a system of channels and routes [*voies*], inclined on one another and following a series of indefinite, and consequently curved and broken angles' (citation of Jean Reynaud's article, 'Ville' in the *Encyclopédie nouvelle* of 1841, vol. VIII, pp. 676–87, in Picon, 2002: 263; my translation). Such a vision of a city, in which space would be organized by a pulsating fluidity of traffic, water, air and people, became a common conception for the Saint-Simonians and effectively brought an end to the tradition of geometrical regularity cultivated since the early Renaissance. Inspired engineers such as Henry Darcy of the ponts et chaussées designed and constructed a network of water supply and sanitation for Dijon based on a 'scientific approach to filtration and flow' (ibid.: 262; my translation) – a project that began in 1834, a decade and a half prior to when Eugène Belgrand began his work in Paris.

Charles Duveyrier, in his *La Ville nouvelle ou le Paris des saint-simoniens* of 1832, echoing Girard's work on the hydrological planning of Paris, described a totally reconstructed Paris with streets that would now twist and bend according to a hydrologically imagined flow of traffic. Duveyrier in fact attempted to apply the same mathematics used for hydrological networks of territorial waterways to calculate the flow of all kinds of traffic within the city. Not only does this mark a clearly territorial conception of the city, but, by applying the mathematics of hydrology, Duveyrier also opened up the possibility of scientifically and technically *regulating* the circulation of traffic within the city. As Picon shows, 'Duveyrier's "*rues sinueuses*" reveal the abandonment of the ideal of geometric regularity in favour of techniques of flow regulation based on analytical calculation and the sciences of engineering' (ibid.: 263; my translation). Regulation – the technical correlate of the Saint-Simonian notion of administration – accompanied the entire Saint-Simonian project, a concept essential for achieving a future world of industrial universalism united by radically expanded application of the knowledge of territory. Indeed, regulation is itself inseparable from the concept of *réseau*, as Picon explains:

> [T]he passage from *regularity* to *regulation* constitutes the birth of a new technical approach to urban problems, an approach that will progressively emancipate itself from questions of the form of the city, which do not take into account the circulations and abstract equations that govern them. (Ibid.: my translation; original emphasis)

Although the core group of Saint-Simonians restricted their work to writings, their legacy was prolific, a legacy perhaps most clearly exhibited in the work of Haussmann. Haussmann's entire project for the reconstruction of Paris, from his selection of engineers, to the financial structure of the banking system created by the Périere brothers, to the political leverage of Napoleon III, was deeply imbued with Saint-Simonian thought. It was the Saint-Simonians who largely foregrounded the programme that Haussmann eventually unfolded. Duveyrier's *Ville nouvelle*, for example, proclaims a programme of '*grands travaux*' aiming to achieve a condition of public hygiene for the whole city, advocating '*distribution générale d'eau dans Paris*'. Echoing Duveyrier, a key influence on the work of Eugène Belgrand was Stéphane Flachat:

> Water for the people of Paris! Water on the squares, in the streets, the houses, on all the floors; fountains springing from all sides, and spreading a salutary freshness throughout the atmosphere! Large baths not only for the rich, but for the people! Free baths where they can come to rest from their work, and soak [*retremper*] their limbs weighted down by fatigue, inundated by sweat! This is the best, the most beautiful, the safest of all protections [*préservatifs*] against an epidemic. (Flachat, 1832, quoted in Picon, 2002: 258; my translation)

In an 1831 issue of *Le Globe*, Chevalier highlighted the need to reform the law on the expropriation of land in order to transform Paris. His call for such a '*coup d'état pacifique*' consisted of an appeal 'to change by order the law of expropriation so as to provide the owner's interest, but to reduce to a very few days the endless delays prescribed by the current legislation' (Chevalier, 1831, quoted in ibid.). A decade and a half prior to Eugène Belgrand's work on the Parisian sewers, Darcy, a staunch Saint-Simonian, had already constructed his network in Dijon. The relationship between Jean-Charles Adolphe Alphand's *Promenades de Paris* of 1867–73 and Duveyrier's visions of '*rues sinueuses*', '*anneaux qui s'interlacent*' is easy to see. And, of course, the construction of the Eiffel Tower or the monumentality constituted by buildings such as Garnier's Opera alongside Haussmann's general scheme of monumental preservation can all be compared with the dreamlike descriptions of the future city by the likes of Duveyrier. As Picon surmises, 'some twenty years before Haussmann and his engineers, the Saint-Simonians proposed to rethink [the space of the city] according to the logics of circulation and services that characterized the emergent thinking of the networks' (ibid.: 245). Haussmann's project (as well as Cerdá's) would not have been possible without the influence exerted by Saint-Simonian thought.

At once organism and milieu, nature and artifice, the city imagined by Saint-Simonian pen altered forever the relationship between itself and the territory. Conceived as a network within a territory – and thus a territory in miniature – the Saint-Simonian city was the first to invert the static, torpid relationship between territory and city that had characterized European space since Hobbes's *Leviathan*. The entrance of territorial technologies and knowledge promised to purge the city of its obsolete rigidity just as incessant circulation would clean the air of miasmas and fill fountains with fresh water. For the Saint-Simonians, the city was no longer the riddle it had been for the architects and engineers of the eighteenth century. Instead, it became the site of a new vocation of social redemption. In the conceptual non-distinction made between city and territory, a paradoxical space opened in which the city, invested with a new techno-spiritual intensity, became a space even vaster than the territories surrounding it (ibid.: 294). Such a paradox can only be explained by the pure potential of this new spatiality opened up by the concept of the *réseau*: 'The Saint-Simonian approach dilated urban space while at the same time shrinking the globe to become the "abode of mankind"' (ibid.: 225). This new space radiated outward from the city through its networks, seemingly consuming the very notion of territory itself. In its place, a new space appeared to span a continuous meshwork of cities across the planet.

From the transcontinental to the architectural in scale, the idea of a single network – a *single spatial logic* – provided a powerful tool for the reconstruction of modern spatiality. It was a concept that promised not only to transcend the political datum of the territory, but also to pierce the formal, material and architectural stagnancy of the city. Architectural discourse had proven insufficient to respond to the epistemological crisis into which the city had fallen; both materially and discursively, it had never developed the means by which to grasp a form of power beyond that which could be represented. As a new configuration of power had been surfacing in Europe over the course of the sixteenth and seventeenth centuries, one that needed no representation but rather manifested itself in the actual circulation of materials in space, it found its correlate in the development of territory. As this *œconomic* form of power deepened its purchase in Europe, it was, therefore, the technology of territory that, by the eighteenth century, answered to the striations of space that it had produced between itself and the cities that dotted its vast, geometrical spaces:

> As an image of society, the territory replaced the image which the architecture of a man such as Blondel had provided, and which had been buttressed by the spirit of *convenience*. Since it delineated a territory that was productive, this image made it possible to escape the ponderousness of urban space. [. . .] It was in this sense that the territory was limitless, and it was from this point of view that it was increasingly to penetrate the town, fashioning it in its own likeness. (Picon, 1992: 254)

A conceptual apparatus born in the territorial technologies of the seventeenth century and abstracted through the utopian universalism of the early nineteenth century, the Saint-Simonian *réseau* helped to redefine the ontological status of the territory in order to answer to this. No longer the definitive political spatiality of the modern world, the territory (as a space) could now be emptied of its political force, reduced to but one of several technological octaves of an apolitical space of unlimited circulation. Yet, far from rendering it innocuous, it was precisely through the abstract scalelessness of the *réseau* that the Saint-Simonians would in fact emancipate territory (as a political technology), allowing its logic to *escape* its epistemologically bound spatial confines. As we will see, the concept of *réseau*, once put into practice, is precisely the device that allows territorial technologies to embed themselves instead at all scales and dimensions of space at once.

The zeal of the Saint-Simonians was not isolated to the small group of followers. Their work was so influential not because of its radical propositions, but because their visions in fact gave shape to an already existing momentum. The Revolution had released an expansive energy captured by the notion of 'society' in its realization of a liberal bourgeois-capitalist order. By inverting the spatial privilege of the city over the territory and the process of reorganization of the state into an increasingly industrial order, this energy had already been put to work by the time their writings were published. It was an energy that, in some sense, surpassed the fantastical idealism that it produced and, in so doing, soon realized the first crisis of its own making. The mass migrations of people into the major European cities that capitalism forced made visible a new kind of political struggle and its intimate relation to the biological frailty of life, populations and the problem of dense, ill-equipped modes of cohabitation. For all these reasons, the generation of administrators, financiers and politicians who followed found the most practicable solutions to these crises in adopting and materializing ideas that were clearly Saint-Simonian in origin. Yet, despite any liberal optimism, although the Saint-Simonian interpretation of circulation via the *réseau* cleared the way for a profoundly new social and economic configuration of space, it was never, as we shall see, able to overcome the fact that this space was first and foremost a political space.

HAUSSMANN AND THE TERRITORIALIZATION OF THE CITY

Haussmann's work is all too well known to be recounted here in full. The absolute prevalence of this figure and his work in the history of the modern city stands as testament to this. Yet this is perhaps part of the problem. In all the countless chronicles of his reconstruction of Paris, the significance of his work within broader spatio-political and epistemological terms is rarely reflected upon. His application within the city of a specifically territorial knowledge and set of techniques born in the spaces outside the city is completely missed by the overestimated dependence on categories such as 'modernism' on the one hand or absorbed into and overlooked by the all-too-common critique of his work in light of humanist and social justice considerations on the other. Of course, to say that he was both influenced and supported by a great number of Saint-Simonian thinkers and ideas does not bring this to light any more either, as this fact is also well known. Rather, what needs elucidation here is a certain theoretical assessment of how Haussmann's reconstruction of Paris introduced a *territorial* model of spatial planning into the space of the city and its organization.

Draped in impressive statistics and illustrated with staggering daguerreotypes, drawings and engravings, the history of Haussmann's project typically (and rightfully so) emphasizes the accomplishment of the first *Plan Général* – the first citywide 'master plan' of another name. What drove Haussmann was, on one level, a clear recognition that the fragmented and self-sufficient *quartiers* that constituted Paris yielded a city that, as such, could not sustain an emergent capitalist world market. Quoting Haussmann, Choay summarises, 'his purpose was to give unity to and to transform into an operative whole the "huge consumer market, the immense workshop" of the Parisian agglomerate' (Choay, 1969: 16). At another level, his ambitions transcended the demands of capitalism alone and pointed towards a future world in which capitalism was but one means to unify it in perpetual movement. Like the Saint-Simonians, Haussmann drew from a teleology based on industry and technology, in which politics was to be superseded by an administrative order charged with the task of maintaining unity. Benevolo would expand on this: '[f]or the first time a complex of technical and administrative provisions, covering a whole city of over a million inhabitants, had been coherently formulated and implemented within a relatively short space of time' (1978a: vol. 1, 63). Siegfried Giedion points to a further ambition of Haussmann's: to 'make the entire Department of Seine-et-Oise a single unit' (Giedion, 1982: 750). The combination of actually wielding this supreme administrative power, underpinned by a zealous 'terrestrial' religion, reveals much more than a simple lust for capitalism. Haussmann's ruthlessness comes perhaps more from a certain messianic drive rooted in his belief in Saint-Simonian ideals. From his first act in office, precisely surveying the existing city and representing it in a single drawing, to his last, the famous *troisième réseau*, the construction of which would have required the support of the entire city, subsequently providing the very conditions of his downfall, Haussmann's work had answered to the general crisis in which the city had languished for a century. His project, although short of establishing a completely new spatial model for thinking the city, nevertheless was the event that would open and make visible the outlines of a certain epistemic transformation of space that presented itself to Europe (and the capitalist world) in the nineteenth century.

Haussmann achieved this unity by launching a programme of '*régularisation*', a series of parallel strategies that began with a new legal definition of the spatial totality of the city and extended to the construction of a uniform architectural typology to be repeated throughout the city. Haussmann first enlarged the boundaries of the city to the old fortifications, a move that both absorbed the suburban landscape of *faubourgs* and normalized this space and that of the old city in an array of 20 *arrondissements*. Reforming the *arrondissements* into administrative units allowed him to establish a decentralized system of control across the entire city, each one appointed with its own *mairie*.

The distinctly territorial disposition of such a strategy was not lost on geographer David Harvey, who rightly recognized a new type of space emerging in the desire to treat it as a totality: 'Within this new and larger space he created a sophisticated hierarchical form of territorial administration [. . .] through which the complex totality of Paris could be better controlled' (Harvey, 2006: 113). By establishing a logic of the whole, Haussmann could devise a radically new approach to the organization of space. Applying Saint-Simonian ideas, Haussmann saw this new space as a kind of homogeneous medium whose order would be given not by individual streets, building plots or the autonomous *quartiers* he so despised, but rather by the overlaying of a pure, schematic series of networks. In his *Mémoires*, he recounts his intentions: 'to cut a cross, north to south and east to west, through the center of Paris, bringing the city's cardinal points into direct communication' (Haussmann, 1890–3: vol. III, 424–5, quoted in Choay, 1969: 18). This scheme was of course accomplished by cutting through the actual material of this grey 'dross' – the 'fractured' and 'disorganized' medieval city fabric – with a series of subsystems, or *réseaux*, repeating the same basic model in each district, underdeveloped site and *faubourg* throughout the space defined by the new city limits, and connecting the whole through a single, unified and multi-scalar network system.

His famous '*trois réseaux*' that constituted his overall strategy aimed to form a comprehensive system of circulation, integrating the entry of rail networks into the heart of the city, diverting the waters of the Seine by channelling them through an expansive new subterranean sewerage system on a scale never before seen, bringing a system of 'ventilation' by connecting the city with two new 'lungs' – the Bois du Boulogne to the west, and the Bois de Vincennes to the east – and constructing a network of gas lamps to provide light throughout the city. All of which, of course, was organized around the addition of 90 miles of new boulevards, which formed the structural basis of his *trois réseaux* and the primary foundation of the overall spatial organization:

> Haussmann's first step was to conceive a network of through streets which have no significance in themselves but are essentially a means of connection. They form new lines of communication, general ones between districts (east, west, north, south), specific ones between certain old or new key points such as railway stations or market places. [...] This overall network of arterial connections constituted what Haussmann described as a kind of 'general circulatory system,' which he subdivided into hierarchized tributary systems, each organized around a plaza, which is no longer a place in it [sic] itself but a traffic node, or what the Prefect termed *nodes of relation*. (Choay, 1969: 17–18)

The much-criticized boulevards,[6] whose great widths and lengths were articulated by a single, homogeneous architecture, not only neutralized a new 'public' stage for the ascendant bourgeoisie, but also offered a completely new scale of experience for the city. Best seen in the *Plan Général* drawn up by Haussmann's collaborator, Alphand, for the publication of his *Promenades de Paris*, the essence of this new order of space emerges. In the plan, having been previously drawn up with exquisite precision using triangulation techniques, the city is reduced to a kind of grey surface into which are carved the multiple boulevards, *rond-points* and squares, each drawn in meticulous detail, lined with trees and textured with differing pavements. Complementing this linear system and suspended amid the grey is an array of monuments, churches, institutions and railway stations, as well as painstakingly illustrated gardens and parks. Emphasizing the singular totality of the city, the wall encircling it takes special pride of place as another detailed element in the composition.

Together, these components provide a counterbalance to the visual dominance of the circulatory network of boulevards, and, in total, this new assemblage lends the only material relief – the only evidence of a signified materiality – to the generalized, unspecified grey substance that otherwise fills the Parisian space, setting the backdrop for the boulevards. Overall, if the city appears as a kind of 'organism', it is appended by the superbly drawn 'organs' ('lungs') in the *bois* adjacent to it. As opposed to the gardens or squares within the city-organism, these new parks exist at an altogether new scale. No longer residing on the exterior of the city, connecting it to cities and destinations within the territory, these bodies appear as major appendages now captured *within* the city, suggesting that this new space emerging in Paris in the mid nineteenth century could overcome the opposition between city and landscape by incorporating large swathes of the latter into the former.

In very brief terms, this schema comprises the work Haussmann implemented in the city itself – what is generally the centrepiece retold in countless architectural and urban histories. Yet this was only one scalar register of his work. Indeed, for nearly every mode of circulation brought into the city and integrated in his *trois réseaux*, he was, at the same time, tying these lines of movement and communication to much greater networks that he and Napoleon III were developing outside the city. In this sense, the planning of Paris took on the character of a centralized node within a series of larger and larger networks of circulation, communication and trade. At the scale of the state of France, Haussmann would help to extend the fledgling railways that existed prior to his appointment as Prefect to Paris into a vast new network of railways throughout the territory, increasing them from just over 1,900 kilometres of rail in 1850 to some 17,400 kilometres only 20 years later (Harvey, 2006: 109). By 1866, Haussmann had extended more than 23,000 kilometres of telegraph cables, and roadways were built and improved to feed the rail network and the system of navigable canals, which would also be expanded (ibid.). Belgrand's famous aqueducts designed under Haussmann would stretch its network out hundreds of miles into the territory to bring fresh water into Paris (ibid.: 251).

The new banking system opened up by the Périere brothers helped to bring French capital out of France, directly investing in the construction of a vast network of railways and telegraphy systems that founded the beginnings of a new international market and effectively brought the Parisian market into direct contact with the global movement of traffic through the newly constructed Suez Canal. The relationship between both scales of networks that unfolded under Haussmann's administration could be seen in the proliferation of large department stores or in the expansion of the Parisian food market, both of which drew on the fluidity and connectedness of the new network of trade that gave the bourgeois consumer in Paris a daily influx of produce from North Africa and the Middle East (ibid.: 111).

Perhaps more importantly, Haussmann's plan exposed the interrelatedness of these multiple scales through a choreographed experience of space, staging great vistas along the network of boulevards, terminating in the architecture of the ring of railway stations – a phenomenology of networked space. Typically billed as the introduction of the 'scenographic' into the city, the system of boulevards did much more, drawing the architecture and activities of city life into direct contact with the circulation throughout the territory and, in turn, bringing the experience of the territory into the city. The oft-repeated example is the vista framed by the tree-lined Boulevard Sébastopol, which, to the south, is punctuated by the realigned dome of the Tribunal de Commerce and, to the north, terminates in the Gare de l'Est (see, for example, ibid.: 100). This arrangement, more than providing the 'theatricality' of monumentality through which Haussmann's work is typically interpreted, had made explicit a certain logic and experience of territory that had entered into and transformed the spaces of the city.

It is no coincidence that the actual making of the plan involved topographical surveys and triangulation techniques (Choay, 1969: 17) developed in the mapping and planning of the territory, which had never before been deployed in mapping the city. Until then, such techniques were used for measuring geological features, navigating the seas, estimating great geographical distances (such as the circumference of the Earth) and, of course, for mapping territorial boundaries and spaces. From the early seventeenth century until the mid nineteenth, an entire history of triangulation extending from antiquity had been put to work in the interest of state reason as a means to construct detailed knowledge of the territory. Triangulation, in a certain sense, was at the historical heart of territory as a political technology. From the early methods of Willebrord Snell, to Jean Picard's measurement of the distance from Paris to Sourdon, to the monumental work by the Cassini family to plot the first *Carte de France*, to the arrival of the Ordnance Survey (see Joyce, 2003: chap. 1), such techniques were fundamental to the advancement of the overall technologies of territory. This knowledge was also instrumental in making the epistemological gulf that had formed over this time between the city and the landscapes that filled the space of territory. The city was primarily controlled by piecemeal interventions and by the introduction of a permanent police apparatus, whereas the landscape of the territory remained fundamentally open to its geometric mode of extractive production. Landscape was always already seen as a neutral space, a substance that could be cut through, arranged and exploited by rational thought; the city, in contrast, was a politically

overdetermined space that was the object of perpetual, often violent, neutralizations. Thus, the application of triangulation techniques to map the city should be
understood in all of its historical, political and epistemological significance: at
once the signature of a new order of knowledge brought to bear on the spatial
assessment of the city, the tools born of territorial planning would impose a radically new spatial condition on the ontological status of the city.

A sign of this transformation, the visual representation of landscape in Alphand's
plan plays a new and significant role, inverting the traditional hierarchy of landscaped elements in the city. In the plan, landscaped elements no longer appear as
exceptional moments within the city, but rather as the primary materiality that
gives structure, order and hierarchy to the plan. Landscape becomes the tool and
signature of a new *territorial* order entering the city as a network of tree-lined
boulevards connecting in lush *places*, *rond-points* and *jardins*, or appearing as vast
tracts of landscape itself in the case of the newly designed *bois*, bringing the pastoral experience of the countryside, with running water, woodlands, mounds, lakes
and fields, into the heart of the city (see Picon, 2010). Such a shift is visible in
Alphand's many engravings of Paris. In them, another clue appears in the representational shifts he invokes between landscape and city: recalling Laugier, the city
appears as a kind of abstract 'nature' – a 'forest' of sorts – through which promenades are cut. Almost all the engravings of *Les promenades de Paris* illustrate a
civilized bourgeois society dwelling not in a bustling city, but rather amid a kind
of tamed nature. In contrast to the level of detail given to trees, vegetation, water,
rocky outcrops, and so on, architecture becomes a kind of abstracted background
condition whose form and details dissolve into a quasi-natural consistency: blocks
of newly constructed apartments appear in some engravings almost as if they were
dense thickets of trees cut through by broad boulevards. The parks and squares act
in this way not to deny the city, as it were, but rather to stage and justify a new
space, one in which the self-evident virtues of landscape pass through the city,
entering and organizing it for the first time. In this way, architecture now begins to
take on an altogether new scale with Haussmann's famous homogeneous facade
regulations. No longer fixed to the scale of a building or even as a series of objects
framing the open spaces of squares, places or parks, Haussmann's architecture,
bearing the distinctive Saint-Simonian character of the *réseau*, becomes relevant at
the scale in which it can make visible the network of monuments and axes that, in
turn, unifies the city as a naturalized machine of capitalist circulation. From the
techniques used to first map the city, to the technologies, principles and hierarchies
of its reconstruction, Haussmann and his team of engineers managed to introduce
the materiality and knowledge of territory as an object no longer in opposition to
the city, but rather as the epistemic means of its modern redemption.

Yet, more than accomplishing this at a technical level alone, Haussmann
brought to bear in the spaces of Paris the entire framework of planning developed
by the engineers of the territory a century prior, imposing new processes and legal

structures on its spaces. The result was that Haussmann's reconstruction of Paris was not laid out in the form of a single optimized, idealized plan; rather, he instituted its reconstruction as a continual *process*. With the addition of the eleven peripheral communes he set up in 1859, Haussmann opened the Office du Plan de Paris. As Benevolo writes:

> [Y]ear by year this office mediated between work carried out and future projects, taking into account changing circumstances; the machinery survived the death of Haussmann and the collapse of the Second Empire, ensuring the coherence of Parisian planning for the whole of the second half of the nineteenth century. (1978a: 75)

It becomes clear that what Haussmann did, in contrast to a kind of single, fixed plan, was to inaugurate a governmental, economic and legal structure that would set in motion an entire apparatus of managed planning, an ongoing framework for the continuous modification, adaptation and growth of the city – in short, the *urbanization* of the city. If the engineers of the eighteenth century had opened up a new domain of planning the territory, giving it its processual dimension, Haussmann had effectively constructed a planning apparatus of the same scope, which he applied for the first time to the spaces of the city.

The space that we see emerging in Alphand's plan and his engravings is more than just a hybrid of the city and territory; it is a spatial order that *privileges* the territorial as a means to reconceive and reorganize the city as a network of landscaped corridors and pastoral spaces in which bourgeois society can become visible, just as the landscaped axes of Versailles had once served to celebrate the grandeur of Louis XIV and his court. More than just an effort to represent the bourgeoisie as the natural ruling class by bringing a concept of nature into the city, or a semiotic attempt to naturalize the circulation of capital (these sentiments are argued extensively by Harvey, 2006), such reorganizations of the space of the city represent a far more profound epistemological transformation. In nearly every account of Haussmann's reconstruction of Paris, we miss the effective power that he deploys by bringing about a spatial order composed of both city and territory. We miss the broader epistemological *coherence* between the various achievements of Haussmann and Napoleon III in Paris (typically depicted as a comprehensive list or series of stand-alone facts; see, for instance, Benevolo, 1978a: 67–75; Harvey, Giedion, Bergdoll, Tafuri and many others follow similar suit). Far from simply constructing a space appropriate to the circulation of capital or the stage on which a new subjectivity could claim its place in history, or even the means by which capitalist social divisions would dominate the experience of modern life, Haussmann and Napoleon III had opened up the city to the territory and vice versa, creating a seamless space of technological administration. As Picon points out,

Figure 6.1 Jean-Charles Alphand, Plan Général de Paris, 1867–73 (Les Promenades de Paris)

[i]nseparable from a circulatory conception of technical and social efficiency, the network, whether territorial or urban, tends to put on the same plane the different points that it connects without seeking to mix them. [. . .] In this perspective, the new avenues and the parks and gardens of the Paris of Napoleon III and Haussmann would not attempt to eliminate the opposition between the bourgeoisie and the workers; it would, in contrast, seek to re-articulate both within the same functional totality. (Picon, 2002: 251; my translation)

Haussmann and Napoleon III had created a paradigm in which the space of the city was made available to *planning* for the first time. Far from providing a rational response to the demands 'naturally' emerging from 'the modern city', as canonical histories of Paris may have it, the two achieved this by applying to the city a specific form of knowledge – a *political technology* (Elden, 2010) – forged over the span of 200 years of absolutist rule. A technology born of the calculus of early modern politics, its purpose was not only to appropriate space by securing borders, but to distribute a geometry of power throughout its homogeneous space in which all resources, population, wealth could be measured and their movements could be controlled. The territory – a spatio-political order, a practice of control and calculation and a form of knowledge – became the principal technology that gave early modern power its spatial and material legitimacy, setting in play a juridico-political and economic *nomos* of power that, by the mid nineteenth century, had expanded its reach into spaces and scales to which its logic had previously been not only impervious, but completely antithetical.

As I will argue in Chapter 7, the urban was discovered in the knowledge and space of territory; it is a territorial logic applied to the city, allowing the city, as it were, to become 'territorial' in nature. And with this, paradoxically, shortly after the city was finally made visible as a theoretical object in its own right, it was simultaneously seen to be obsolete, insufficient. Its eclipse by a wholly new category – the urban – would follow. The world that would open out as a result of this synthesis would revolve around precisely what territorial knowledge had achieved: the ability to facilitate endless, managed circulation across increasingly abstract, quantified and securitized landscapes of production and reproduction. Yet this would not be the accomplishment of Haussmann's work, despite its transformative breadth. To understand this, we need to return to the work of Cerdá.

NOTES

1   By the term 'secularize', I mean to refer to Agamben's reading of the famous Löwith–Blumenberg debate on secularization (see Wallace, 1981) in which he concludes that secularization is in fact not a concept but a signature that 'move[s] and displace[s] concepts and signs from one field to another [. . .] without redefining them semantically'. As such, Agamben (2011: 4) argues that secularization

    can be seen as a 'performance of Christian faith that, for the first time, opens the world to man in its worldliness and historicity. The theological signature operates here as a sort of trompe l'oeil in which the very secularization of the world becomes the mark that identifies it as belonging to a divine *oikonomia*' (see Agamben, 2011: 2–4).

2   'Now the empire of man over things is founded on the arts and sciences, for nature is only to be commanded by obeying her' (Bacon, 1884: 115).

3   In fact, as Picon argues, it is precisely because the idea of the network gives itself equally to representational qualities and to a framework that can be used as a tool of development (see Picon, 2002).

4   Many of the Saint-Simonians were affiliated with or matriculated within the École des ponts et chaussées.

5   This is a work completely based on fluid mechanics in which, by the regularization of Paris's ancient aqueducts, Paris can be divided into 12 *quartiers* according to a system of 12 canals serving each.

6   To name a very few of these works, see Baudelaire (1995), Clark (1990), Harvey (2006), 'Paris, capital of the nineteenth century' (Benjamin, 1999), Lefebvre (1991) and Hazan (2010).

7

Circulation Unbound:
The Urban

Although, for many historians, Haussmann's reconstruction of Paris bears all the signatures of a broad set of socio-economic and aesthetic transformations playing out in nineteenth-century Europe, such readings perhaps conceal a more profound epistemological shift that underpins them all. The becoming-territorial of Paris would open up a new spatial imaginary that would exceed any singular achievement of Haussmann's project. Yet, as profound as this may have been, the problem remains that it is difficult to generalize Haussmann's work itself as a 'paradigm' of modern urbanization, despite the fact that many still do (see Chapter 1 of this book). Contemporary urbanization simply cannot be reduced to some legacy of so-called 'Haussmannization' without disregard for the specific spatial, political and technological complexities bound together in the much broader transformations of space that we have seen unfolding across scales and around the world since the nineteenth century. Furthermore, as transformative as it was, Haussmann's project remained incomplete precisely in the terms of its becoming-territorial. Cerdá would certainly have recognized all this. Although he too was inspired by Haussmann's spectacular work of opening the old city up to broad, straight boulevards and his 'regularization' efforts, he was also deeply critical of this strategy's limitations. For Cerdá, reforming the city as Haussmann had done was not only unjust, it was insufficient. Haussmann's project, despite its totality in itself, would remain, for Cerdá, a half-project.

Unlike Haussmann's work, Cerdá's project in Barcelona was a kind of test case for a far more *politically idealistic* project. Because he saw little distinction in the material form of the city and the politics of absolutism, he also believed that politics itself could be overcome by reordering space and the relationships of habitation – in the creation of a new material configuration of life. Cerdá's attempt to construct a spatio-technological apparatus aimed at dismantling the state can be expressed as a system mobilized against the division between territory and city, as territory had been the principle spatio-political technology of the state – a project, we could say, of depoliticizing territory by literally inhabiting it, *by making it domestic.* His work was inspired by Haussmann's reconstruction of Paris, but he was also fascinated by many of the cities in the Americas that were built on generic, colonial gridiron plans, all of which displayed, even in his time, the ability to extend without limits into the territory beyond. For Cerdá, the idealism embedded in his *urbe* was that it was *both city and territory* while being neither at the same time – a spatiality that existed in excess of both.

The previous chapters charted the epistemological rise of circulation in Europe during the sixteenth and seventeenth centuries by reading the material changes registered in the space of its cities, in the corridors of communication between them, in the vast maritime networks of colonial trade and in written treatises and laws. This condition manifested itself in Europe through the works of municipal administrations and police apparatuses deploying control and piecemeal embellishments to the city and its circulatory infrastructure. In its colonial space, however, the very same epistemological shift provoked the emergence of a new type of 'city' altogether – one that departed from the colonial settlement type. If the attempt to assess the rise of circulation charted the analysis and construction of traffic as the object of city and state administration and as a correlate of a new horizon of closed, circular motion, this chapter will turn its attention to this same phenomenon as it developed in the colonial spaces that Europe controlled.

In order to assess how the spatiality of *raison d'état* developed by privileging circulation, we have to examine the spaces it gave rise to both within Europe and outside it. If the European city, burdened by existing landownership complications, coped with the new demands of circulation by introducing a police apparatus to manage traffic and control the spaces of exchange, in the colonies, a very different condition held. I will follow the rise of a new paradigm realized on the scaffold of the colonial settlement – a device or *grid* of territorial occupation founded initially (at least in its early modern appearance) on a *purely administrative* form of power. Precisely because of its absolute 'rationality' – a condition intensified by the apparent lack of legal and political obstacles in the 'New World' – it was able to respond to the demands of traffic *at many scales simultaneously*, extending its control into the surrounding landscape. This model proved crucial not in its ability to manage circulation, but rather in its inherently territorial capacity as a mechanism of appropriation, distribution and production. As opposed to the European city of the time, this model was able to offer a radically new form of knowledge in itself that lay largely dormant in the 'empty' spaces outside European consciousness for almost two centuries, until Cerdá reappropriated its potential in the process of *urbanización*.

The colonial settlement tends to be historically qualified by its assemblage of models and principles from the history of classical and Renaissance treatises, through the Roman *castrum* or drawing from the *bastide* towns in southern France, constructing what was impossible to execute in Europe (see, for example, Benevolo, 1978b, and Stanislawski, 1947). What this history misses is that, in its materialization, the colonial settlement offered an abstracted grid optimized not only for its clear, disciplined administrative organization, but because it also provided a rationalized pattern of extendable circulation *between land and settlement*. For this reason, despite a previous century and a half of the universal, gridded colonial settlements, it would not be until the late seventeenth century that this new figure would become legible as a paradigm adapted to the demands of a world increasingly ruled by the modern, territorial state and its nascent capitalist economy. In other words, it would not be until circulation was fully realized as an organizational principle of space that this new paradigm would arise within a figure already constructed by an administrative logic for the appropriation, distribution and production of land, thus bringing together a form of cohabitation with the establishment and administration of territory. This paradigm is best illuminated by the plan of Philadelphia, created by William Penn and Thomas Holme in 1682.

Penn and Holme's plan for Philadelphia offered a fundamentally new type of territorial inhabitation for the early modern world. The clearest example of a proto-urban system, it was a model that would reveal a rational spatial configuration perfectly suited to the economic administration and circulation of resources, inhabitants and agricultural produce between its surrounding lands, the settlement and the Atlantic network of trade of which it was a crucial port. Endowed with both ideological permanence and pragmatic schemes of self-sufficiency, Philadelphia was among the first settlements to encompass the scale of both the city and the larger agricultural region into which its control extended, creating a unique, integrated relationship between the two.

The novelty of Penn and Holme's scheme was in its deployment of a single, trans-scalar extension of its grid, which could incorporate and parcel agricultural, rural and civic lands in a single seamless, interdependent and, above all, *calculated* spatial system: Philadelphia is one of the first cities planned with the aim of consolidating both cultivated lands, rural plots and city blocks in a single, expandable grid. Yet it was not only a geographical device that incorporated large-scale planning and the laying out of a city. More importantly, as we shall see, its spatial order was based on a calculated distribution that directly related a given number of settlers to an agricultural yield, expressing this relationship in terms of private property and foreshadowing the essence of 'population' as an administrative category. That Cerdá paid tribute to Philadelphia's grid was no mere gesture. In it, he found a dormant paradigm, a project created in the 'empty' spaces of America the potential of which had yet to be comprehended as the basis for a far greater project of reconstructing the space of the post-Revolution world.

This chapter will show how the synthesis of the 'urban' in Cerdá's work resulted in a new paradigm of spatio-political order that transcends the political qualities exposed in the initial chapters of this book: in those chapters, I characterized the urban as a biopolitical apparatus with a mode of control that revolved around the various technologies and channels of circulation, reducing the city to a machinic continuum comprising spaces of life's enhancement (production) and those of its preservation (reproduction). In subsequent chapters, I established how, previous to its deployment within the city, circulation came to be a principal subject and object of absolute power in the West. I examined how, by the seventeenth century, it had become constituent in the ordering of state space – how circulation became a key principle in the construction of *territory*.

In this chapter, I return to Cerdá to re-examine his attitude towards circulation (*vialidad*) – the fundamental 'cause' of urbanization – with regard to this history in order to advance a further understanding of urbanization beyond that of its biopolitical capture of life. Although Cerdá presents *vialidad* as the origin of every design decision he made for the *urbe*, which, as I have argued, is the basis on which the *urbe* introduces a new biopolitical space of administration, such an emphasis is unable to shed light on the territorial nature that the urban simultaneously demonstrates. Thus, the purpose of this chapter will be to see circulation not as a principle of design, but rather as *the signature of a territorial spatial order* making its entrance for the first time in the space of the European city; it is the signature, in other words, of the reorganization of political power in space. In this way, we will begin to see the complexities of the urban, whose form of power exercises itself simultaneously in domestic and territorial registers and whose order is no longer dependent on a set of oppositions (interior/exterior, territory/city, nature/artifice, land/sea, etc.), but rather on its singularity as a universal and totalizing *space-process* that coordinates territories of production and reproduction.

FROM RECONSTRUCTION TO 'REFORM AND EXTENSION'

If Haussmann constructed a radically new approach to the city by drawing in part on the French tradition of territory – a tradition whose formal legacy can be traced to Le Nôtre – Cerdá countered his contemporary, critically building on this model by invoking another, much less overt tradition of territory. Cerdá's work was certainly inspired by the transformations of Paris. Although there is no evidence that he knew the actual role played by Haussmann himself (he never mentions his name),[1] Cerdá had spent time visiting the city between 1856 and 1858, during the initial years of Haussmann's project (Cerdá, 1999: 359–60). Viewing the task of reform as based largely on the implementation of systems of circulation both above ground and below, he took inspiration from many technical details of the design of systems of water, gas and telegraphy conduits designed by Belgrand, Haussmann's director of water and sewers, all of which helped inform his overall concept of *vialidad*.

More generally, Cerdá was moved by the overall effect of the reforms Haussmann brought about in Paris, principally the tactical advantages of cutting through the ancient city with a network of broad, straight boulevards. A military man himself, Cerdá applauded the regularization efforts that Haussmann had inaugurated in their well-known capacity to neutralize insurgency, which had been so rampant during the first half of the century.

> In modern cities there is an imperative need which we can never forego: the need for internal defense and preservation of public order, the first guarantee of civilized nations, which has obliged the Emperor Napoleon to open up spacious streets, thus destroying the confused maze of ancient Paris. (Cerdá, 1859a, quoted in Cerdá, 1999: 133)

Keen to view the form of the city as a direct outcome of technology, Cerdá reasoned that the advanced capacities of firearms and artillery of his day had necessitated the straightening and widening of all major streets within a city, making both the use of firearms as well as the movement of the army throughout the city more effective in quelling any resistance to 'public order':

> And even ... assuming that there were streets longer than the range of a cannon, this would be no reason [to] counsel that such streets be interrupted, since it would be easier to advance artillery along a straight way, where no opposition could be met which would not be overcome in passing, than along winding streets which would throw up stumbling blocks to it at every street corner. (Cerdá, 1863, quoted in Cerdá, 1999: 134)

Of course, the type of 'public disorder' that Cerdá had identified was another name for the irruptions of insurgency that had proliferated across Europe in the shadow of the French Revolution. It is impossible to grasp the nature of this new form of struggle that coursed throughout and beyond Europe outside the radical transformations that transpired in the form of the state itself.

The nineteenth-century formation of the nation-state was in part constructed in opposition to the sovereign state that had preceded it. Fuelled by an idealism around internationalism (Mattelart, 2000), it brought with it a wholly new understanding of the figure of the enemy and thus of war as well. What was once seen clearly as a political adversary, a permanent threat situated externally to the state, the notion of the enemy in the nineteenth century was transcribed as an exceptional figure – just as war itself would become extraordinary – an *insurgent* born within the state's population (see Foucault, 2003: 256–7). As Cerdá clearly recognized, in this transformation, the site of such 'struggles' had been displaced from battlefields in the countryside that stretched along the borders of the territory to the streets of the city. For this reason, the city itself would need to adopt radical new strategies, technologies and forms that could diminish the threat of such warfare: 'since the disruptive elements existing today cannot be destroyed instantly and in every detail, it is essential that the Government should, at all costs, set aside the appropriate resources to smother any attempt at disorder at its origins' (Cerdá, 1860b: 560, quoted in Cerdá, 1999: 134). And he was well aware of the effect that introducing broad, straight boulevards into the heart of his own Barcelona had had in depoliticizing the spaces previously occupied by revolutionaries (see Cerdá, 1991 (1859): § 1423).[2] His admiration for what had been possible in Paris in the name of 'public order' was evident:

> Only very recently has a powerful government undertaken with heroic valor the reform of its capital city and of some outlying towns. And even though as a matter of fact it was only attempting to solve the problem of public order, it has also resolved the problem of humanity, for the mysterious linkage of all major social issues is such that solving one problem almost always amounts to solving the others. (Cerdá, 1860a: § 8, quoted in Cerdá, 1999: 361)

Yet Cerdá, possibly following Saint-Simon, saw that eliminating the spaces in which insurgency could find tactical advantage was not enough; a second, far more effective way to confront 'public disorder' was to ensure the universal provision of private property. The equation between private property and neutrality could not have been more self-evident: such a programme, taken on by a liberal administration, could 'thereby increase the number of property owners within the town and, consequently, the guarantees of peace and public order' (Cerdá, 1991 (1859): § 1051). It was in part around this point that Cerdá would launch a sharp critique of the approach of Haussmann and Napoleon III.

Despite his admiration for the scale and ambitions of Haussmann and Napoleon's project, Cerdá saw in it a tremendous amount of injustice, which helped him develop his *Teoría* as a response. Cerdá had grave concerns about the fact that no adequate provisions of housing had been considered for the many thousands of people who had been displaced by the *grands travaux*.

> It seems impossible that any administration could be capable of undertaking a major urban reform without first providing comfortable housing in ample time for the families which are going to be dislodged. And yet the administration which passes for the best organized, the most paternal and even the most officious, the one which not infrequently descends to the minutiae of the tutelage or care of the individual, the French administration of the second half of the nineteenth century, undertook the demolition of hundreds of buildings in order to reform Paris without a care for the fate of thousands of souls ejected from their homes. (Cerdá, 1991 (1861): § 1349)

Cerdá, as we know, took great interest in the conditions of the working class and he believed vehemently that, in his time, the material, political and economic conditions had arrived in which to achieve a universal status of social equality, at least across the major European states. He saw only an 'inexcusable cruelty' in the gratuitous eviction of countless families without access to new housing. Even more insidious for Cerdá was that the initial need for reform always occurred in areas of the city where population densities were highest.

> Therefore, since the population is already known to be overcrowded whenever a reform is undertaken, ejecting a part of this population from their homes and actively beginning demolition without first building, outside the precinct which is to be improved, the same number of dwellings as is to be vacated, will produce by violence a much greater concentration and crowding of families than we are trying to eliminate. (Cerdá, 1991 (1861): § 1348)

The notion of density is highly significant: for him, density, as we have seen, is a key parameter with which the general crisis of the city could be made visible. Yet here we see it has taken on a more diagnostic role: density is a measure that makes it possible to know in which locations urban reform is needed. Density thus also acts as a measure by which to assess the very processes of reform itself, which Cerdá's critique of Haussmann's administration reveals. This pragmatic concern led Cerdá to one of his most significant conclusions that surpassed the model of so-called Haussmannization as a paradigm of modern urbanization – that reform can only happen if it is accompanied by *extension*: 'This is why the idea of reform is inextricably linked to that of extension, for it would be impossible to bring about the desired rarefaction without spreading the buildings out further' (ibid.). And, because reform (and thus extension) will become synonymous with urbanization, the index of density will also play a crucial role in the form that urbanization takes under Cerdá's pen as a parameter with which to distribute a population across the territory, achieving a uniform density of 40 square metres of urban space (*urbe*) per person (see Chapter 1 of this text).

Having discovered the intimate relationship between reform and extension that was at the core of his theory of urbanization, Cerdá uncovered an even deeper flaw in Haussmann's project: it was not simply the injustices that Haussmann and Napoleon III had inflicted upon the Parisian population that bothered him. Rather, he saw this as a symptom of a greater lack of foresight and planning that plagued their entire reconstruction of Paris.

> [S]uch a system or, as we have been bold enough to label it repeatedly – with or without the permission of the blind admirers of the French Administration – such a lack of system, flies in the face of a sense of justice which we could never subdue. (Cerdá, 1991 (1861): § 1183)

For Cerdá, calculation, foresight and a more systematic planning mechanism were all prerequisites for achieving a just practice of reform. Having
discovered that no such system (in particular, an economic calculation) had
been put in place in Paris, his initial admiration for the project turned to
despondency.

> We found nothing there [in Paris] but the omnipotent will of one man who
> says: *Let this be done!*, and it is done. At the sound of his voice, the public
> treasury opens up, the Municipality of Paris contracts massive loans, and the
> economic question is not of the slightest importance. (Cerdá, 1860a: § 9)

He continues:

> [A]s the French Administration proceeded with such a lack of foresight, we
> might almost say lack of humanity, there should be no surprise at our belief
> that the costs that would be incurred and the means that should be
> employed to meet them had not been calculated in advance. (Cerdá, 1991
> (1861): § 1181)

This was not to favour a more timid, cautious programme of reform over that
carried out by Haussmann: Cerdá's criticism of the Parisian project should be
read as a claim that Haussmann had not gone far enough. The far more radical
scope of 'reform' Cerdá was after required an equally radical construction of, as
we have seen, a massive governmental apparatus, integrating economic, legal,
administrative, political and technical planning – a system capable of sustaining
reform not as a project, but rather as a *process-based framework* applicable anywhere. His criticisms were not limited to Paris: Cerdá often complained that
other similar projects taking place in Spain had either been too meagre or otherwise limited to serving the interests of a particular class or individuals. In all
cases, he found that:

> the method followed in them is not the offspring of any system nor of any
> general thought, for which reason it sets no precedent. [. . .] Through
> measures of this type, a government may escape the hardships of the
> moment, but it creates no system nor permanent legislation, nor does it
> establish principles that might subsequently be applied to other similar
> cases, which is exactly what appeals to us and what we have set out to
> achieve, and what interests governments and societies. (Cerdá, 1991
> (1861): § 1199–200)

This ambition would lead Cerdá to set out his 'five bases' of urbanization that
would constitute the core of his masterwork, the *Teoría general de la urbanización*, laying the groundwork for a universal model of urban reform. And,
because 'reform' should never happen without extension, any model seriously

interested in reform would need to incorporate a coordinated calculus of *planning* – not merely an office to oversee it – in order to achieve a just, equitable outcome. The universality of this model is thus not attributed to the technical, spatial parameters alone, which constitute the more visible aspect of Cerdá's work, but must be seen as the complex system of planning that integrates the economic, administrative, legal and political concerns necessary to realize the spatio-technical model. Such an 'urbanizing science' would allow the new promise of 'reform' to unfold beyond the series of isolated projects throughout Europe that had taken shape in his time, but rather as a universal *process* named *urbanización*.

Cerdá's break from Haussmann comes in his insistence on reform *as a complex calculation*, rather than a surgical mode of improvement. The consequence of this meant that the process of reform should not only respond to the transformation of cities, but that it had to incorporate a calculus of growth as a condition of the modern city itself, thus uniting reform with extension. The realization of this was of course fundamental to Cerdá's abandonment of the concept of the city in favour of the *urbe*, a spatio-technical correlate of the governmental apparatus designed to modulate its infinite expansion. Attention has already been given to the way this apparatus, developed as an isometric grid, was able to respond to a population as a bio-economic quantity to be separated into spaces of life's preservation and enhancement and distributed across the qualitatively 'empty' countryside surrounding the city. This organization of space, architecture and infrastructure both enables and is the product of a specifically modern form of administrative governance over a population that makes sovereignty at once invisible and totalizing by bringing all of life into permanent contact with its administrative modes of controlled circulation. Although the spatio-technical strategy that Cerdá had created was based on a calculus of *vialidad*, sanitation, private property and an overall statistical distribution of population and services across space, it drew from a family of historical precedents that allows us to see an entirely different scale of political calculation, outside the biopolitical, that lies at the heart of his project of *urbanización*: the colonial settlement. In other words, if Haussmann had introduced a territorial logic into the organization of the city, by reinterpreting the European tradition of colonial settlements within the space of nineteenth-century Europe, Cerdá in effect allowed the city (or rather the *urbe*) to become a *territorial* apparatus by other means.

Many commentators have highlighted connections between Cerdá's *urbe* and the history of colonial settlements in the Americas.[3] Most have drawn attention to the study he did in his *Teoría de la construcción de las ciudades* of 1859 in which he charts street widths, block dimensions and populations of a set of exemplar cities from around the world whose form is at least partially determined by a grid. In this study, he focuses in particular on the cities of the Americas. Although he pays tribute to cities such as Buenos Aires, perhaps in an effort to distance himself from the Spanish history of colonization in Latin America, he lauded in particular the cities of North America, whose forms are, of course, predominantly organized around the grid. What struck his interest was the way in which cities planned as grids could both accommodate growth by expanding outward, while also being able to efficiently absorb high traffic flow within an ample, rationalized street grid. In stark contrast, the cities of Europe, built on top of medieval layouts, had had to resort to constructing massive underground networks of transportation to cope:

> [F]aced with the alternatives of having to consider establishing a new system of underground communications, as is happening in Paris and London, or giving the streets now being planned a width not for present-day needs, but for the likely needs of the future, as is happening in the modern cities of the North American Union – faced with these alternatives, I repeat, I believe it is preferable, from the perspectives of both health and economy, to opt for the latter system. (Cerdá, 1855, § 109, quoted in Cerdá, 1999: 183)

Of especial interest for Cerdá was the city of Philadelphia, which, in his own words, was 'the most regularly beautiful city, not only in the United States, but in the world' (Cerdá, 1991 (1859): § 1400), a contemporary plan of which he included in his 'Atlas' at the end of the above volume. It is not clear to what extent Cerdá was acquainted with William Penn and Thomas Holme's plan of 1682, but the similarities between it and his own plan for Barcelona (not to mention the *urbe* more generally) are striking. From the dimensions of the blocks to the overall layout of the grid and its distribution of dwellings and open spaces, there are many obvious resemblances between the two plans. However, it is when we examine Penn and Holme's plan in more detail, as well as the highly systematic logic that drove its design, that deeper similarities begin to emerge.

PHILADELPHIA

Unlike other colonial projects tied up with the interests of a single trading company or bound to the political directives of the colonizing powers, Pennsylvania had been given over to William Penn as payment to cancel a debt held by Charles II. As a result, Penn colonized the province with a degree of autonomy not typically seen in the two centuries of early European colonial exploits; Pennsylvania became the site in which a radically new approach to colonization took place – one not only anticipating Cerdá's ambitions, but widely appreciated as having set a precedent for modern planning in general.

Having received the great tract of land in America, Penn set about drafting his plan for colonizing this land by first founding the town of Philadelphia. Originally established as a 'holy experiment' by the affluent Quaker, providing solace for those seeking religious tolerance, Philadelphia took on broader ambitions in the

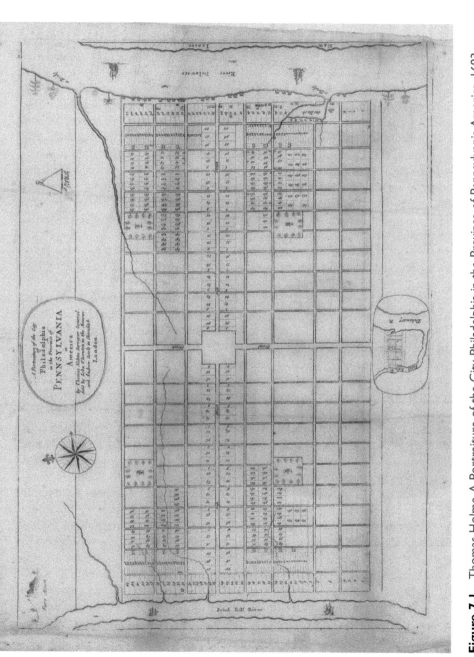

Figure 7.1 Thomas Holme, A Portraiture of the City Philadelphia in the Province of Pennsylvania America, 1683 (*A Letter from William Penn, proprietary and governour of Pennsylvania in America, to the committee of the Free Society of Traders of that province, residing in London, by William Penn*)

setting out of a paradigm of town planning built on the prospect of affording economic opportunities to those wishing to settle. The first major American city to be planned as a grid, Penn and Holme's plan extended a symmetrical grid of 22 blocks deep by 8 blocks across, over a section of land that sat between the Schuylkill and Delaware Rivers.

Originally set to be only half the size, Penn insisted on stretching the grid from river to river, anticipating substantial future growth. The resulting grid, two miles in length and just under a mile in breadth, is structured by uniform streets 50 feet wide and bisected in both directions by two major streets, each 100 feet wide, the two of which meet in a large open square in the centre. The plan is then punctuated by four additional public squares of the same dimension and roughly centred in each quadrant of the grid. Initial plots were laid out in the blocks symmetrically along the banks of each river, gradually decreasing in density as they proceeded inward, where they eventually line the major transverse road alone. Such a distribution would simultaneously encourage a systematic growth distributed throughout the town and maintain the town's unity throughout. As Penn had witnessed the outbreak of the plague in 1665 and the Great Fire of the following year, his plan can be seen as a spatial response to each, incorporating measures that would deter both disease and fire from besetting his city. As such, each house was to be located in the plot so as to have ample gardens, orchards or fields flanking each side of it, 'that it may be a green country town, which will never be burnt and always be wholesome' (Hazard, 1850: 530).

Beyond being a site of religious freedom and tolerance, Philadelphia was, for Penn, an early capitalist venture in land development. Not beholden to any single trading company, an ambition of Penn's had been to prepare a settlement in which trade and commerce would flourish.[4] Philadelphia would be a new centre for Quakers, as well as others seeking economic opportunities outside a Europe torn apart by decades of religious civil war. And, because of the way in which Pennsylvania had been acquired, Philadelphia would benefit from its relative independence. Such an ambition was clear even before any plan had been drafted, with Penn diligently seeking to attract a host of like-minded purchasers, trade societies and other wealthy adventurers. His personal enthusiasm for the project aside, Penn clearly saw the colony as an investment. He regularly corresponded with potential settler-investors in England, reporting on the natural wealth of the land, the rapid growth of the city, the seasonable conditions of the area and the general desire for a prosperous life that had been created around the bustling town of Philadelphia (Reps, 1965: 165–7). Much like a modern speculator, he measured the success of the town's development by the growth ('improvement') in property and land value:

> The Improvement of the place is best measur'd by the advance of Value upon every man's Lot. I will venture to say that the worst Lot in the Town, without any Improvement upon it, is worth four times more than it was when it was lay'd out, and the best fourty. (Penn, 1685, quoted in Reps, 1965: 167)

Of course, real-estate speculation was only one side of the economic model of development Penn had in mind. More than this, his colony was to serve as a central hub in the network of colonial trade. For this reason, when planning Philadelphia, Penn also planned the large tract of lands surrounding it. Purchasers were legally bound to invest in agricultural land in addition to town plots, as Penn understood the notion of 'improvement' to be a single economic idea comprising multiple coordinated activities. In 1681, he published the conditions of settlement, which followed his general scheme of colonization in which purchasers of land would be proportionally allocated 10 acres of city land for every 500 acres of 'liberty lands' (agricultural plots) purchased. In this way, the development of the city would be tied in with the sale and development of a proportion of productive, agricultural land outside and contiguous to the city, at a ratio of 1:50. Although this actual proportion changed (Reps, 1965: 163–5), it set in motion a system in which the laying out of Philadelphia would be synchronized with the planning of the region, including the founding of other rural townships and the division and ordering of agricultural lands.

> That the land in the town be laid out together, after the proportion of ten thousand acres of the whole country; that is, two hundred acres, if the place will bear it; however, that the proportion be by lot, and entire, so as those that desire to be together, especially those that are by catalogue laid together, may be so laid together both in the town and country. (Hazard, 1850: 517)

Like Philadelphia, the townships in the surrounding 'liberty lands' would follow a similar layout and would reflect the same ratios of population, land area of township and area of associated productive lands:

> Our Townships lie square [. . .] Five hundred Acres are allotted for the Village, which, among ten families, comes to fifty Acres each: This lies square, and on the outside of the square stand the Houses, with their fifty Acres running back, where ends meeting make the Centre of the 500 Acres as they are to the whole. Before the Doors of the Houses lies the high way, and cross it, every man's 450 Acres of Land that makes up his Complement of 500, so that the Conveniencey of the Neighbourhood is made agreeable with that of the land. (Penn, 1685: 261–73, quoted in Reps, 1965: 165)

These 'liberty lands' were to be the source from which a great wealth was to be reaped, and Philadelphia served as the central port where it could be exported to circulate in the colonial network of trade routes. For this reason, Penn went into great detail setting out the ordinances regulating the division, ownership, governance and production of the rural lands in order to ensure that all lands were planned and looked after, that no settler remained idle and no land lay fallow.

For those purchasers who failed to produce, Penn even provided disciplinary measures, one concession stating:

> [t]hat every man shall be bound to plant or man so much of his share of land as shall be set out and surveyed, with three years after it is so set out and surveyed, or else it shall be lawful for new comers to be settled there-upon, paying to them their survey-money. (Hazard, 1850: 518)

Although he went to great lengths to attract 'purchasers' of land, Penn took care that the order of the overall system of settlement that he had planned would remain intact. Like Cerdá would do, Penn placed great faith in setting out a system that ensured the most productive, agreeable and orderly distribution of people, resources, services, goods and labour in the colonial world. For this reason, the development of the entire settlement (Philadelphia, its townships and 'liberty lands') needed to follow a rational order in which town, township and farmland could be systematically related. At the same time, it needed to privilege a system of movement within and between towns. Thus, the planning of the surrounding 'liberty lands' followed an overall orthogonal network of divisions, laid out over the countryside, that reproduced the grid of the city at a larger scale. As Benevolo notes, '[t]his arrangement [. . .] shows that the grid plan system was not associated with any particular scale, but was already used as a generic instrument applicable in any scale' (1978b: 1025). This grid would be articulated by a well-planned, hierarchical grid of streets, roads and highways: with a keen sense of future development, Penn required that the establishment of public rights of way was to precede private development and to take priority over private interests. Giving clear authority to the surveyor over the purchaser, the allocation of private land would take place only after the laying out of city streets and highways between cities:

> But it is to be noted, that the surveyors shall consider what roads or highways will be necessary to the cities, towns, or through the lands. Great roads from city to city not to contain less than forty feet in breadth, shall be first laid out and declared to be for highways, before the dividend of acres be laid out for the purchaser, and the like observation to be had for the streets in the towns and cities, that there may be convenient roads and streets preserved, not to be encroached upon by any planter or builder, that none may build irregularly, to the damage of another. In this custom governs. (Hazard, 1850: 518)

Both town and countryside would function as a single system of extraction, cultivation and production, all bound together by a precise system of circulation.

This systematic logic would also embody a temporal calculation. Just as Cerdá observed almost two centuries after Penn and Holme's plan had been laid out, Philadelphia's streets were still much wider than their European counterparts, and the plan provided for even wider streets, yielding more than ample service to the traffic of the time (Reps, 1965: 172). Its incorporation not only of oversized streets, but of the major streets bisecting the city, and those stretching out into the countryside, offered a radically new approach to the laying out of colonial settlements. Indeed, from his first move doubling the city to the division and ordering of the countryside in conjunction with the development of the town, to the control of the region's overall development, to his persistent consideration for 'after Commers', Penn always took a visionary stance to accommodate the future through the organization of the colony, offering the first example where 'improvement' was in fact an early form of coordinated, multi-scalar 'planning'.

In the words of historian John Reps, '[i]n no other colony did the problems of city and regional planning receive such attention' (ibid.: 158). The relationship between town and countryside that Penn had articulated can best be seen in the Mapp of ye Improved Part of Pensilvania in America of 1687 (the date is estimated by Reps; ibid.), where, anticipating Thomas Jefferson's Land Ordinance of 1785, the ordering of space is achieved as a coherent whole by a single orthogonal structure creating order at multiple scales.

The consistency of the various scales of this system with one another, through the abstract logic of the grid, reveals the degree of controlled calculation operating at the heart of this spatio-economic system. In fact, it is likely that Penn's planning of Pennsylvania, based on a 'proportionate ownership in town and country' (Johnson, 1976, 39), served as a model not only for Jefferson, but for an entire tradition of multi-scalar grid-based colonial plans that developed over the seventeenth and eighteenth centuries in the Americas, integrating planning of the town with that of the countryside, from Oglethorpe's plan of Savannah to Vallejo's plan of Sonoma, to name but a few exemplar cases.

Indeed, Jefferson, echoing Penn, would construct his entire Land Ordinance system as a single grid that telescoped the spatial organization of individual plots with the distribution of townships, counties and states, integrating a spatial administrative apparatus capable of accounting for private property, local and national jurisdiction, and a network of circulation through a single device of spatial organization.

Perhaps this explains why Jefferson would call Penn 'the greatest law-giver the world has produced' (Pennsylvania Historical and Museum Commission, n.d.), and why Benevolo would later reflect similarly on Penn's work: 'The historical result of these experiments was the generation of the traditional grid plan, which was no longer an exclusively urban device but could also be applied to the surrounding region, on a landscape or indeed a geographical scale' (Benevolo, 1978b: 1026).

Many of Penn's principles can be seen in more reduced form in the tradition of colonial settlements a century before him, consecrated in the Laws of the Indies. From the provision of wide streets for purposes of defence to the incorporation of an expansive grid set up to anticipate growth, even to the setting out of common land and farmlands in proportion to the number of settlers (see Nuttall, 1921),

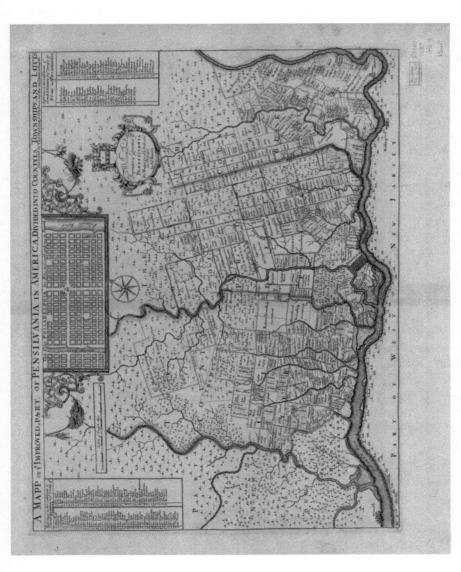

Figure 7.2 Thomas Holme, A Mapp of ye Improved Part of Pensilvania in America. Divided into Countyes, Townships and Lotts, 1687

Source: Library of Congress

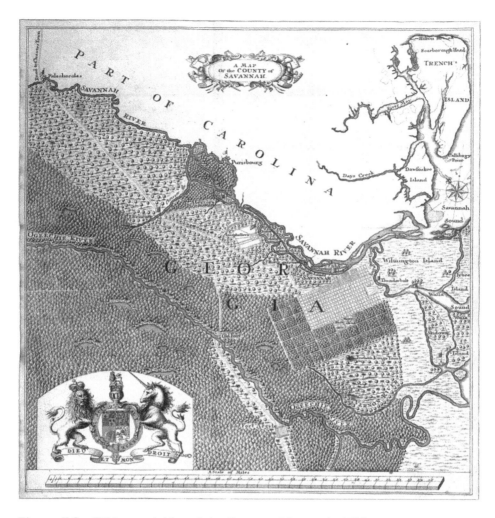

Figure 7.3   T.F. Lotter, A Map of the County of Savannah, 1735

a humbler assessment may see Penn and Holme's plan of Philadelphia as merely a shining example in a long tradition, knowledge of which had circulated between all imperial powers of Europe since the end of the fifteenth century. However, there is a fundamental difference that makes this work paradigmatic of a truly new tradition. Although the ordinances of the Laws of the Indies had set out the spatial and administrative logic for occupying lands, distributing settlers through a division of land and producing wealth, it was organized through a uniform, centralized grid that lacked any systematic means of controlling the town's growth beyond simply extending its grid endlessly outward. It also lacked a defined disposition in its organization of the countryside outside its boundaries.

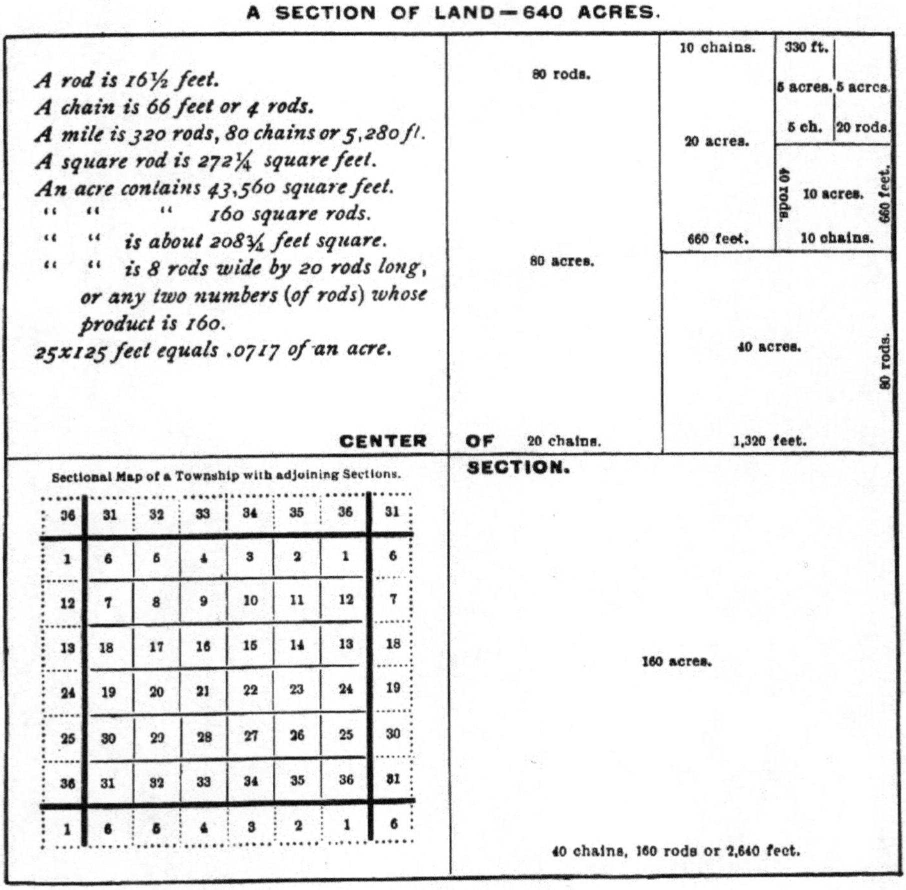

A SECTION OF LAND—640 ACRES.

		10 chains.	330 ft.	
A rod is 16½ feet.	80 rods.		5 acres.	5 acres.
A chain is 66 feet or 4 rods.				
A mile is 320 rods, 80 chains or 5,280 ft.	20 acres.		5 ch.	20 rods.
A square rod is 272¼ square feet.				
An acre contains 43,560 square feet.			10 acres.	
" " " 160 square rods.				
" " is about 208¾ feet square.	660 feet.		10 chains.	
" " is 8 rods wide by 20 rods long,	80 acres.			
or any two numbers (of rods) whose				
product is 160.		40 acres.		
25x125 feet equals .0717 of an acre.				

A rod is 16½ feet.
A chain is 66 feet or 4 rods.
A mile is 320 rods, 80 chains or 5,280 ft.
A square rod is 272¼ square feet.
An acre contains 43,560 square feet.
" " " 160 square rods.
" " is about 208¾ feet square.
" " is 8 rods wide by 20 rods long,
or any two numbers (of rods) whose
product is 160.
25x125 feet equals .0717 of an acre.

CENTER OF SECTION.

20 chains. 1,320 feet.

40 rods 10 acres. 660 feet

80 rods

Sectional Map of a Township with adjoining Sections.

36	31	32	33	34	35	36	31
1	6	5	4	3	2	1	6
12	7	8	9	10	11	12	7
13	18	17	16	15	14	13	18
24	19	20	21	22	23	24	19
25	30	29	28	27	26	25	30
36	31	32	33	34	35	36	31
1	6	5	4	3	2	1	6

160 acres.

40 chains, 160 rods or 2,640 feet.

Figure 7.4 Diagram of Thomas Jefferson's territorial grid established by the Land Ordinance of 1785

Control over the growth and development of the town was in fact limited to the internal disposition of the town, the rules for building houses and the codes of conduct that presided, and so on. The provision for commons and farmlands was, in that way, contingent on the structure of the settlement at any one moment. Its spatial organization had nothing to do with the organization of land outside its grid: it was an expansive logic based on a modular understanding of the settlement, which treated the countryside around it as infinite and, therefore, spatially insignificant in the planning of the overall settlement. This perception of the settlement was reflected in that the knowledge of its layout, the rules of its spatial distribution of buildings, streets and plazas and its centralized mode of growth were all contained in the pedagogical device of the plan itself, which was to be literally taught to new settlers by being made publicly visible at all times (ibid., §127, 751).[5] Despite the plan's role as a device for appropriating land for the Crown, the Spanish settlements themselves remained restricted in scope, unable to incorporate and deploy a *territorial knowledge* in their plan and development over time; all provisions, ordinances and forms of control would, in that sense, remain bound to the epistemic scale of the city in its early modern sense.

This should come as no surprise for, as we know, the modern conception of territory would not fully come to light as a developed political technology of the state until the seventeenth century. What makes Penn's experiment in the province of Pennsylvania so different from anything that had preceded it is precisely the presence of a territorial knowledge that permeates all levels of its planning. This is shown in the multiple dimensions of calculation that coordinate its abstract, *scaleless* grid capable of combining multiple registers of economic production and circulation with an early knowledge of the population (as property owners and producers) in a single spatial apparatus that deliberately makes no great epistemological distinction between the city and the countryside – a character that surely caught Cerdá's interest nearly two centuries later, with his theory of 'ruralized urbanization' – offering insight into an emerging *urban* spatiality.

> It can be seen that country life and city life are opposites to one another, like nature and reason, body and soul, woman and man. [. . .] It is necessary for country and city life to meet within the latter, in the same way that body and spirit meet within man. (Cerdá, 1991 (1859): §§ 1479–80)

Stuart Elden's work on territory focuses on its discursive development as a technology of the early modern European state, emphasizing the knowledge built around the coordination of techniques of economic measurement (land) and political-strategic control (terrain) over space that make this spatio-political figure possible. Certainly, a parallel deployment of such technologies pertained in the spatial and administrative techniques that stamped order on to the appropriated territories of the colonized world. Although I do not wish to raise questions of territory within colonial spaces in great depth here, I would like to explore a certain aspect of its expression in a parallel manner to that in which previous chapters have depicted territory in Europe through practices of its spatial rationalization, focusing primarily on circulation.

It may be that the cartographic knowledge used to map and divide space and the techniques of quantifying the land in its economic and strategic consistency, or the surveying techniques used to measure, mark out and make it productive, were the same whether the object of such knowledge was colonial space or European (see Edney, 2009). However, the actual practices of occupying and controlling the 'empty' land of the Americas differed radically from those used to order the interiors of a landscape of competing European state territories, precisely because, to the colonizers, they lacked the same ontological qualification of interiority so crucial for the territorial state.

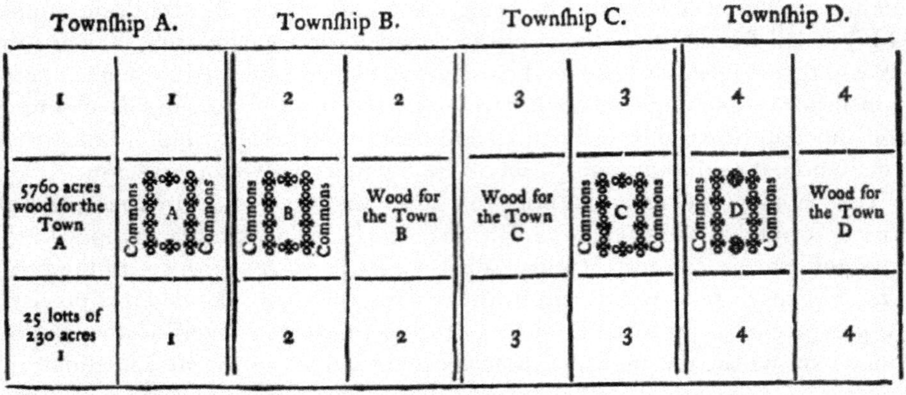

Townſhip A.			Townſhip B.		Townſhip C.		Townſhip D.	
ɪ	ɪ	2	2	3	3	4	4	
5760 acres wood for the Town A	Commons ▓ A ▓ Commons	Commons ▓ B ▓ Commons	Wood for the Town B	Wood for the Town C	Commons ▓ C ▓ Commons	Commons ▓ D ▓ Commons	Wood for the Town D	
25 lotts of 230 acres ɪ	ɪ	2	2	3	3	4	4	

Figure 7.5   Henry Boucequet, Plan for a frontier camp, 1765

In that sense, we must recognize that a principal figure in the establishment of an order and the control of the space of the New World would be of necessity the colonial settlement itself. Even before the notion of territory had been consolidated in the cognitive spaces of *raison d'état*, one can read a territorial imperative in the very structure of the early colonial settlement and the knowledge deployed in its founding. In the early sixteenth century, the Spanish began to pillage the Americas without a strategy to colonize them or a principle by which to found new settlements (see Stanislawski, 1947). It can be argued that the towns they built already had a 'proto-territorial' imperative that operated only at a symbolic level, as the primary figures marking out the property of the kingdom over a vast, homogeneous, 'empty' space, and because, as colonial settlements multiplied across ever vaster swaths of land, they naturally began to establish strategic and economic cartographies of their ever-expanding surrounds, mapping out swamps, rivers, passes, coastal waterways, resources and fertile lands. In this sense, they naturally accumulated knowledge and techniques that we might call 'territorial'. The knowledge advanced by this form of occupation would develop in response a rationalized practice of its own with the Laws of the Indies, and yet, by the mid seventeenth century, a clearly new articulation of this technology emerged in the rationalized spatial calculus of Penn and Holme's Philadelphia. Penn and Holme's ordering of the province of Pennsylvania represents the first conception of a settlement that responded to a territorial epistemology.

In a space apparently free of national histories, property divisions, religious allegiances, constitutions, feudal disputes and centuries-old conflict, there were very few recognizable mechanisms by which spatial order could be asserted beyond literally occupying space itself. The 'unplanned' violence that the early Spanish Conquistadores had used was soon transformed into a highly calculating practice by which the territories of the colonial world were defined less by the setting out of precise borders, and more *from inside out*. That is to say, unlike in Europe, such territorial definition would not conceptually start with its space being measured through a defined border and fortified, and then its 'empty' interior being structured through a hierarchical geometry of circulation, resources and cities. Instead, it had to conceive of itself, by default, from the colonial settlement, moving outward into the infinitely 'empty' spaces beyond. Whereas the epistemological shift to territory saw the European city reduced to an element placed within a mechanical territorial hierarchy – its space contracting in on itself, marking an ever sharper distinction between its brittle streets and theatrical squares and the fluid, rationalized territorial space outside its walls – the same shift saw the colonial settlement in the Americas, with its geometrical, abstract spatial relationships, become an incredibly agile figure for appropriating, distributing and producing new territories outside Europe.

URBANIZATION AND COLONIZATION

The question remains, however: in the reconception of the modern city, why would a European engineer of the nineteenth century take such interest in and seem to emulate many of the principles effectively born in sixteenth- and seventeenth-century colonial settlements? It might seem odd that someone obsessed with the future and committed to ideas such as 'progress' would find such a central paradigm in the colonial world of centuries past. Although it is beyond the scope of this book to speculate on the depth of Cerdá's knowledge of colonial history and, certainly, how much this knowledge would have influenced his work, there is a strong correlation between the two at many levels that warrants further investigation.

It cannot escape observation that the tradition of colonization in the Americas, and especially that of the English, yielded the elements of a space designed entirely to suit an administrative rationale – one with which Cerdá's Saint-Simonian inclinations would have certainly shared affinities. The majority of settlements in the New World had been built according to administrative ordinances that, beginning with the Laws of the Indies in 1573, produced a *generic* form intended to be repeated wherever colonial land needed to be strategically secured or economically expanded. Unlike the tradition of Renaissance cities in Europe, built upon the 'inadequate' fabric of the medieval towns and overburdened by a history of political excesses, the colonial grid that populated the Americas was born of and thrived on a power that needed no political representation. Even if initially controlled by the state, trade showed itself to be power in practice, something certainly more evident in the history of English or Dutch imperialism. Furthermore, the colonial settlement was an entity whose existence only made sense as an interchange within a global space of economic circulation – a node within a space of the free sea, unburdened by territorial borders or formal, political geometries. All of these can be seen to have shared much in common with Cerdá's ideas of a borderless world of endless circulation. For this reason, we should see the family of spatio-administrative experimentations that took place in the wake of Penn and Holme's Philadelphia as a crucial set of proto-urban formations relevant to our history of the urban.

The New World was a space in which an experiment in new spatial configurations that were not possible in Europe could take place. But, although it was an 'exterior' to European space, the so-called New World was never a space whose perception and experience could be completely detached from those of Europe. Rather, the coexistence of the two was founded on the dependency of one on the other, binding the two spaces in a single dialectic, interior and exterior, centre and periphery, that would perpetually fold in on itself, reproducing exterior in interior and vice versa. In that sense, with the absolutist legacy succeeded by the development of the nation-state, the irresistible drive to 'fill' the equally 'empty' spaces of the territory it left behind with the essentialist contours of 'the nation' would have made any reference to colonization, as paradoxical as it may seem, all the more pertinent.

In a letter written during the final year of his life, Cerdá made precisely this intention explicit. Writing to the Marquis of Corbera in 1875,[6] Cerdá elaborated on a final, synthetic theory of his entire life's work, revealing the inherently *geopolitical* ambitions he had invested in his theory of urbanization. He referred to this as the *general colonisation 'de nuestro pais'* (of our country). In this letter, he developed his earlier theory of 'ruralized urbanization', explaining that both the process of urbanization and 'ruralization' should be seen as two faces of a single project of colonization. To accomplish this, he proposed subdividing the space of the state into seven categories of territorial jurisdiction, ranging in scale from the basic division between 'rustic' and urban land contained within the municipal, to the township, the province and the principality and finally arriving at the scale of the nation – all of which could be reduced to a single, telescopic system subject to simultaneous processes of urbanization and ruralization. In other words, by conceiving the entire space of the modern territory using the dichotomy of urban/rural, he could propose a single corresponding system of governance that would oversee the spatial transformation of the entire nation. The *two* spaces that the territory consists of (urban and rural) would be unified as a single system through a hierarchy of circulation, just as he had prescribed in the development of his theory of urbanization. He elaborated this hierarchy as a 'theory of irradiation' (Tarrago Cíd, 2007), which made explicit the interrelations between all scales through a total system of circulation and dwelling: urbanization at the scale of the planet.

Thus, a certain resonance between the spatiality of the Saint-Simonians, which had been a central influence on Cerdá (Bergdoll, 2000: 261–2),[7] and that of the colonial network that took shape over the course of three centuries prior should not come as a surprise: Both spatialities reveal 'urban' characteristics. Whether fully conscious or not of the historical, political and spatial complexities of the colonial world,[8] it is no coincidence that Cerdá took at least superficial inspiration from this history. Perhaps with a silent nod to Penn and Holme,

Cerdá had finally made explicit the true trajectory of urbanization as a single spatial logic operating at multiple scales to rationally and apolitically order the totality of the territory. In his constant overturning of every opposition, like Penn, he would reinterpret the difference between rural and urban not as two distinct spheres, but rather as a single, unified process composed of two simultaneous processes – urbanization and ruralization – each occurring within the other: inasmuch as the rural was to be urbanized, the urban too was to be 'ruralized' by the incorporation of measured parcels of rural land within the structure of each *intervia*. At once network and grid, urban and rural, interior and exterior, respite and movement, biopolitical and territorial, a new spatial order had been summoned forth in the political spaces opened up in the contingencies and chaos of nineteenth-century Europe. The means by which to constitute this space, as it turns out, was through a directed project of *colonizing* the spaces of the state with the same territorial technologies cultivated over three centuries in both Europe and the New World, washed over with the domestic moralism of liberal society.

TECHNOLOGIES OF TERRITORY AND THE BIRTH OF THE URBAN

Discussing the relationship between the network of roads and the emergence of the police, Foucault suggested that the seventeenth-century territory was planned as though it were a large town, a process that he loosely called the 'urbanization of the territory' (Foucault, 2009: 336). Although I take Foucault's point, clearly a much more radical 'urbanization of the territory' happened two centuries later, only once the city had been 'territorialized' first. The complex processes and spatial concepts at work in constituting the urban (or urbanization) can only begin to be grasped when Cerdá's work is placed in dialogue with Haussmann's, and then this entire set of experiments is brought into context within a far broader history of circulation. This is what makes Cerdá's work so crucial today.

Piling critique and analysis on Haussmann is, first of all, very easy to do as the violence exacted on the whole of Paris by his reconstruction project is more than obvious. But more than this, in crediting Haussmann as the 'inventor' of modern urbanism, our current historiography yields an all too simplistic framework for critically understanding contemporary modes of urbanization, forcing one to focus solely on the most blatant instances of social violence and injustice that any large-scale project of urban transformation will effect. By focusing on the socially divisive forces that Haussmann's conservatism played into, the question of the systematic forces that in fact *cut across* socio-economic classes, not only encompassing the entire urban population, but erecting in space the structures and channels of a new political order altogether, goes completely unquestioned.

Of course, we should not rush to write *the* history of urbanization around Cerdá either: as with all of Cerdá's work, we should never take it to be the origin of a certain spatial concept, just as we should not take him as the inventor of these ideas. Rather, we should see Cerdá as a man whose socio-political inclinations, paired with his keen sensibility towards the broader changes taking place in his time, allowed him to build a body of work by condensing a whole host of ideas, concepts and ideologies that had themselves been circulating for some time. His work, in that sense, should be seen as a kind of diagram of a set of principles that had become visible through the cyclical fervour of the production of ideas and the precipitation of crises that had given shape to notions such as 'progress' during the nineteenth century. The dialogue between him and his unidentified counterpart, Haussmann, had made visible a certain set of techniques, technologies and forms of knowledge from which a new spatial order could be, and indeed was, constructed – a project whose profound epistemological significance was grasped in full by Cerdá and whose consequences we are only now becoming aware of.

Although the nearly planetary repercussions of this spatiality would only begin to be felt more than a century later,[9] evidence of its becoming could already be seen in the mid to late nineteenth century with, on the one hand, the 'territorialization' of the city and, on the other, the 'urbanization' of the territory. If the latter may be seen in the proliferation of exuberantly limitless schemes to radiate calculated, rationalized urban space across 'empty' land,[10] the former can be seen even prior to Haussmann's interventions in Paris, with the introduction and proliferation of specialized 'city atlases' – anonymously produced, layered compositions of maps, statistics and information, a system of representation formerly used to describe entire regions of the world (Picon, 2003). Such atlases introduced an entirely new knowledge of the city through the use of 'deep territorial' techniques to map the geological, hydrological and archaeological composition of cities (ibid.: 141–3) and cartographic and statistical techniques of the Ordinance Survey (see Joyce, 2003: chap. 1), useful in the development of multiple maps of socioeconomic distributions, real-estate values and medical conditions in the city.

This new mode of representing the city, depicted as a multilayered entity by an anonymous set of technicians, confirms a move away from the epistemological framework of artistic, architectural knowledge that had for centuries placed emphasis on the representational and the aesthetic. But, more than this, such a cartographic depiction of the city would, of course, be useful in terms of controlling its space as well. If the above-ground maps of these atlases projected a new cartography of real estate, property circulation and socio-economic dispositions, those below ground were committed to exposing a certain 'nature' that lay below the streets. The opposition between the two helped to expose and defuse the 'underground' as a realm of danger and fear (Picon, 2003), and the maps above ground opened themselves up to the new expansive forces of liberal capitalist development. Although the juxtaposition of above- and below-ground conditions attempted to naturalize both realms, such *territorial* knowledge was deployed not in order to 'perfect nature', as it had for the engineers of the ponts et chaussées, but rather to control it.

Indeed, the construct of the city atlas was itself an effort to produce a sense of total control over the city as an object of governmental knowledge and administration, and led significantly to its radical transformation as outlined above (ibid.: 140). Such techniques would naturally lend themselves to the city being conceived, much as the territory had been depicted, as a geometric, isotropic space 'emptied' of qualitative difference and open to a calculative, administrative knowledge. 'Geometric models [used in mapping the city] assumed that space was continuous and uniform in all directions, and therefore uniformly subject to mathematical laws' (Joyce, 2003: 35). Fundamental to this epistemological shift in the city was the notion that Patrick Joyce calls 'functional equivalence': 'the notion that space was reducible to formal schemata or grids, in which the elements of the schemata could be reproduced as equivalents one of another' (ibid.). Value and quantity, just as the atlases reveal, are now indistinguishable, transforming the city into a grid of private property and its continuous circulation. And likewise, beyond the space of the city, just as the Saint-Simonians had anticipated, space was now open to the universal mathematics of circulation, as the maps of Joseph Minard would later reveal.

The fluid circulation of money, goods and people had seen space transform itself into a perpetual means of analysis and a form of regulation over an economic system of international power nurtured under the values of the liberal nation-state.

The imbalance in power that had maintained the rift between territory and city marked the endpoint of a history of the opposition between city and countryside, humankind and wilderness, the world of civility, ritual and politics and that of mystery, myth and the natural world. By the nineteenth century, a new conception of space had emerged that would overturn this ancient order. The urban would see the territory as the natural domain it could rightfully claim as its own – the spatial horizon into which it would now perpetually expand and the technological rationale that would in turn expand across its spaces. No longer conditioned by its opposition to the space outside its bounds, the urban would propose a radically new spatial order that is better described as both material organization *and* the mode of its production, both concrete order *and* process.

Very few have considered urbanization as a mode of spatial organization, producing a space that departs from that of the city. Urbanization persists as a category unworthy of its own theory – perhaps a subcategory of architectural history. Still today, urbanization remains a kind of neutral horizon of cohabitation rooted in the prehistorical origin of human settlement and thus the inevitable future of the human condition. Perhaps this explains why even the most rigorous of historians only make mention of Cerdá in the context of his plan for Barcelona, ignoring almost completely his prodigious efforts to theorize urbanization. It is lost on most historians how such an artefact as the *Teoría* could in fact be far more important than the actual execution of a single plan. Indeed, this is precisely what makes Cerdá's work so important today: Despite his best intentions to naturalize urbanization, Cerdá did theorize the urban (*urbe*) as an entirely new

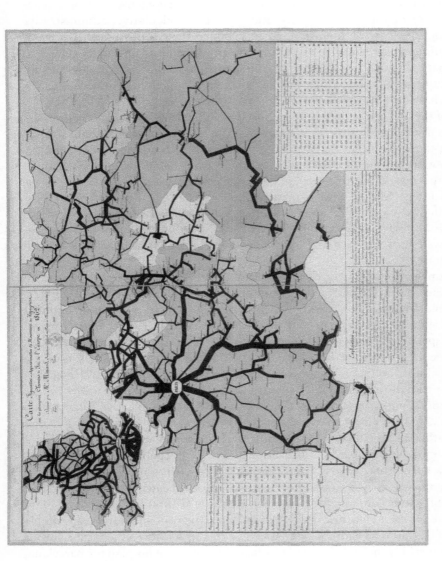

Figure 7.6 Charles-Joseph Minard, Carte Figurative et approximative du mouvemens des voyageurs sur les principaux chemins de fer de l'Europe en 1862 (Figurative and Approximate Map of the Movement of Passengers on the Main Railways of Europe in 1862), 1865

Source: Régnier et Dourdet, Paris. Bibliothèque nationale de France. Reproduced with permission from la Biblio-

Figure 7.7 Comisión Especial de Ensanche de Barcelona, Apertura y urbanización de la Gran Via de les corts Catalanes (Opening and Urbanization of the Gran Via de les Corts Catalanes), 1928

spatial order of cohabitation. The general neglect of this work in the modern history of the city leaves a gaping hole in an all-too-uniform history. It has allowed us to forgo the very possibility of theorizing a historico-epistemological break between the city and the urban, perpetuating instead an ambivalent narrative of urbanization as natural process.

Any critical understanding of the urban has until recently remained beyond the horizon of scholarly interest. Only today is such an understanding becoming evident in light of the crisis of climate change and its obvious relationship to rampant 'planetary urbanization'. Indeed, the *Teoría* is perhaps the clearest depiction of the urban ever written – an ideal diagram of the concrete, historical reality that continues to unroll across the Earth today. Because Cerdá devises it as a collusion between the technical and the governmental, it is the most legible register of a spatial order that corresponds to the emergent political form of modern liberalism of the nineteenth century. In its spatio-administrative consistency, the *Teoría* shows how urban space (the space of the *urbe*) could become not only responsive to the demands of capitalism, but, more importantly, a primary means of exerting a new form of biopolitical control over a population, all while transposing domesticity to become a territorial technology.

We are fated to comprehend the urban as but a type of 'city', displaying all the benefits of scientific and statistical knowledge and planned according to the capacities of ever-newer technologies – a city that will arrive as the outcome of centuries of technological development coupled with the loosening of absolutist rule over a 'natural' society. Our history revels in the objective facts of newness insofar as such facts reflect the basic integrity of a myth of historical continuity. It fails to register the urban on an epistemic level exactly because it has never allowed for a relationship between spatial order and political form to carry any historical importance. Perhaps this explains why today we so easily accept the 'fact' of the 'urban age' as our collective destiny, without ever grasping the true depth of such a proposition.

NOTES

1 Cerdá continually attributes the work of Paris's reconstruction to Napoleon III, never making mention of Haussmann (see Cerdá, 1999: 360n).

2 Here, Cerdá recounts how the Plaza de la constitución, which had previously served as an assembly point for '*malcontentos*' to stage parades and uprisings, had been transformed by the cutting of broad thoroughfares, forcing them to seek other, less exposed locations to assemble.

3 See, among others, Soria y Puig's comments in Cerdá (1999), Ortíz (1977) and Martí Arís (2009).

4 This was made clear in a separate settlement that he had commissioned for Burlington, New Jersey: 'Our purpose is, if the lord permit, with all convenient expedition, to erect and build one principal town; which by reason of situation must in all probability be the most considerable for merchandize, trade and fishery in those parts' (Reps, 1965: 158).

5 'The other building lots shall be distributed by lot to the settlers, those lots next to the main plaza being thus distributed and the lots which are left shall be held by us for assignment to those who shall later become settlers, or for the use which we may wish to make of them. And so that this may be done better, the town which is to be laid out should always be shown on a plan.'

6 *La carta al Marqués de Corvera*. For a lengthy explanation of the ideas expressed in the letter, see García-Bellido García de Diego (2000).

7 It is likely that Cerdá was acquainted with much more Saint-Simonian literature than the writings of the Reynaud brothers alone.

8 Cerdá only seems to praise the contemporary cases studied, not their historical formation.

9 Many architects and planners of the late nineteenth and early twentieth centuries, from Hilberseimer to Le Corbusier to Doxiadis and others, had recognized the inadequacy of the term 'city' in describing their contemporary urban condition. None offered to theorize this distinction.

10 In addition to Cerdá's proposals, there were arguably many others that appeared after his that could be seen to follow a similar limitlessness. Projects such as Otto Wagner's Großstadt of 1911, Ludwig Hilberseimer's project of *Großstadtarchitektur* of 1927 or Constantinos Doxiadis's Ecumenopolis of 1961 are a very few that exemplify this tendency.

Bibliography

Adams, R.E. (2014a) 'Lefebvre and Urbanization', *Society & Space*, http://societyandspace. org/2014/04/21/lefebvre-and-urbanization-ross-exo-adams/ (accessed 26 July 2018).

Adams, R.E. (2014b) 'The Burden of the Present: On the Concept of Urbanisation', *Society & Space*, http://societyandspace.org/2014/02/11/the-burden-of-the-present-on-the-concept-of-urbanisation-ross-exo-adams/ (accessed 26 July 2018).

Adams, R.E. (2016) 'An Ecology of Bodies', in *Climates: Architecture and the Planetary Imaginary*. Zurich: Avery Review/Lars Müller.

Agamben, G. (2005) *The Time that Remains: A Commentary on the Letter to the Romans*. Stanford: Stanford University Press.

Agamben, G. (2009) *The Signature of All Things: On Method*. Trans. by L. D'Isanto and K. Attell. Brooklyn, NY: Zone Books.

Agamben, G. (2011) *The Kingdom and the Glory: For a Theological Genealogy of Economy and Government*. Trans. by L. Chiesa and M. Mandarini. Stanford: Stanford University Press.

Agnew, J. (2005) 'Sovereignty Regimes: Territoriality and State Authority in Contemporary World Politics', *Annals of the Association of American Geographers*, 95 (2): 437–61.

Alphand, J.-C. A. (1867–73) *Les Promenades de Paris*. Paris: J. Rothschild.

Amin, A. and Thrift, N. (2002) *Cities: Reimagining the Urban*. Oxford: Polity Press.

Arendt, H. (1958) *The Human Condition*. Chicago: University of Chicago Press.

Aureli, P.V. (2008) *The Project of Autonomy: Politics and Architecture within and against Capitalism*. Illustrated edn. New York: Princeton Architectural Press.

Aureli, P.V. (2011) *The Possibility of an Absolute Architecture*. Cambridge, MA: MIT Press.

Bacon, E. (1975) *Design of Cities*. London: Thames & Hudson.

Bacon, F. (1884) *Novum Organum, or the True Suggestions for the Interpretation of Nature*. London: William Pickering.

Barbon, N. (1690) *A Discourse of Trade*. www.marxists.org/reference/subject/economics/barbon/trade.htm (accessed July 2011).

Baudelaire, C. (1995) *The Painter of Modern Life and Other Essays*. Trans. by J. Mayne. London: Phaidon Press.

Benevolo, L. (1975) *The Origins of Modern Town Planning*. Trans. by J. Landry. Cambridge, MA: MIT Press.

Benevolo, L. (1978a) *History of Modern Architecture: The Tradition of Modern Architecture*. Cambridge, MA: MIT Press.

Benevolo, L. (1978b) *The Architecture of the Renaissance*. London: Routledge & Kegan Paul.

Benevolo, L. (1980) *The History of the City*. Trans. by G. Culverwell. Cambridge, MA: MIT Press.

Benevolo, L. (1993) *The European City*. Trans. by Carl Ipsen. Oxford: Blackwell.

Benevolo, L. (1994) *La captura del infinito*. Trans. by M. García Galán. Madrid: Celeste.

Benjamin, W. (1999) *The Arcades Project*. Trans. by H. Eiland and K. McLaughlin. Cambridge, MA: Belknap Press, Harvard University.

Bergdoll, B. (2000) *European Architecture 1750–1890*. Illustrated edn. New York: Oxford University Press.

Berlin, I. (1969) *Four Essays on Liberty*. Reprint edn. Oxford: Oxford University Press.

Botero, G. (1956) *The Reason of State*. Trans. by P.J. Waley and D.P. Waley. New Haven, CT: Yale University Press.

Botero, G. (2012) *On the Causes of the Greatness and Magnificence of Cities*. Ballerini, L. and Ciavolella, M. (eds). Trans. by Geoffrey Symcox. Toronto: University of Toronto Press.

Brenner, N. and Schmid, C. (2013) *Implosions/Explosions: Towards a Study of Planetary Urbanization*. Brenner, N. (ed.). Berlin: Jovis.

Browne, T. (1928–31) *The Works of Sir Thomas Browne*. 6 vols. London: Faber & Gwyer.

Bruno, G. (1891) 'De Rerum Principiis', in Fiorentino, F., Tocco, F., Vitelli, H., Imbriani, V. and Tallarigo, C.M. (eds), *Opera latine conscripta*. Florence: Le Monnier.

Busquets, J. (2006) *Barcelona: The Urban Evolution of a Compact City*. Barcelona: Actar.

Busquets, J. and Corominas, M. (2009) *Cerdà and the Barcelona of the Future: Reality versus Project. Exhibition catalogue. 20 October 2009–28 February 2010*. Centre de Cultura Contemporània de Barcelona (CCCB), Barcelona, Spain.

Bylebyl, J.J. (ed.) (1979) *William Harvey and His Age*. Illustrated edn. Baltimore, MD: Johns Hopkins University Press.

Cabanis, P.J.G. (1843) *Rapports du physique et du moral de l'homme*. Paris: Fortin, Masson.

Cantillon, R. (1959) *Essai sur la nature du commerce en général*. Reprint, reissue edn. Higgs, H. (ed.). Trans. by H. Higgs. London: Frank Cass.

Castells, M. (1979) *The Urban Question: A Marxist Approach*. Cambridge, MA: MIT Press.

Castells, M. (1999) 'Grassrooting the Space of Flows', *Urban Geography*, 20 (4): 294–302.

Castells, M. (2000) *The Rise of the Network Society*. 2nd edn. Oxford: Blackwell.

Castells, M. (2010) 'Globalisation, Networking, Urbanisation: Reflections on the Spatial Dynamics of the Information Age', *Urban Studies*, 47 (13): 2737–45.

Cavalletti, A. (2005) *La città biopolitica: mitologie della sicurezza*. Milan: B. Mondadori.

Cerdá, I. (1851) *Diario de las sesiones del Congresso de los Diputados*. Madrid: Imprenta Nacional. (Reissued in 1977 by 2C.)

Cerdá, I. (1859a) *Juicio crítico de la exposición pública de planos y proyectos para la reforma y ensanche de Barcelona, mandada por Real Orden de 17 Septiembre último e inaugurada por el Exemo. Auyntamiento en 29 de Octubre de 1859*. Anonymous leaflet.

Cerdá, I. (1859b) 'Ordenanzas municipales de la construcción para la ciudad de Barcelona y pueblas comprendidos en su ensanche', first published in 1991 in *Teoría de la construcción de las ciudades. Teoría de la construcción de las ciudades aplicada al proyecto de reforma y ensanche de Barcelona: Cerdà y Barcelona*. Madrid: Ministerio para las Administraciones Públicas.

Cerdá, I. (1860a) *Pensamiento económico*. Presented to the Ministry of Development, 23 January 1860, first published in Cerdá, I. (1991) *Teoría de la construcción de las ciudades. Teoría de la construcción de las ciudades aplicada al proyecto de reforma y ensanche de Barcelona: Cerdà y Barcelona*. Madrid: Ministerio para las Administraciones Públicas.

Cerdá, I. (1860b) *Reforma y ensanche. Cartas de un amigo de allá a otro amigo de acá*. Anonymous leaflet.

Cerdá, I. (1863) 'La Calle', *Revista de Obras Públicas*, Madrid, XI (4–6), February/March.

Cerdá, I. (1867) *Teoría general de la urbanización, y aplicación de sus principios y doctrinas a la reforma y ensanche de Barcelona*. Madrid: Imprenta Española.

Cerdá, I. (1991 (1855)) *Ensanche de la ciudad de Barcelona. Memoria descriptiva de los trabajos facultativos y estudios estadísticos hechos de orden del Gobierno y consideraciones que se han tenido presentes en la formación del ante-proyecto para el emplazamiento y distribución del nuevo caserío*. Madrid: Ministerio para las Administraciones Públicas.

Cerdá, I. (1991 (1859)) *Teoría de la construcción de las ciudades aplicada al proyecto de reforma y ensanche de Barcelona: Cerdà y Barcelona*. Madrid: Ministerio para las Administraciones Públicas.

Cerdá, I. (1991 (1861)) *Teoría de la viabilidad urbana y reforma de la de Madrid*. Madrid: Instituto Nacional de la Administración Pública and Ayuntamiento de Madrid.

Cerdá, I. (1991 (1863)) *Necesidades de la circulación y de los vecinos de las calles con respecto a la vía pública urbana y manera de satisfacerlas*. Madrid: Instituto Nacional de la Administración Pública and Ayuntamiento de Madrid.

Cerdá, I. (1999) *Cerdá: The Five Bases of the General Theory of Urbanization*. Illustrated edn. Soria y Puig, A. (ed.). Trans. by B. Miller and M. Fons i Fleming. Madrid: Electa.

Cesalpino, A. (1593) *Quaestiones peripatetica*. Book V. Venice.

Chevalier, M. (1831) 'France. De l'Expropriation pour cause d'utilité publique', *Le Globe*, 15 November.

Chevalier, M. (1832) *Religion saint-simonienne. Politique industrielle. Système de la Méditerranée*. Paris: Bureaux du Globe.

Child, J. (1693) *A New Discourse of Trade: Wherein is Recommended several weighty Points relating to Companies of Merchants, the Act of Navigation, Naturalization of Strangers, and our Woollen Manufactures, The Ballance of Trade, And the Nature of Plantations, and their Consequences in Relation to the Kingdom, are seriously Discussed. And some Proposals for erecting a Court of Merchants for determining Controversies, relating to Maritime Affairs, and for a Law for Transferrance of Bills of Depts, are humbly Offered*. London: John Everingham.

Choay, F. (1969) *The Modern City: Planning in the 19th Century*. Illustrated edn. New York: G. Braziller.

Choay, F. (1997) *The Rule and the Model: On the Theory of Architecture and Urbanism*. Illustrated edn. Cambridge, MA: MIT Press.

Clagett, M. (2001) *Greek Science in Antiquity*. Mineola, NY: Dover.

Clark, T.J. (1990) *The Painting of Modern Life*. London: Thames & Hudson.

Condorcet, J.-A.-N. C. (1795) *Outlines of an Historical View of the Progress of the Human Mind*. London: J. Johnson.

Cowen, D. (2014) *The Deadly Life of Logistics: Mapping Violence in Global Trade.* Minneapolis: University of Minnesota Press.

Cresswell, T. (2006) *On The Move: Mobility in the Modern Western World.* New York: Routledge.

Cusanus, N. (1954) *Of Learned Ignorance.* Trans. by G. Heron. London: Routledge & Kegan Paul.

Davenant, C. (1771) *The Political and Commercial Works of that Celebrated Writer, Charles D'Avenant, LL. D., Relating to the Trade and Revenue of England, The Plantation Trade, The East-India Trade, And African Trade.*, vol. I. Whitworth, C. (ed.). London: R. Horsfield, T. Becket, P.A.De Hondt, T. Cadell and T. Evans.

De La Mare, N. (1729) *Traité de la police, où l'on trouvera l'histoire de son établissement, les fonctions et les prerogatives de ses magistrats, toutes les loix et tous les règlemens qui la concernent.* Amsterdam.

Doxiadis, C. (1968) *Ekistiks: An Introduction to the Science of Human Settlements.* Oxford: Oxford University Press.

Duveyrier, C. (1832) 'La Ville nouvelle ou le Paris des saint-simoniens', in *Paris, ou le livre des cent-et-un.* Paris: Ladvocat, pp. 315–44.

Edney, M. (2009) 'The Irony of Imperial Mapping', in Ackerman, J.R. (ed.), *The Imperial Map: Cartography and the Mastery of Empire.* Chicago: University of Chicago Press, pp. 11–45.

Elden, S. (2007) 'Governmentality, Calculation, Territory', *Environment & Planning D,* 25 (3): 562–80.

Elden, S. (2010) 'Land, Terrain, Territory', *Progress in Human Geography,* 34 (6): 799–817.

Elden, S. (2013) *The Birth of Territory.* Chicago: University of Chicago Press.

Esposito, R. (2008) *Bíos: Biopolitics and Philosophy.* Minneapolis: University of Minnesota Press.

Flachat, S. (1832) 'Politique. France. Le choléra. Assainissement de Paris', *Le Globe,* 2 April.

Forty, A. (2000) *Words and Buildings: A Vocabulary of Modern Architecture.* New York: Thames & Hudson.

Foucault, M. (1994) *The Order of Things: An Archaeology of the Human Sciences.* New York: Vintage Books ed. Random House.

Foucault, M. (2002) *The Archaeology of Knowledge.* Trans. by A.M. Sheridan Smith. Abingdon: Routledge.

Foucault, M. (2003) *Society Must Be Defended: Lectures at the Collège de France, 1975–1976.* Bertani, M., Fontana, A. and Ewald, F. (eds). Trans. by Macey. New York: Picador.

Foucault, M. (2009) *Security, Territory, Population: Lectures at the Collège de France 1977–1978.* Senellart, M., Ewald, F. and Fontana, A. (eds). Trans. by G. Burchell. London: Palgrave Macmillan.

Foucault, M. (2010) *The Government of Self and Others: Lectures at the Collège de France, 1982–1983.* New York: St Martin's Press; Houndmills: Palgrave Macmillan.

Frank, R.G. Jr. (1979) 'The Image of Harvey in Commonwealth and Restoration England', in Bylebyl, J.J. (ed.), *William Harvey and His Age.* Illustrated edn. Baltimore, MD: Johns Hopkins University Press.

French, R.K. (2006) *William Harvey's Natural Philosophy.* Cambridge: Cambridge University Press.

Galli, C. (2010) *Political Spaces and Global War*. Sitze, A. (ed.). Trans. by E. Fay. Minneapolis: University of Minnesota Press.

Gandy, M. (2014) *The Fabric of Space: Water, Modernity, and the Urban Imagination*. Cambridge, MA: MIT Press.

García-Bellido García de Diego, J. (2000) 'Ildefonso Cerdà y el nacimiento de la urbanística: la primera propuesta disciplinar de su estructura profunda', *Scripta Nova*, 61, 1 April, www.ub.edu/geocrit/sn-61.htm (accessed August 2012).

Garnier, T. (1989) *Une cité industrielle: étude pour la construction des villes*. New York: Princeton Architectural Press.

Giedion, S. (1982) *Space, Time and Architecture: The Growth of a New Tradition*. Cambridge, MA: Harvard University Press.

Girard, P.S. (1843) *Mémoires sur le canal de l'Ourcq et la distribution de ses eaux*. Paris: Chez Carilian-Gœury & Dalmont.

Gottmann, J. (1990) *Since Megalopolis: The Urban Writings of Jean Gottmann*. Gottmann, J. and Harper, R.A. (eds). Baltimore, MD: Johns Hopkins University Press.

Graham, S. and Marvin, S. (2001) *Splintering Urbanism: Networked Infrastructures, Technological Mobilities and the Urban Condition*. London: Routledge.

Grupo 2C. (2009) *La Barcelona de Cerdà*. Barcelona: Flor del Viento.

Habermas, J. (2010) *The Structural Transformation of the Public Sphere: An Inquiry into a Category of Bourgeois Society*. Trans. by T. Burger and F. Lawrence. Cambridge: Polity Press.

Harvey, D. (1996) 'Cities or urbanization?', *City*, 1 (1–2): 38–61. DOI: 10.1080/13604819608900022

Harvey, D. (2001) *Spaces of Capital: Toward a Critical Geography*. New York: Routledge.

Harvey, D. (2006) *Paris, Capital of Modernity*. New York: Routledge.

Harvey, D. (2008) 'The Right to the City', *New Left Review*, 53: 23–40.

Harvey, D. (2009) *Social Justice and the City*. Athens, GA: University of Georgia Press.

Harvey, W. (1847) *The Works of William Harvey, M.D.* Trans. by R. Willis. Printed for the Sydenham Society by C. & J. Adlard, London.

Haussmann, G.-E. (1890–3) *Mémoires du Baron Haussmann*. Paris: Victor-Havard.

Hazan, E. (2010) *The Invention of Paris*. Trans. by David Fernbach. London: Verso.

Hazard, S. (1850) *Annals of Pennsylvania, from the Discovery of the Delaware: 1609–1682*. Philadelphia.

Hilberseimer, L. (1960) 'City Architecture: The Trend toward Openness', in R. Pommer, D. Spaeth and K. Harrington (eds). (1988) *In the Shadow of Mies: Ludwig Hilberseimer Architect, Educator, and Urban Planner*. New York: Rizzoli International.

Hilberseimer, L. (2013) *Metropolisarchitecture and Selected Essays*. Illustrated edn. Anderson, R. (ed.). Columbia University.

Hobbes, T. (1845) *The English Works of Thomas Hobbes of Malmesbury, vol. VII*. Molesworth, Sir W. (ed.). London: Longman, Brown, Green, & Longmans.

Hobbes, T. (1986) *Leviathan*. Reprint edn. New York: Penguin.

Hsiang, J. and Mendis, B. (2013–14) *The City of 7 Billion: An Index*. Hong Kong/Shenzhen Biennale 6 December 2013–28 February 2014.

Huntley, F.L. (1953) 'Sir Thomas Browne and the Metaphor of the Circle', *Journal of the History of Ideas*, 14 (3): 353–64.

Isin, E.F., Osborne, T. and Rose, N.S. (1998) *Governing Cities: Liberalism, Neoliberalism, Advanced Liberalism*. Toronto: Urban Studies Programme, Division of Social Science, York University.

Johnson, H.B. (1976) *Order Upon the Land: The U.S. Rectangular Land Survey and the Upper Mississippi Country*. Illustrated ed. London: Oxford University Press.

Jordan, D.P. (1995) *Transforming Paris*. New York: Free Press.

Joyce, P. (2003) *The Rule of Freedom: Liberalism and the Modern City*. London: Verso.

von Justi, J.H.G.V. (1782 (1756)) *Grudsätze der Policeywissenschaft: in einem vernünftigen, auf den Endqweck der Policey gegründeten, Zusammenhange und zum Gebrauch Academischer Vorlesungen abgefasset*. 3rd edn. Göttingen: Wittwe Vandenhoek.

Kaika, M. (2004) *City of Flows: Modernity, Nature, and the City*. New York: Routledge.

Kant, I. (1991) *Kant: Political Writings*, vol. 2. Illustrated, revised edn. Reiss, H.S. (ed.). Cambridge, New York: Cambridge University Press. (Original publication date: 1784.)

Keynes, G. (1966) *The Life of William Harvey*. New York: Oxford University Press.

Koselleck, R. (1988) *Critique and Crisis: Enlightenment and the Pathogenesis of Modern Society*. Reprint, illustrated edn. Cambridge, MA: MIT Press.

Koselleck, R. (2004) *Futures Past: On the Semantics of Historical Time*. Illustrated edn. New York: Columbia University Press.

Koselleck, R. (2006) 'Crisis', *Journal of the History of Ideas*, 67 (2): 357–400.

Koyré, A. (1994) *From the Closed World to the Infinite Universe*. Reprint edn. Baltimore, MD: Johns Hopkins University Press.

Lazzarato, M. (2014) *Signs and Machines: Capitalism and the Production of Subjectivity*. Los Angeles: Semiotext(e).

Laugier, M.-A. (1977) *An Essay on Architecture*. Illustrated edn. Trans. by W. Herrmann and A. Herrmann. Los Angeles: Hennessey & Ingalls.

Le Corbusier (1987 (1929)) *The City of To-morrow and Its Planning*. Mineola, NY: Dover.

Le Corbusier (1991 (1930)) *Precisions on the Present State of Architecture and City Planning*. Trans. by E.S. Aujame. Cambridge, MA: MIT Press.

Lefebvre, H. (1991) *The Production of Space*. Trans. by D. Nicholson-Smith. Malden, MA: Blackwell.

Lefebvre, H. (2003) *The Urban Revolution*. Illustrated edn. Trans. by R. Bononno. Minneapolis: University of Minnesota Press.

Le Goff, J. (1989) 'Head or Heart? The Political Use of Body Metaphors in the Middle Ages', in M. Feher (ed.), *Fragments for a History of the Human Body, Part III*. New York: Zone Books, pp. 12–27.

Le Maître, A. (1682) *La metropolitée, ou, De l'établissement des villes Capitales, de leur utilité passive & active, de l'Union de leurs parties, & de leur anatomie, de leur commerce, &c*. Amsterdam: Chés Balthes Boekholt for Jean van Gorp.

Lévy, M. (1844) *Traité d'hygiène publique et privée*. Paris: Chez J.-B. Baillière.

Locke, J. (1821) *Two Treatises on Government*. London: Whitmore & Fenn.

Locke, J. (1849 (1690)) *An Essay Concerning Human Understanding*. 30th edn. London: W. Tegg.

Loftus, A. (2012) *Everyday Environmentalism: Creating an Urban Political Ecology*. Minneapolis: University of Minnesota Press.

Lowry, S.T. (1974) 'The Archaeology of the Circulation Concept in Economic Theory', *Journal of the History of Ideas*, 35 (3): 429–44.

McFarlane, C. (2011) 'The City as Assemblage: Dwelling and Urban Space', *Environment & Planning D: Society & Space*, 29 (4): 649–71.

Martí Arís, C. (2009) 'Cerdà: Un Puente Entre dos Civilizaciónes', in *La Barcelona de Cerdà*. Barcelona: Flor del Viento.

Martin, R. (2014) *Aesthetics, Politics and the City*. Minneapolis: University of Minnesota Press.

Martin, R. (2016) *The Urban Apparatus: Mediapolitics and the City*. Minneapolis: University of Minnesota Press.

Martini, F.D.G. (1967) *Trattati di architettura ingegneria e arte militare*. Maltese, C. (ed.). Milan: Il Polifilo.

Marx, K. (1992) *Capital: A Critique of Political Economy, Volume I*. London: Penguin Classics.

Marx, K. (1993) *Capital: A Critique of Political Economy, Volume II*. London: Penguin Classics.

Marx, K. and Engels, F. (2001) *Revolution in Spain*. Honolulu: University Press of the Pacific.

Mattelart, A. (1996) *The Invention of Communication*. Trans. by S. Emanuel. Minneapolis: University of Minnesota Press.

Mattelart, A. (2000) *Networking the World: 1794–2000*. Minneapolis: University of Minnesota Press.

Merrifield, A. (2014) *The New Urban Question*. London: Pluto Press.

Migne, J.P. (Ed.) (1855) *Patrologia Latina*, CCX, *Patrologiae Cursus Completus*. Paris.

Mintz, S.I. (1952) 'Galileo, Hobbes, and the Circle of Perfection', *Isis*, 43 (2): 98–100.

Misselden, E. (1623) *The Circle of Commerce or, The Ballance of Trade*. London.

Morris, A.E.J. (1994) *History of Urban Form: Before the Industrial Revolutions*. London and New York: Routledge.

Mumford, L. (1937) 'What Is a City?', *Architectural Record*, 82 (November): 92–6.

Mumford, L. (1961) *The City in History: Its Origins, Its Transformations, and Its Prospects*. New York: Harcourt, Brace & World.

Myers, A.C. (1912) *Narratives of Early Pennsylvania, West New Jersey and Delaware, 1630–1707*. New York.

Neilson, B. (2012) 'Five Theses on Understanding Logistics as Power', *Distinktion: Scandinavian Journal of Social Theory*, 13 (3): 323–40.

Neilson, B. and Rossiter, N. (2010) 'Still Waiting, Still Moving: On Labour, Logistics and Maritime Industries', in Bissell, D. and Fuller, G. (eds) (2011), *Stillness in a Mobile World*. London: Routledge, pp. 51–68.

Nicolson, M.H. (1950) *The Breaking of the Circle: Studies in the Effect of the 'New Science' upon Seventeenth-Century Poetry*. Evanston, IL: Northwestern University Press.

Nietzsche, F.W. (2001) *The Gay Science*. Williams, B.A.O. (ed.). Trans. by J. Nauckhoff and A. Del Caro. Cambridge and New York: Cambridge University Press.

Nuttall, Z. (1921) 'Royal Ordinances Concerning the Laying out of New Towns', *The Hispanic American Historical Review*, 4(4).

Onians, RB. (1951) *The Origins of European Thought: About the Body, the Mind, the Soul, the World, Time, and Fate*. Cambridge: Cambridge University Press.

Oresme, N. (1956) *The De Moneta of Nicholas Oresme and English Mint Documents*. Trans. by C. Johnson. London: Thomas Nelson & Sons.

Ortíz, A. (1977) 'Perspectiva y Prospectiva desde Cerdá: Una Linea de Tendencia', 2C *Construccion de la Ciudad*, (6–7).

Osborne, T. and Rose, N. (1998) *Governing Cities: Liberalism, Neoliberalism, Advanced Liberalism: Urban Studies Programme working paper, no. 19.* Toronto: Urban Studies Programme Division of Social Science York University, pp. 1–29.

Pagel, W. (1950) 'Giordano Bruno and the Circular Motion of the Blood', *The British Medical Journal*, 2 (4679): 621.

Pagel, W. (1951) 'William Harvey and the Purpose of Circulation', *Isis*, 42 (1): 22–38.

Painter, J. (2010) 'Rethinking Territory', *Antipode*, 42 (5): 1090–118.

Park, R. (1967) *On Social Control and Collective Behavior.* Chicago: Chicago University Press.

Patte, P. (1769) *Mémoires sur les objets les plus importants de l'Architecture.* Paris.

Peak, L., Patrick, D., Reddy, R.N., Sarp Tanyildiz, G., Ruddick, S. and Tchoukaleyska, R. (eds). (2018) 'Placing planetary urbanization in other fields of vision' [Special issue], *Environment & Planning D: Society & Space*, 36 (3): 373–610.

Pearson, A.C. (1917) *The Fragments of Sophocles.* Cambridge: Cambridge University Press.

Penn, W. (1685) *A Further Account of the Province of Pennsylvania*, in Myers, A.C. (1912) *Narratives of Early Pennsylvania, West New Jersey and Delaware, 1630–1707.* New York.

Pennsylvania Historical and Museum Commission. (n.d.) Online archive, www.phmc. pa.gov/Archives/Pages/default.aspx (accessed 26 July 2018).

Petty, W. (1899) *The Economic Writings of Sir William Petty Together with the Observations upon the Bills of Mortality more Probably by Captain John Graunt.* Cornell: Cornell University Press.

Picon, A. (1992) *French Architects and Engineers in the Age of Enlightenment.* Illustrated edn. Cambridge: Cambridge University Press.

Picon, A. (2002) *Les saint-simoniens: raison, imaginaire et utopie.* Paris: Belin.

Picon, A. (2003) 'Nineteenth-Century Urban Cartography and the Scientific Ideal: The Case of Paris', *Osiris*, 18 (Science and the City): 135–49.

Picon, A. (2009) 'The Engineer as Judge: Engineering Analysis and Political Economy in Eighteenth Century France', *Engineering Studies*, 1 (1): 19–34.

Picon, A. (2010) 'Nature et ingénierie: le parc des Buttes-Chaumont', *Romantisme*, 4 (150): 35–49.

Plato (1997) *Complete Works.* Illustrated edn. Cooper, J.M. and Hutchinson, D.S. (eds). Indianapolis, IN: Hackett.

Pope, A. (1996) *Ladders.* Princeton, NJ: Princeton Architectural Press.

Quesnay, F. (1730) *Observations sur les effets de la saignée.* Paris: Charles Osmont.

Quesnay, F. (1736) *Essai sur l'œconomie animale.* Paris: Guillaume Cavalier.

Quesnay, F. (1758) *Maximes générales du gouvernement économique.* Paris: Pierre Trabovillet.

Quesnay, F. (1972 (1758)) *Tableau économique.* Kuczynski, M. and Meek, R. (eds). London: Macmillan.

Rabinow, P. (1989) *French Modern: Norms and Forms of the Social Environment.* Chicago: University of Chicago Press.

Raphson, J. (1702) *Analysis Aequationum Universalis.* 2nd edn.

Reps, J.W. (1965) *The Making of Urban America: A History of City Planning in the United States.* Illustrated ed. Princeton, NJ: Princeton University Press.

Robinson, D.M. (1946) 'The Wheel of Fortune', *Classical Philology*, 41 (4): 207–16.

Rousseau, J.-J. (1998) *The Social Contract: or Principles of Political Right*. Trans. by H.J. Tozer. London: Wordsworth Editions.

Roy, A. (2015) 'What Is Urban about Critical Urban Theory?', *Urban Geography*. DOI: 10.1080/02723638.2015.1105485

Saint-Simon, H. (1975) *Henri Saint-Simon (1760–1825): Selected Writings on Science, Industry, and Social Organisation*. Taylor, K. (ed.). London: Taylor & Francis.

Schmitt, C. (1997) *Land and Sea*. Unabridged, reprint edn. Washington, DC: Plutarch Press.

Schmitt, C. (2005) *Political Theology: Four Chapters on the Concept of Sovereignty*. Chicago: University of Chicago Press.

Schmitt, C. (2006) *The Nomos of the Earth in the International Law of the Jus Publicum Europaeum*. Trans. by G.L. Ulmen. New York: Telos Press.

Schmitt, C. (2007) *The Concept of the Political*. Trans. by G. Schwab. Chicago: University of Chicago Press.

Schmitt, C. (2008) *The Leviathan in the State Theory of Thomas Hobbes: Meaning and Failure of a Political Symbol*. Illustrated edn. Trans. by G. Schwab and E. Hilfstein. Chicago: University of Chicago Press.

Schmitt, C. (2011a) 'The Großraum Order of International Law with a Ban on Intervention for Spatially Foreign Powers: A Contribution to the Concept of Reich in International Law (1939–1941)', in T. Nunan (ed.), *Writings on War*. Cambridge and Malden, MA: Polity.

Schmitt, C. (2011b) *Writings on War*. Nunan, T. (ed.). Cambridge and Malden, MA: Polity.

Schumpeter, J.A. (1972) *History of Economic Analysis*. Schumpeter, E.B. (ed.). New York: Oxford University Press.

Scott, T. (2012) *The City-State in Europe, 1000–1600*. Oxford: Oxford University Press.

Serra, A. (1613) *Breve trattato delle cause che possono fare abbondare li regni d'oro e d'argento dove non sono miniere. Con applicaxioni al Regno di Napoli. Diviso in tre parti*. Naples: Lazzaro Scorriggio.

Sitte, C. (1889) *City Planning According to Artistic Principles*, in Collins, G.R. and Collins, C.C. (eds.) (2006) *Camillo Sitte: The Birth of Modern City Planning*. Mineola, NY: Dover.

Skinner, Q. (1978) *The Foundations of Modern Political Thought: The Age of Reformation*. Cambridge: Cambridge University Press.

Skinner, Q. (1998) *The Foundations of Modern Political Thought: The Renaissance*. Cambridge: Cambridge University Press.

Sloterdijk, P. (2013) *In the World Interior of Capital*. Trans. by W. Hoban. Cambridge: Polity Press, p. 34.

Small, R. (1983) 'Nietzsche and a Platonist Tradition of the Cosmos: Center Everywhere and Circumference Nowhere', *Journal of the History of Ideas*, 44 (1): 89–104.

Smith, A. (2008) *An Inquiry into the Nature and Causes of the Wealth of Nations*. Sutherland, K. (ed.). Oxford and New York: Oxford University Press.

Smith, N. (1990) *Uneven Development, Nature, Capital and the Production of Space*. Oxford: Basil Blackwell.

Smith, N. (2005) *The New Urban Frontier: Gentrification and the Revanchist City*. London: Routledge.

Soja, E. (1998) *The City: Los Angeles and Urban Theory at the End of the Twentieth Century*. Illustrated, reprint edn. Soja, E.W. and Scott, A.J. (eds). Berkeley: University of California Press.

Soja, E.W. (2000) *Postmetropolis: Critical Studies of Cities and Regions*. Illustrated, reprint edn. Oxford: Blackwell.

Stanislawski, D. (1947) 'Early Spanish Town Planning in the New World', *Geographical Review*, 37 (1): 94.

Steinberg, P.E. (2009) 'Sovereignty, Territory, and the Mapping of Mobility: A View from the Outside', *Annals of the Association of American Geographers*, 99 (3): 467–95.

Storper, M. and Scott, A.J. (2016) 'Current Debates in Urban Theory: A Critical Assessment', *Urban Studies*. DOI: 10.1177/0042098016634002

Swyngedouwe, E. (2004) *Social Power and the Urbanization of Water: Flows of Power*. Oxford: Oxford University Press.

Swyngedouwe, E. (2006) 'Circulations and Metabolisms: (Hybrid) Natures and (Cyborg) Cities', *Science as Culture*, 15 (2): 105–21.

Tafuri, M. (1980) *Theories and History of Architecture*. Trans. by G. Verrecchia. New York: Granada.

Tafuri, M. and Dal Co, F. (1986) *Modern Architecture*. Illustrated edn. New York: Electa/Rizzoli.

Tarlow, S. (2010) *Ritual, Belief, and the Dead Body in Early Modern Britain and Ireland*. Illustrated edn. Cambridge and New York: Cambridge University Press.

Tarrago Cíd, S. (2007) 'Ildefonso Cerda visto por Javier García-Bellido: Aproximación a un encuentro', *Arquitectura, Ciudad y Entorno*, August.

Taubes, J. (2004) *The Political Theology of Paul*. Stanford: Stanford University Press.

Telesio, B. (1586 (1965–76)) *De rerum natura iuxta propria principia*. 3 vols. De Franco, L. (ed.). Florence: La Nuova Italia.

Toscano, A. (2014) 'Lineaments of the Logistical State', *Viewpoints Magazine* (28 Sept.), https://viewpointmag.com/2014/09/28/lineaments-of-the-logistical-state/ (accessed 26 July 2018).

Tribe, K. (1978) *Land, Labour and Economic Discourse*. London: Routledge & Kegan Paul.

Urry, J. (2007) *Mobilities*. Cambridge: Polity Press.

Vauban, S.L.P. (1737 (1675)) *De l'Attaque et de la defense des places*. Chez Pierre de Hondt.

Walaeus, J. (1673) *De motu chyli et sanguinis ad Thom. Bartholinum*, in T. Bartholin, *Anatomia ex Caspari Bartholini Parentis Institutionibus*. Leiden.

Wallace, R.M. (1981) 'Progress, Secularization and Modernity: The Löwith–Blumenberg Debate', *New German Critique*, 22: 63–79.

Webster, C. (1979) 'William Harvey and the Crisis of Medicine in Jacobean England', in J.J. Bylebyl (ed.), *William Harvey and His Age*. Illustrated edn. Baltimore, MD: Johns Hopkins University Press.

Williams, R. (1973) *The City and the Country*. New York: Oxford University Press.

Winter, T.N. (2007) 'The *Mechanical Problems* in the Corpus of Aristotle', *Faculty Publications, Classics and Religious Studies Department*, Paper 68, http://digitalcommons.unl.edu/classicsfacpub/68 (accessed 4 May 2012).

Wirth, L. (1938) 'Urbanism as a Way of Life', *American Journal of Sociology*, 44 (1): 1–24.

Wittkower, R. (1971) *Architectural Principles in the Age of Humanism*. Reprint edn. New York: W.W. Norton.

Index

'ADAMS SHATTERS CONVENTIONAL URBAN THOUGHT TO REVEAL THE CIRCULATORY LOGICS AT THE HEART OF URBANIZATION. A TRULY EYE-OPENING BOOK.'
PHILIP STEINBERG, DURHAM UNIVERSITY

'THIS PATH-BREAKING INTERVENTION URGES US TO RETHINK OUR MOST BASIC ASSUMPTIONS REGARDING THE SITE, HISTORY AND PURPOSE OF ''URBAN'' RESEARCH. AN ESSENTIAL BOOK FOR ANYONE CONCERNED TO UNDERSTAND AND SHAPE THE CONTEMPORARY URBAN CONDITION.'
NEIL BRENNER, HARVARD UNIVERSITY

'IN THIS TIMELY AND POWERFUL RETHEORIZATION OF URBANIZATION, ADAMS OFFERS A CONCEPTUAL TOOLBOX FOR UNDERSTANDING HOW POWER FUNCTIONS WITHIN CITIES AND POPULATIONS AND UPON SUBJECTS.'
FELICITY SCOTT, COLUMBIA UNIVERSITY

Circulation & Urbanization is is a foundational investigation into the history of the urban. Moving beyond both canonical and empirical portrayals, the book approaches the urban through a genealogy of circulation – a concept central to Western political thought and its modes of spatial planning. Locating architectural knowledge in a wider network of political history, legal theory, geography, sociology and critical theory, and drawing on maritime, territorial and colonial histories, Adams contends that the urban arose in the nineteenth century as an anonymous, parallel project of the emergent liberal nation state. More than a reflection of this state form or the product of the capitalist relations it fostered, the urban is instead a primary instrument for both: at once means and ends.

Combining analytical precision with interdisciplinary insights, this book offers an astonishing new set of propositions for revisiting a familiar, yet increasingly urgent, topic. It is a vital resource for all students and scholars of architecture and urban studies.

ROSS EXO ADAMS is Assistant Professor of Architecture and Urban Theory at Iowa State University.

SOCIETY & SPACE SERIES

ISBN 978-1-4739-6331-3

www.sagepublishing.com
Los Angeles | London | New Delhi | Singapore | Washington DC | Melbourne

by Wendy Scott | Cover image © Bas Princen-Alley (Skywalk)

9 781473 963313

Circulation & Urbanization

SOCIETY AND SPACE SERIES

The *Society and Space* series explores the fascinating relationship between the spatial and the social. Each title draws on a range of modern and historical theories to offer important insights into the key cultural and political topics of our times, including migration, globalisation, race, gender, sexuality and technology. These stimulating and provocative books combine high intellectual standards with contemporary appeal for students of politics, international relations, sociology, philosophy, and human geography.

Series Editor: Professor Stuart Elden, University of Warwick

Migration, Ethics & Power: Spaces of Hospitality in International Politics by Dan Bulley

Geographies of Violence by Marcus A. Doel

Surveillance & Space by Francisco R. Klauser